Disability Praxis

'A masterful intervention in disability theory and praxis that is particularly pertinent for an age of austerity, pandemic and rising living costs.'
—Robert Chapman, author of *Empire of Normality: Neurodiversity and Capitalism*

'A brilliant and much needed contribution to current debates in disability politics – offering a timely corrective to the most recent approaches to disability that have taken a neoliberal turn.'
—Ioana Cerasella Chis, University of Birmingham

'Look no further for a comprehensive analysis of the disabled movement which also intelligently looks at how disability can fit into the modern world.'
—Joshua Hepple, activist, writer and disability equality trainer

'An essential read for the activist and the lay person who is interested in disability. Bob offers a Marxist materialist critique, identifying the limitations of the movement's emphasis on decontextualised legal rights rather than a deeper resistance to wider oppression of disabled people within capitalist society. The book clarified a lot of the main issues for me.'
—Marian Brooks-Sardinha, carer and retired lecturer

Disability Praxis

The Body as a Site of Struggle

Bob Williams-Findlay

First published 2024 by Pluto Press
New Wing, Somerset House, Strand, London WC2R 1LA
and Pluto Press, Inc.
1930 Village Center Circle, 3-834, Las Vegas, NV 89134

www.plutobooks.com

British Library Cataloguing in Publication Data
A catalogue record for this book is available from the British Library

ISBN 978 0 7453 4098 2   Paperback
ISBN 978 1 78680 804 2   PDF
ISBN 978 1 78680 805 9   EPUB

Typeset by Stanford DTP Services, Northampton, England

Simultaneously printed in the United Kingdom and United States of America

Contents

We do not organise because we are people first, nor because we are physically impaired. We organise because of the way society disables physically impaired people, because this must be resisted and overcome. The Union unashamedly identifies itself as an organisation of physically impaired people, and encourages its members to seek pride in ourselves, in all aspects of what we are. It is the Union's social definition of disability which has enabled us to cut out much of the nonsense, the shame and the confusion from our minds.

Disability Challenge 1 (Union of the Physically
Impaired Against Segregation – UPIAS, 1981)

Acknowledgements

I would like to take this opportunity to thank those people who directly and indirectly contributed to the writing and presentation of *Disability Praxis*. The book would never have materialised if disabled people had not had the strength and willpower to engage in a global emancipation struggle. My own journey began with Carol encouraging me to make contact with Paul and Judy Hunt. Paul Gilroy played a similar role while we wrote *The Empire Strikes Back: Race and Racism in 1970s Britain* (published in 1982). He suggested I attended a Liberation Network of People with Disabilities meeting, and as a result, I became directly involved in the British Disabled People's Movement. Merry, Kirsten and Chris, influenced my early thinking. Maria, Alun, Dave, Geraldine and many others supported me in the establishment of the Birmingham Disability Rights Group. I had the privilege to campaign alongside key people within BCODP and DPI, such as Jane, Rachel, Mike, Anne, Richard and Lucile. Meeting Ed, Judy and Theresa also drove me on.

Alongside developing my campaigning skills, I also learnt how to analyse the ideas behind our movement. Within the pages of *Disability Praxis* are disability scholar activists such as Vic, Mike, Len, Marta and Debbie, who helped shape my thinking. I have also been able to complete the book due to encouragement and support from Ioana, Luke, Milo, Susan, Sandra and Rob. Rowan helped with the final stages of tidying up the book.

Thanks should also go to my publisher, Pluto Press, and in particular staff members, Nicki, Neda, Melanie, Jeanne and Robert. Finally, Cindy and Tamara were there when I needed them.

Preface

I was approached by Pluto Press to produce a book exploring disability politics within the context of their history and potential for assisting in shaping the future. When accepting this challenge, I wanted to be quite transparent in my approach; offering a critical critique alongside signposting towards ideas and concepts that have the potential of assisting the development of a new disability praxis.[1] Looking at how I might approach the subject, I was mindful of Vic Finkelstein's assertion that the '"radical" social model of disability provides an overarching view of disability and cannot be placed alongside selected elements as if they were of equal value.'[2] This led to him being critical of Mike Oliver's view, 'that the "social model of disability" and "civil rights", alongside with "independent living" are harmonious components in our struggle for emancipation.'[3]

While I agree that the 'radical' social model of disability provides an overarching view of disability, I believe it is still possible and valid to identify four specific cornerstones of British disability politics. The idea of a cornerstone is that it acts as an important quality or feature upon which a particular thing depends or is based. I used a series of blogs to outline what I see as the four cornerstones alongside a critique of specific issues surrounding how both influenced the development of disability politics and praxis as they emerged over a twenty-year period. Since writing these blogs, I have revised how I want to present these four cornerstones. In my original thinking, the social approach towards defining disability was divided into two elements – firstly, the historical and material grounding of both the social interpretation and social model of disability, and secondly, the ideas developed by the Union of the Physically Impaired Against Segregation (UPIAS). I also made a distinction between developing a disability culture and forging a political identity. In this book, I have combined them.

A crucial aspect of praxis is to engage in reflection before attempting to move forward. Whatever people's opinion is of this book, I hope it will be accepted as a genuine attempt to contribute to the struggle for disabled people's emancipation.

Bob Williams-Findlay
Birmingham
July 2023

PART I

Are There Four Cornerstones of Disability Politics?

1

Setting the Scene

INTRODUCTION

I elected to divide this book into two parts. The first part explores what I have described as the four cornerstones of British disability politics, which are: the fundamental principles of disability, the self-organisation of disabled people, campaigning for de-institutionalisation and the promotion of self-directed living, disability culture and identity. The first cornerstone is concerned with addressing disability as a social and not a personal phenomenon. It is important to stress that at no time should the social interpretation of disability be expected to explain/provide answers for all the experiences disabled people might have and talk about. What is provided are insights into the historical positioning of people who have been subjected to disablement, and it offers a framework for engaging in an emancipation struggle. The second cornerstone is the importance of self-organisation to the Disabled People's Movement. The third cornerstone involves political issues around de-institutionalisation and the tensions, and contradictions that exist within promoting self-directed living. The term 'self-directed living' has been used to cover the many ways disabled people have described having control over their lives.[1]

Finally, I will seek to justify why I see the fourth cornerstone as being the development of disability culture and a political disability identity. This will involve a discussion on the importance of forging individual and collective identities to contest what it means to be a disabled person in society. In addressing both self-organisation and issues around culture and identity, consideration has been given to whether or not disability politics can be viewed as 'identity politics'. The differing ways in which disability is viewed and approached has implications for how society and disabled people understand who and what they are, both individually and collectively. This in turn has implications for us when considering the question of identity politics in relation to disabled people.

Disability politics is about changing the relations various groups of people have with given societies. It has always involved both ideas and action. By presenting 'four cornerstones of disability politics', I am merely suggesting that:

- the fundamental principles of disability;
- the self-organisation of disabled people;
- the advocating of de-institutionalisation and the promotion of self-directed living,* and
- the development of a counter-hegemonic culture and political collective identity

are interconnected to form the basis of disability politics in Britain and were influential worldwide. Although I am exploring them as separate issues, I view them as forming the base upon which disability politics was founded.

I am mindful of the fact that Frances Hasler once stated that the social model of disability was 'the big idea of the disability movement'.[2] This is similar to something Mike Oliver claimed and was then challenged by Vic Finkelstein. Vic wrote: 'Mike maintains that these advances were founded on three big ideas: "the social model of disability, independent living and civil rights". I don't agree. I don't see how "components" of a model can be given equal value to the model itself!'[3]

Whether or not one speaks of 'components' or 'cornerstones', there is an interconnectedness between the ideas and actions which forged and maintained disabled people's emancipation struggle. This said, I also want to acknowledge what Judy Hunt writes in her book:

> The foundation of UPIAS was an important event for the subsequent development of the movement for it placed disability under thorough scrutiny, for the first time. The UPIAS policy statement posed several distinctive concepts that had not been clearly stated before.[4]

This is why I call the first cornerstone the headstone because I believe constructing a socio-political challenge to the social oppression of disabled people is the driving force behind disability politics. By placing disability

---

* I have used the term 'self-directed lives' here because I want to discuss later in the book what 'choice and control' mean in terms of understanding integrated, independent, and inclusive living.

under scrutiny, UPIAS paved the way for the development of the radical social interpretation of disability and in due course what was to become the social model of disability. These developments need to be placed in context because, through this process, we can begin to explore how and to what extent the ideas they generated are grounded within what I refer to as 'disability politics'.

The second part of the book considers issues that are relevant to creating a new disability praxis. The style of the presentation will therefore alter from offering a critique of past and present disability politics and praxis towards trying to explore theoretical considerations for future praxis. I will discuss one of the thorns in the side of both British and global disability politics: the question of the positioning of impairment in the analysis of disabled people's oppression, which continues to be an extremely contested area of debate. It is impossible to do justice to the various positions or critiques within Disability Studies, therefore the historical relationship between disability politics and Disability Studies will be largely sidestepped.

When discussing impairment in this book, I will not do so only in relation to rejecting how disability is viewed as 'an individualised problem' caused by the nature and degree of an impairment, but I will at the same time argue that impairment is in one sense the basis for people with impairments' social oppression. This approach to positioning impairment within disability politics, however, is in keeping with the arguments made by Paul Abberley, who argued:

> To claim that disabled people are oppressed involves, however, arguing a number of … points. At an empirical level, it is to argue that on significant dimensions disabled people can be regarded as a group whose members are in an inferior position to other members of society because they are disabled people. It is also to argue that these disadvantages are dialectically related to an ideology or group of ideologies which justify and perpetuate this situation.[5]

Accepting Abberley's framework should not in any way be seen as undermining my support for breaking the direct causal link between impairment and disability as advocated by UPIAS. The distinction made between impairment and disability remains a crucial aspect of radical disability politics, however, it is still an abused concept more often than not. The distinction is based upon viewing impairment as the real or perceived altered state of a body or mind caused by injury, disease, or other socially related factors, and disability, which is the imposed social restrictions created by unequal and differential treatment.[6] Chapter 6 outlines Abberley's ideas on what needs addressing in order to develop a theory of disability as oppression.

Chapter 7 builds upon this discussion by contrasting two different concepts that can be used to investigate the impairment side of this relationship: impairment effects and impairment reality. The former concept was developed by the disability studies scholar Carol Thomas, based on her belief that

> ... the social model needs to be set to one side – since it is only a model and a shorthand statement – so that we can get on with the task of developing a social relational theory (or theories) of disability. Moving away from a preoccupation with the social model should facilitate a departure from the current rather futile arguments about whether impairment does or does not cause disability. It would encourage a more constructive theoretical engagement with the significance of impairment and impairment effects in the lives of disabled people, while enabling the various dimensions of disability – socially imposed exclusions and disadvantages – to take centre stage.[7]

I will explain my opposition to this before presenting an alternative which centres on what I call 'impairment reality'. This term focuses on what is or can be 'knowable' about the consequences of a person's impairment.

Chapter 8 introduces the question of the dialectics of disability which is rarely openly discussed within disability politics, despite being evident within the social interpretation of disability as developed by UPIAS and Vic Finkelstein. Paul Abberley, in my opinion, has been one of the few disabled scholar activists who has talked about it explicitly. Without consideration of the dialectics of disability, I believe there remains too many unanswered questions in relation to disabled people's engagement with the development of policies, movements and transformative agendas. In this book, it is not my intention to discuss any specific policy in detail, although some policies will be referred to; instead I want to consider some of the issues that impinge upon policy development. Chapter 8 will also consider issues around the emancipation struggle which relate to the diverse makeup of groups who are subjected to disablement. The roots of the British Disabled People's Movement stem from the ideas and actions of people with physical impairments. It is necessary to not only acknowledge this, but also to question whether or not the emancipation struggle has a shared agenda. Nonetheless, this book primarily features issues facing people with physical impairments; however, intersectional issues will be raised.

A conscious decision was taken not to include discussions on specific sites of struggle where disabled people encounter disabling barriers or social restriction, such as health, education, work, housing, transport. It was felt each area would require a chapter in its own right to do the subject justice. Chapter 9 introduces a discussion on developing a radical eco-social approach; one that fights for a new system capable of producing and sustaining community-based services. This chapter explores various debates around how to transform disabled people's position within society and argues that by drawing from natural ecosystems – which are defined as the network of interactions among organisms and between organisms and their environment – it is possible to look at ways of interconnecting with social environments and therefore pay explicit attention to the social, institutional and cultural contexts of human interaction with environments. It suggests ordinary lifestyles are interdependent; what happens in households, streets, communities, cities and the planet, impacts upon us all. However, disablement excludes and marginalizes disabled people from or within the participation processes. Adopting a radical eco-social approach situates removing disabling barriers and social restrictions within a framework which addresses all the systems that impact upon human existence.

At the heart of the final chapter is an enquiry into what extent the British Disabled People's Movement saw itself as being involved in the struggle for emancipation; or had they simply set their sights on social inclusion? The meaning I am attaching to 'emancipation' is that it is 'the process of giving people social or political freedom and rights.'[8] This enquiry, I believe is central to the debate within this book in terms of the relationship between theory and praxis. Did the Disabled People's Movement under-develop disability praxis by abandoning the foundations upon which disability politics were built? In reality, disability politics and disability praxis should be synonymous with each other, but the truth is that 'disability politics' have taken a myriad of forms which mean most elements of 'praxis' were neglected. As we shall see, some questioned to what extent the Movement developed any 'theory' at all.

In this book, I outline my definitions of disability politics and praxis; however, I acknowledge that differing perspectives on what disability is, results in alternative approaches. Central to this book, and to disability politics, is the need to acknowledge that 'what disability is' is contested on many fronts. One ramification of the differences that exist in defining disability is that people who are impaired often see themselves differently from one another, as well as being treated differently by other people. Part of the argument I will further is that, despite views to the contrary, the *nature* of disabled people's oppression is unlike other forms of oppressive practice.[9]

In later chapters in the book, I discuss differing definitions and defending the political assertion made by the Union of the Physically Impaired Against Segregation that disability is best understood as being 'imposed social restrictions placed on top of our impairments'.[10] In taking this approach, it is my intention to contest the definition of 'disabilities' offered within the World Health Organization's International Classifications of Functioning.[11] A crucial element of disability praxis must be how to address people's experience of oppression. Oliver put forward a specific methodology when he stated:

> Using the generic term [disabled people] does not mean that I do not recognise differences in experience within the group but that in exploring this we should start from the ways oppression differentially impacts on different groups of people rather than with differences in experience among individuals with different impairments.[12]

Given the scope of the book, it will only be possible to signpost these differential experiences of oppression alongside issues concerned with intersectionality. Intersectionality refers to the way in which different types of discrimination or oppression are linked to and affect each other.[13]

I am using the term 'disabled people' to refer to different groups of people who are subjected to differing forms of unequal and differential treatment on account of how given societies address the issue of impairment and, as a consequence, encounter social restrictions. Nevertheless, it is the oppressive social relations that they have with, and within society, that defines their collective political identity. Unless it appears in a quotation, I will not be employing the term, 'people with disabilities', in line with my rejection of the WHO's ICF.

It is my intention to make a distinction in this book between what I see as radical disability politics and what has been called idealist disability politics. By radical disability politics, I mean political activity that is anti-capitalist and seeks transformative change; as opposed to a politics of those disabled people focused solely on securing 'rights', challenging negative 'attitudes', and striving for social inclusion.

Alison Sheldon explained that:

The idealist or 'rights' interpretation of the social model, whilst generally acknowledging the realities of the materialist model, understands
disability to be the irrational product of deep-rooted cultural beliefs, attitudes and prejudices. Hence the claim that: people with impairment are
disabled, not just by material discrimination, but also by prejudice. This
prejudice is not just interpersonal, it is also implicit in cultural representation, in language and in socialization. Such analyses have definite appeal
for western researchers reporting on disability in the majority world. This
has major implications, both ideologically and practically ... .[14]

I believe the major implications identified by Sheldon need to be addressed
against a backdrop where disability politics are at its lowest ebb since the
early 1970s when Paul Hunt and a handful of others began to explore the
true nature of their exclusion from mainstream society. There are disabled
activists plugging away in Britain who are more than aware that we require
a new strategy to further our resistance to disabling government policies
and practices, but there is a complete lack of resources and political will
to self-organise. Despite the emergence of organisations such as Disabled
People Against Cuts (DPAC) in 2010, and a number of disabled activists
arguing for a platform to initiate a discussion among disabled people around
the need for various attempts to re-group the remnants of the movement,
little progress has been made. This is extremely frustrating for those who
still believe in the need for a Movement and the need to explore once again
the core political understandings that gave it life in the first place.

We have witnessed both the highs and the lows of the British Disabled
People's Movement (DPM) and now there is a growing awareness that there
is the need to appraise our past in order to contribute towards building fresh
perspectives if disability politics are to survive. Crucially, there is an urgent
need to politically assist disabled activists in building bridges between the
past and present, with the aim of influencing our futures. In truth, it is likely
that we will have more questions than answers, but by opening up a dialogue
and considering the central questions which bring us together politically, we
can start the process of piecing together a large-scale strategy.

As one of the 'old guard' of the Disabled People's Movement, I believe I
have a responsibility to pass on the legacy of our Movement, but in doing so,
I must attempt to explain to future generations both the negative as well as
the positive aspects of our disability praxis. By disability praxis, I mean 'the
process by which a theory or ideas relating to the struggle against disable-

ment is enacted, embodied, or realized'. 'Praxis' may also refer to 'the process of using a theory or something that you have learned in a practical way'.[15]

It is important to acknowledge that British disability politics cannot be discussed in isolation. From the earliest stages and through its height, the British DPM influenced and was influenced by disabled people in other countries. UPIAS was in close communication with disabled militants in Japan, Sweden and Germany, as well as the American Independent Living Movement. The integration campaigns of disabled people in the post-colonial world made a deep impression on the thinking of leading disabled activists in Britain. In return, the British DPM gave the international organisation of disabled people – the Disabled People's International (DPI) – its social definition of disability – that is, a framework in which disabled people the world over could identify with and enable them to view their struggles in a radical context.[16]

It is not possible to discuss disability politics and praxis without reference to academic theory; therefore, I will refer to the academic literature and positions relevant to the arguments being put forward.

WHAT IS PRAXIS?

The understanding of 'praxis' I use in this book is indebted to the work and the methodology of Paulo Freire, an educator and philosopher who worked with oppressed sections of Brazilian society. His approach towards learning resonates with the work undertaken by those engaged in various forms of disability politics which I have witnessed over the last forty years. He developed a specific, critical pedagogy, which is a method and practice of teaching. Critical pedagogy is viewed as a philosophy of education that sees teaching as a political act. This of course includes challenging students to examine the power structures and status quo of their surroundings.

In *Pedagogy of the Oppressed*, Freire, proposed a pedagogy with a new relationship between teacher, student and society. The relevance of his work lies in his methodology, where he viewed praxis as 'reflection and action directed at the structures to be transformed'.[17] I suggest that the methodological approach, if consistently adopted, not only shapes 'a new relationship between teacher, student and society', but applies equally to relationships between scholar activists, disabled communities and society. The processes of learning, of course, can go beyond the 'classroom' or the boundaries of education.

Freire saw praxis as a cyclical process with four stages: theory, reflection, action and reflection. Further insights from Freire's pedagogical approach to praxis continue to be of value to those engaged in Disability Studies and disability politics, as they have been to the thought of oppressed people's liberation struggles.[18]

A common definition of praxis, a Greek word initially meaning activity engaged in by free people, is that it is 'practice, as distinguished from theory'.[19] While in its original, Ancient Greek context, this distinction reflected a widespread view that thinking and acting were separate human activities, the term took on a more social and transformational meaning in nineteenth-century philosophy.[20]

Disability praxis, in my reading, is a process of critically appraising and taking action in relation to disabled people's social oppression. In relation to developing praxis, Freire believed it was insufficient for people to simply come together in dialogue in order to gain knowledge of their social reality. Talking about issues is inadequate; people must act together upon their environment in order critically to reflect upon their reality and to transform it through further action and critical reflection. This raises many questions for academics, researchers, activists, social movements and communities.

Among the biggest challenges within disability politics is that of breaking disabled people free, materially and ideologically, from how they are both seen and treated. In this sense, a vital role of disability politics is to empower disabled people to 'examine the power structures and status quo of their surroundings'. Dominant ideologies are strong, and many disabled people are isolated or herded together within institutions thereby unable to truly develop a sense of self and an acceptance of self-worth. The need for oppressed people to unlearn as well as learn is a central question for any type of social movement, but I would suggest it is an essential aspect of developing disability politics. In my opinion, there are several Freirean concepts that could be applied or adapted to provide tools that could be useful in constructing a clearer transformative disability praxis.

SETTING THE SCENE: HOW DID WE GET HERE?

Before exploring the four cornerstones of British disability politics, I want to place this exercise in the context of where British disabled people find themselves currently.

I wish to start our journey at the end rather than at the beginning by stating that the Disabled People's Movement, as a social movement, does not exist as it once did. I will consider the nature of our Movement in later chapters, but here I want to acknowledge that:

- There are still elements of disability politics visible in the discussions and campaigning taking place.
- There are still several disabled people's organisations working away on various fronts.
- Resistance to austerity has been going on for over a decade, but I would argue there is no longer a collective consciousness around the central ideas that UPIAS and other disabled activists put forward in the 1970s and 1980s.

Attempts to kickstart the Movement from 2012 onwards have failed and one of the causes for this failure is the fact that the radical ideas contained within UPIAS's 'interpretation' of disability no longer informed disabled activists' praxis from the early 1990s onwards. The current situation in which disabled people in Britain find themselves is without a doubt one of the most oppressive in living memory. Many disabled people are experiencing cuts to services and social security benefits which they rely upon to live self-directed lives, whilst others fear that the reduction in services will ultimately lead to them being forced back into residential care. Tony Blair's Labour government set the framework that the coalition government of Conservatives and Liberal Democrats and the successive Conservative governments have built upon during the so-called 'Age of Austerity'.[21]

At this moment in time, disabled people and the limited number of organisations under their control are like the rest of the country; caught in limbo having to deal with the aftermath of the Covid-19 pandemic which saw thousands of older and disabled people die needlessly in residential homes.[22] If this is not enough to contend with, people living in Britain remain unsure still of the full impact of Brexit and this has specific implications for disabled people. In addition, the contradictions and tensions within neoliberal capitalism has seen an increase in fascist and right-wing regimes across the globe. Since 2010, the British state has become increasingly authoritarian. Disabled people across the globe, as well as in Britain, are considering the implications of climate change and pending ecological disaster; many disabled people and activists feel invisible and marginalised within the narratives and dialogues surrounding planning for the future.[23]

TIME TO RE-DISCOVER DISABILITY PRAXIS

We must admit that many disabled activists have either lost sight of, or have never been introduced to, the Disabled People's Movement's disability politics' cornerstones. As a result, there are huge differences of opinion on what we seek to achieve and how best to resist our oppressors. Just at the time when people with impairments are living disabled lives in the age of austerity, there appears to be a lack of joined-up thinking at a strategic level and an absence of collective political leadership within our ranks. Without a doubt, a struggle is taking place, but are disabled people adequately equipped to defend ourselves from further onslaughts, or united enough to take disability politics into the mainstream arena? This is not to deny the importance of groups such as DPAC and others; however, we are entering a new political phase which suggests campaigning against austerity measures is presently little more than a form of firefighting. The type of campaigning currently taking place is part of a resistance movement, not an adequate basis upon which to re-build the type of politics required by disabled people in their struggle for social and political emancipation.

To be in a position to articulate the type of disability politics and praxis required, we must remind ourselves of how the Disabled People's Movement came into being and what established it as a 'social movement'. By using this backdrop, we will be in a better position to introduce and interrogate key concepts and arguments that have shaped disability politics along the way. There is an opinion among some activists that for too long, disabled people who aligned themselves with the Movement have avoided frank discussions of the differing political views on how to improve the lives of disabled people. These disagreements still exist, and their significance is beginning to surface again. This situation needs to be addressed if disabled people are going to defend themselves against the violent ideological attacks falling down upon their heads. These discussions will not be easy, but by being open and transparent, we will be able to see what unites and what divides us because others have used and abused our concepts. John Ping reported on a conference held in September 2012 where Jenny Morris 'warned that both Labour and coalition governments had used the language of the disability movement to "create policies that are actually creating significant disadvantages for us"'.[24] I have written a number of critiques of the late 1990s onwards and wrote in 2015:

Since the mid-1990s we have seen the development of Janus politics where disability charities, parts of the voluntary sector and certain disabled people's organisations have launched a new Disability Movement that speaks of rights on the one hand, whilst seeking to serve the neoliberal agenda on the other. The [National Disabilities Conference] is populated by individuals and organisations who want to foster the Big Society and buy a piece of the action as the services are hived off – it is an auction and disabled people's lives will be placed under the hammer.[25]

By 'Janus politics' I was referring to looking back to the concepts developed by the Disabled People's Movement, such as Independent Living, and transforming them by inserting *new meaning* to fit the market economy, for example, as was done with 'Personalisation'.[26] The arena of disability politics has gone through a series of makeovers since the 1980s. Whilst Jenny was right to warn of our language being subverted, there is also an urgent need to re-evaluate the ideas that emerged from the Disabled People's Movement and look upon them with fresh eyes. Many of our concepts need to be claimed back, some require re-positioning to serve a purpose in the twenty-first century, and there are perhaps ideas in need of re-discovery if the struggle for disabled people's emancipation is to continue and gain real momentum. Few disabled activists have seriously addressed the stinging criticism levelled at the Disabled People's Movement by one of its creators, Vic Finkelstein, who correctly predicted the divisions that would emerge as disabled politics moved away from its radical roots. In this book, I will highlight the shift away from the radical interpretation of disability.

At the moment, disabled people have their backs to the wall. Whatever lies ahead in the future years, one thing needs to be clearly established: the role of disability politics in disabled people's lives cannot be taken for granted and must be fought for against whatever forces seek to undermine them. There has not been a better time for disabled activists to take stock of the situation, to re-group behind core principles and aims, in order to build a strategy for furthering disabled people's emancipation. I hope this book can contribute to this task.

2

The First Cornerstone:
The Fundamental Principles
of Disability

IDENTIFYING THE FUNDAMENTAL PRINCIPLES OF DISABILITY

The growth of what has come to be known as the British Disabled People's Movement is covered to some extent in the following chapter, but here I want to indicate how its birth is viewed. Jane Campbell and Mike Oliver in their book, talk about the awareness created by the challenge to dominant ideology, the forging of new identities, the development of the social model of disability, and the activism connected with self-determination. They write:

> The origins of these fundamental changes, it seems to us, can be found in the 1960s with the coming of the 'age of influence', where disabled people began to organise around issues of income, employment, rights, and community living rather than institutional care. It continued in the 1970s with the passage of the Chronically Sick and Disabled Persons Act (1970) and the formation of the Union of Physically Impaired Against Segregation.[1]

Perhaps surprisingly, they fail to mention the founding of the Disablement Income Group (DIG) here, although they do speak about DIG later in their book. DIG was a British disability pressure group formed in 1965 in Godalming, Surrey. It is considered to be one of the first pan-impairment pressure groups in Britain, and was created to campaign for the introduction of a full disability income through the social security system for all disabled people.[2] Many of the early activists within the Disabled People's Movement cut their teeth within DIG, including Paul Hunt and myself. I tend to share Steven Dodd's view that while there is truth in the claim made by Jane Campbell and Mike Oliver that DIG was a 'false start', we should not discount its instructive experience for disabled people seeking to drive forward political change. Dodd refers to the fact that Vic Finkelstein, one of the key figures behind the formation of the Union of the Physically Impaired Against Segregation (UPIAS), said that UPIAS arose out of dissatisfaction with DIG, directing criticism at DIG and its failure 'to see disability broadly'.[3]

Tensions emerged within DIG, as activists like Paul Hunt articulated the view that disability is not a single issue. The major difference between those who went on to form UPIAS and others within DIG, was that they saw combating disability not as tackling a single issue, but addressing the full range of barriers and discrimination that disabled people encountered. Hunt's view that disabled people should have control over their own lives, and that disability is not a single issue, not only led to his dissatisfaction within DIG. Judy Hunt recalls that:

> The internal turmoil in DIG culminated in a policy conference in 1973 … This proved to be an important turning point. Among the various presentations two campaign approaches, put to the conference, offered very different strategies for solving poverty among disabled people.[4]

Peter Townsend and Paul Hunt were well-established DIG members, yet saw the road ahead very differently. Townsend took a traditional stance, which linked disabled people's experience of poverty with their functional incapacity. As a result, he saw the medical and welfare service professionals as the ones with the expert knowledge to decide levels of compensation on behalf of the State.[5]

In sharp contrast, Hunt represented disabled people who viewed poverty as linked to disablement, which resulted in the absence of independence brought about by a myriad of external causes. He saw disabled people themselves as the driving force for social change via self-determination, in the form of 'making the decisions about how to increase their opportunities for social participation.'[6]

This ideological and strategic division led Townsend to pursue his agenda by forming the Disability Alliance, and Hunt writing a series of letters calling for a new consumer group to be set up.[7] These letters indicated the direction of travel UPIAS was to take. There was a call for action to improve residential centres, homes and hospital units, and for ideas around what alternative forms of care could be developed to satisfy the needs of physically impaired people. Crucially, the letters enquired about what 'changes in society are required if severe disability is either to be eradicated or to become no bar to full social participation?'[8]

The letters were aimed primarily at disabled people who were themselves actual or potential recipients of institutional care, as Hunt and Finkelstein believed the recipients' ideas on the situation were more important than anyone else's, as they were rarely listened to by administrators, planners and politicians. This was the backdrop to the view that if 'severely handicapped people were able to get together to work out proposals for change, they could obtain national publicity and say whenever their future was being discussed.'[9]

Judy Hunt informs us that:

> From the outset, a strong lead was given to the discussions by two members in particular ... Hunt drew on his considerable breath of understanding gained from struggles for self-determination in institutions, his concept of disability as oppression and his involvement with the other contemporary disability campaigns. Finkelstein brought his experience of social movement politics from his engagement in the struggles against oppression.[10]

Crucial to our understanding of the roots of British disability politics is the need to see how this duo worked through praxis, bringing together ideas, reflection and action. We are told that both were well grounded in Marxism and socialist literature, which supplied them with the skills to be analytical in their approach towards general social issues. They were able to draw inspiration from each other and lead other members to think about disability in ways not considered before.[11]

UPIAS recruited from people who were physically impaired, and this was done initially through those who had read Hunt's letters, or via word of mouth. The first two years of setting up the organisation centred on debating the nature of disability, especially the significance of institutional living for understanding the unequal and differential treatment disabled people encountered. This debate was mainly conducted through internal circulars in order to ensure confidentiality and to allow members to feel able to speak openly. The debates were challenging and charged; therefore it was vital that participants felt supported and not subjected to possible intimidation. This did draw criticism from external forces and UPIAS was accused of being both exclusive and secretive; however, operating this way was viewed as vital and considered a success.[12]

In 1974, UPIAS was formally established and with a public profile it was able to reveal its policy statement. From its first paragraph, UPIAS sets out its focus:

> So despite the creation today of such an enormous capacity, which could help overcome disability, the way this capacity is misdirected means that many physically impaired people are still unnecessarily barred from full participation in society. We find ourselves isolated and excluded by such things as flights of steps, inadequate public and personal transport, unsuitable housing, rigid work routines in factories and offices, and a lack of up-to-date aids and equipment.

Disability was seen as something to overcome, the core issue being that many physically impaired people were (and still are) unnecessarily barred from full participation in society. The statement then proceeds to give examples of the causes for exclusion and marginalisation. The mainstay of disabled people's exclusion and marginalisation was seen in the first instance as arising from the provision of segregated services:

> The Union of the Physically Impaired believes that the reality of our position as an oppressed group can be seen most clearly in segregated residential institutions, the ultimate human scrap-heaps of this society … The cruelty, petty humiliation, and physical and mental deprivation suffered in residential institutions, where isolation and segregation have been carried to extremes, lays bare the essentially oppressive relations of this society with its physically impaired members.

On page five of their policy statement, UPIAS clearly outline their challenge to dominant ideologies and practice when they declare:

> We as a Union are not interested in descriptions of how awful it is to be disabled. What we are interested in, are ways of changing our conditions of life, and thus overcoming the disabilities which are imposed on top of our physical impairments by the way this society is organised to exclude us.[13]

While UPIAS was, and remained, a relatively small organisation of disabled people, it did seek to place these concerns onto the political agenda. This, of course, resulted in conflict and, in order to try to prevent this from getting out of hand, a meeting between UPIAS and the Disability Alliance was organised. It was from this meeting that the Fundamental Principles emerged.

This document has two aims: firstly, to tease out differences and similarities between the organisations. Secondly, it enabled UPIAS to present what subsequently became the social interpretation of disability. Initially, the Alliance said they agreed with the draft document; however, the transcript of the meeting is painful to read. History shows the Alliance was incapable of breaking with seeing dysfunctional bodies as the direct cause of social disadvantage and the role of professionals as being one of mitigating against this situation. UPIAS, on the other hand, wanted to see if it could push the Alliance to adopt an alternative perspective:

> Fundamental principles to which we are both in agreement: disability is a situation, caused by social conditions, which requires for its elimination, (a) that no one aspect such as incomes, mobility or institutions is treated in isolation, (b) that disabled people should, with the advice and help of others, assume control over their own lives, and (c) that professionals, experts and others who seek to help must be committed to promoting such control by disabled people.[14]

The fundamental principles UPIAS was seeking to establish was that disability ought to be viewed and analysed as a social, not a personal, phenomenon:

> Our own position on disability is quite clear, and is fully in line with the agreed principles. In our view, it is society which disables physically impaired people. Disability is something imposed on top of our impairments, by the way we are unnecessarily isolated and excluded from full participation in society. Disabled people are therefore an oppressed group in society.[15]

How people with physical impairments were excluded from or marginalised within mainstream social activities was the basis for their collective experience of social oppression. This was seen as both material and ideological. The shift in seeing disability as a social and not as a personal phenomenon is rooted in the significant reconfiguration of Amelia Harris' triad definition of disability.[16]

UPIAS, however, in the first edition of *Disability Challenge* sum up their social interpretation in this way:

First, we are members of a distinct group with our own particular physical characteristics (physical impairment) and second, that society singles this out for a special form of discrimination (disability). This perspective differs radically from the 'expert' medical or social scientific view, that disability arises out of the individual and his or her physical impairment. Our analysis leads us to declare that it is the way our society is organised that disables us.[17]

The notion that 'physical disability' is a special form of discrimination has been challenged in a number of ways. What we also witness is a tendency to view discrimination and oppression as being one in the same within the writing of UPIAS members. However, whilst it is difficult to separate discrimination and oppression because in many situations they may contain elements of both discrimination and oppression, I believe a distinction can be made:

> Discrimination is the treatment of a person specifically based upon their (perceived) membership of a certain group. It can, itself, be fairly innocuous and free from any prejudice, to being positive. For example, many types of 'affirmative action' involve positive discrimination … Oppression differs from discrimination in that oppression is always negative. It is also exercised by one more powerful group (class of people) over another, and is often long-lasting … .[18]

The relationship between discrimination and oppression is a constant theme running through my critique of disability politics and the arguments around developing a new praxis. What is key to understanding disabled people's social oppression and encountered forms of discrimination is to discover appropriate ways of addressing how specific societies respond to impairment-related issues and existing social relations. So, whilst it was Finkelstein and UPIAS who shaped the social interpretation of disability, it was Mike Oliver who assisted in taking this particular cornerstone to the next level of elaboration.

A HISTORICAL MATERIALIST APPROACH TOWARDS DISABILITY

There have always been people who, because of injury, disease or genetic makeup, have had bodies that are not fully functional. Research shows that the treatment of people with impairments has varied greatly down the ages and within different cultures; however, it was not until the development of the capitalist mode of production was there a systematic approach to classifying individuals into distinctive groups. Brendan Gleeson explains:

> ... an important critique has been developed of the root cause of disablement – the capitalist system. Disability in its current form is said to have emerged at the time of the industrial revolution, with the growth of the commodity labour market a key factor in the process of disablement ... [thus] the fundamental relationships of capitalist society are implicated in the social oppression of disabled people.[19]

In the third chapter of his book, *The Politics of Disablement*, Oliver writes:

> A framework derived from historical materialism does, at least, add to our understanding of what happened to disabled people with the coming of industrial society ... historical materialism is not just about placing social relationships within a historical setting. It also attempts to provide an evolutionary perspective on the whole of human history, and of particular relevance here are the transitions from feudal through capitalist to socialist society.[20]

There are very few historians or theorists who adhere to a historical materialist approach and, as Nirmala Erevelles informs us, the historical records tend to conform to the dominant modes of writing history.[21] Oliver singles out Finkelstein's three stages of the historical development of disability because 'he located his account within a materialist framework and developed an evolutionary model, broadly along the lines of the three stages of the historical materialist model mentioned above, though without using the same terminology.'[22]

It is the idea of the transformation of people with impairments into 'disabled people' which lies at the heart of the fundamental principles of disability.

CONCEPTS AND CONCERNS

A crucial issue for historical materialists like Oliver is that:

> In Marx's view, to understand the nature of human beings one must understand their relationship to the material environment and the historical nature of this relationship in creating and satisfying human needs.

However, as societies develop and become more complicated, the environment itself will become more complicated, and comprise more socio-cultural constraints.[23]

The ownership of the means of production, along with having systems to distribute, via an exchange, the products that are made, are viewed as the foundations of any society's economic base and subsequently, its superstructure. Hence, the baseline for historical materialism then is the role played by the means of production in sustaining human life.

Oliver refers to how Finkelstein considered the historical processes that have shaped the social construction of disability as a specific category in modern society from within a materialist framework.[24] In his work, Finkelstein employs the terms 'Phase One' and 'Phase Two' which are said to correspond to the periods of the transition from feudalism to capitalism and the established capitalist system itself. The third phase was viewed as the present struggle to transform society. The relationship between the economic base and the superstructure of a society is often debated and a crucial element of this debate has been an examination of the role of 'ideology'. Within Oliver's argument, the role of ideology plays a central part in shaping the 'solution', therefore, it is important to understand this concept and how it is employed.

How then should we view ideology? Through various structures, economic, political, social, and cultural, the groups holding power can exercise maximum control with minimum conflict by using ideology – sets of values, conceptions of the world, belief and symbol systems – to legitimate the current social order. At times, this can be coercive, but more often than not it seeks to be consensual. For many Marxists, ideology is connected to power and power relations, but as John Lye points out:

Power is not a unitary force or phenomenon, nor an exclusively 'political' phenomenon. Power and power relations are woven throughout all our practices and ideas – power is exercised in every relationship, group, and social practice, and it is not necessarily detrimental … [However,] one must not forget that social order relies, in varying degrees, but ultimately, on the ability of one person or group to coerce another person or group, and that the basis of Law, however rationalized, is the authorized use of force.[25]

Power relations, not just at an obvious political level, but also within social and cultural contexts, play a major role in shaping disabled people's lives. The creation of dependency and the devaluing of their lifestyles bring together ideological and material conditions which result in power being exercised against them. Thus 'care' [sic] is often a double-edged sword, as it can empower and disempower at the same time.

Oliver turns to Gramsci whom he sees as providing a 'specific link' between social structures and ideologies through the distinction he makes between ideology which is viewed as 'organic' and subsequent 'arbitrary' ideologies.[26] Oliver views the concept of hegemony as developed by Gramsci as a means of addressing the issues of power and dominant ideologies; he refers to it as becoming more all-embracing than ideology because 'It is the sheer taken-for-grantedness of hegemony that yields its full affects – the "naturalness" of a way of thinking about social, economic, political and ethical issues.'[27]

How the body is viewed, the medicalisation of it, and the social consequences that flow from the 'common-sense' assumptions made about disabled people's social worth and lifestyles assist to maintain capitalist society's hegemonic power. Disability politics must involve praxis capable of disturbing, disrupting and ultimately destroying it.

Oliver puts forward the argument that 'disability as a category can only be understood within a framework ... which suggests that it is culturally produced and socially structured.'[28]

In other words, at different historical moments, people with a variety of different impairments have been subjected to specific forms of social restriction. The significance of this point cannot be stressed enough as the implications are far-reaching. To begin with, there is no universal definition or 'view' of what 'disability' is down the ages. As a consequence, it can be argued, it is not possible to generalise the experiences of people with impairments.

Given this, a focus must be placed on the historically specific nature of particular economic factors and social structures, alongside a consideration of which groups of people with impairments were considered 'different' and why. There are a number of problems which need to be acknowledged. Within mainstream academic circles, the issue of disability is at best ignored as a subject; therefore, as Oliver points out: 'most anthropologists have internalised the personal tragedy theory ... and have therefore seen disability as a non-problematic category.'[29] It is not simply a problem of how disability is or is not defined; to support the argument that views of disability are historically specific and socially constructed as well as created, there is a need to produce empirical evidence.

A major difficulty for Oliver, and indeed anyone wishing to take issue with him regarding disability as culturally produced and socially structured, is the fact that there is inadequate empirical evidence to enable a comparative study of capitalist development in a variety of countries. However, there remains an issue with regard to how to view disability from a historical perspective. Some sociologists argue that disability can only be properly understood as a social construction.[30] However, as Oliver points out, seeing disability as a specific social construct is not enough; one must make an examination of the ideological underpinnings and the material conditions which brought them into play.

The central focus of the historical materialist approach as a contribution to a 'social theory of disability' is a radical critique – a structured account – of how the economic and social structures of capitalist society have led to people-with-impairments' exclusion from, and marginalisation within, mainstream capitalist society. These processes have been made possible by dominant ideologies and socio-political practices which not only socially construct 'disability as a personal tragedy', but at the same time create the material conditions that transform people with impairments into 'disabled' people. Disability, therefore, becomes a 'product' of capitalism.

The importance of Erevelles' work is that she adds new depth to our discussion by pointing out:

> ...while historical materialism focuses on the concrete reality of labor in its changing historical context that constitutes the materiality of human existence, the Marxist method of the dialectic ... enables us to examine the 'process' by which our social reality is constructed at any historical moment as well as the 'social relations' that go to constitute this social reality.[31]

The significance of this, she argues, is that by adopting a historical materialist approach: 'we can (re)insert the category of disability into social history and mark its uneven development – the shifts, the changes, and the movements – the dialectic – that has accompanied the historic construction of disability within historically specific economic structures ... '.[32]

What we need to ask is: have the historical materialists like Oliver and Finkelstein done enough to interrogate these 'shifts, changes, and movements'? In their defence, little assistance has been forthcoming from British historians because 'The positivistic adherence to the visible and immediately verifiable "facts" of the past was reinforced by an almost unquestionable acceptance of the basic tenets of nineteenth-century liberalism.'[33]

If we accept that history is more than 'facts' about significant individuals or groups at a precise moment in time, it can be argued there remains a need to confront the lack of clarity around the notion of 'the history of disability'. Many academics have focused on specific impairment groups, for example, Ryan and Thomas, Szasz, and Scull.[34] However, all of these accounts have been subjected to criticism on the basis of flawed empirical evidence, or for over-generalising people's experiences.

For both Finkelstein and Oliver, the Industrial Revolution appears to be the watershed for changing disabled people's material and social conditions. A number of historians would, however, question the wisdom of such an assertion. A. L. Beier, for example, writes:

> Thus England began the Tudor and ended the Stuart age with a great army of needy persons, possibly the majority of the country's inhabitants. Who were the poor? Statutes distinguished the disabled and the able-bodied, but it was more complicated than that. Instead we may divide them into the settled and the vagrant poor, contrasting groups receiving different treatment.[35]

Finkelstein, by contrast, locates the separation of 'the disabled' poor and the 'able-bodied' poor [sic] as being post-Industrial Revolution. Carol Thomas acknowledges the significance of the transition from feudalism to capitalism in terms of offering 'fertile ground for thinking about the creation of classes of people, including "the feebleminded", cripples, "in-valids", deemed redundant and dependent on the grounds of their incapacity to present themselves as wage labourers.'[36]

Nevertheless, she goes on to say that whilst the historical materialist approach to explaining the root cause of social exclusion that constitutes disability has potential, it still requires considerable development due to the fact that 'The historical analysis itself requires verification in terms of empirical evidence: what did people with impairments "do" in pre-capitalist and pre-industrial communities, what were their social roles and status?'[37]

The lack of concrete empirical evidence does concern people sympathetic to the arguments put forward by historical materialists, but do these historical lapses really matter if it cannot be shown that they weaken the theoretical methodology being employed? Having such evidence would strengthen the argument; however, this alone does not challenge the basic assumptions made.

Oliver set himself the task, in sociological terms, of explaining how dominant ideologies and subsequent social practices emerged within the nineteenth century to present a 'grand theory' of disability, which categorised it as an 'individual, personal tragedy'. The basis of his argument is that all phenomena, including social categories, 'are produced by the economic and social forces of capitalism itself'.[38] However, Oliver does not view the way 'disability' is defined or culturally produced as solely relating to a specific mode of production. Importance is also given to core values within a given society, the weight of the relationship between the two – mode of production and core values – having been debated as far back as Marx and Weber.

Using existing 'historical accounts', Oliver speaks of the changing landscape; the transformation from rural to urban, and from land worker to individual wage labourer. He cites Morris as placing all kinds of people with impairments at the bottom of the labour market.[39] He states social perceptions of various impairments are not informed by the mode of thought alone, but needs to include consideration of the mode of production and social relations. Whilst racism and disability are very different social phenomena and constructs, the work of Stuart Hall on racism offers an important insight into the manner in which previous cultural and ideological traces can be deposited in the present form.[40] This perspective is recognised by Oliver, but to the extent that this is addressed adequately in terms of his explanation of how peripheral ideologies were developed needs some consideration.

Oliver sees the hegemony that defines disability in capitalist society as being 'constituted by the organic ideology of individualism, the arbitrary ideologies of medicalisation underpinning medical intervention and personal tragedy theory underpinning social policy'.[41]

Goodley refers to the social model as anti-hegemonic because it challenges the dominant ideas associated with disability. For Oliver, the central plank of his argument is that social relations under capitalism are governed by the necessity of individuals to sell their labour, thus becoming a commodity. In the process, the collectivist methods of working and communal life were broken down and replaced. How to manage the arrival of the new 'individual' and corresponding lifestyles was deemed problematic within the capitalist free market, and at the same time led to new ways of both 'seeing' and 'constructing' the problems of order and control. Oliver draws upon the work of Foucault to describe how the roles of the institution and, subsequently, medical professions created the ideological underpinning of how individuals who were 'unable to sell their labour' were both seen and treated. Thus 'This process of exclusion was facilitated by focusing on the body, of the individual, and populations, and with the rise of capitalism, the main group who came to focus their gaze on the body, was the medical profession.'*[42]

This of course describes the 'medical gaze' as Foucault calls it. Oliver's usage of Foucault is extremely selective and as a result, other types of 'gaze' are subsequently ignored. It also leaves him open to criticism, for example, as Hughes argues, 'Yet, despite the considerable emancipatory value in this mode of explanation, impairment [the body] is left out of its frame of reference and has no part to play in the constitution of [disability as] oppression.'**[43]

Meanwhile, McElroy writes, 'But the medical gaze of the eighteenth century differed from that of the twentieth century. Therefore, the eighteenth-century human body was different from the twentieth-century one because the body is defined by the ruling episteme.'[44]

It is not just the shift in the medical gaze we need to consider. Equally as important is an understanding of the social and ideological conditions which shaped the nineteenth century, and how people with impairments came to be viewed not only through the medical profession's eyes. Elsewhere I argue:

> The harsh realities it produced created economic and social upheavals which brought about, in turn, moral panics around the fear of illness, disease and depravity ... [Hence,] contours around what was considered 'normal' were drawn and those groups thought to be polluting society ... were withdrawn from the public gaze.[45]

Lennard Davis suggests that the word 'normal' only entered the English language around 1840.[46] The notion of 'normality' only emerged during the nineteenth century and was at first linked to various forms of standardisation; however, within Victorian times, it took on a new 'morality' which shifted it onto the ideological terrain where it met favour with social Dar-

---

* Michel Foucault is perhaps best known as a theorist of power. Foucault analysed several different types of power, including sovereign power, disciplinary power and biopower. Within Disability Studies, S. Tremain, ed., *Foucault and the Government of Disability* (Ann Arbor: University of Michigan Press, 2005), brings together interdisciplinary, international work on disability from a variety of theorists who use Foucauldian approaches.

** To a certain extent, this claim by Hughes is addressed in the second part of this book.

winists and the eugenics movement.* Moore outlines another influence: 'In the late 19th and early 20th centuries, concern was expressed at the degeneration of the national or "racial" stock … a "moral panic" sprang in large from apprehension felt by middle class people on encountering teeming inner city populations … .'[47]

In my early work, I suggested people with impairments were not necessary the focus of attention of the 'public gaze' but were caught up in a generalised moral panic and the creation of the eugenics movement.[48] The rise of large-scale charities to deal with these 'social problems' and the growth of the eugenics movement were also contributory factors.[49]

Oliver's argument is often criticised for the lack of consideration given to the diverse cultural experiences of people with impairments from a historical perspective. An example of this is the nineteenth-century pathologising of homosexuality,[50] the social and medical implications being that it was viewed as both a form of deviance and a medical issue, thus placing it outside of 'normality'. Where my work also differs from Oliver is that I see the various wars at the end of the nineteenth century and beginning of the twentieth as crucial factors in giving the dominant ideologies associated with disability their final hegemonic push through medical practices. Oliver refers to Gramsci to explain how these ideologies became 'common sense', thus influencing social policy and welfare care. My argument is that this took place primarily after the First World War, due to advances in medical technology and shifting social responsibility onto the individual with an emphasis on regaining 'normality'. The State's response towards ex-servicemen has been questioned.[51]

Oliver's argument does raise an interesting question in relation to UPIAS's definition of disability. It could be argued that he is actually suggesting that it is precisely how people with impairments are 'taken into account' which ultimately leads them to be *not* being taken into account, thus marginalising them within and excluding them from mainstream social activities. This is the same argument I outlined earlier, and it is more than a semantic difference, as it relates to the nature of disabled people's social oppression itself.[52]

There appears to be little evidence to undermine the argument that capitalist economic and social relations significantly altered the positioning of people with impairments within society. Whether Oliver's argument is considered valid or not depends upon the extent to which one accepts the view

---

* Normal in the sense of 'ordinary' became common in English from about 1840, the Oxford English Dictionary noted in 1907.

that the nineteenth century cemented the disabling nature of the capitalist mode of production in comparison with the feudalist one, the degree to which the 'personal tragedy' approach gained hegemony and how, in turn, these factors transformed the 'helpless' idiot or cripple into the 'disabled' individual. The nineteenth century certainly provided the basis for how disabled people were hitherto seen and treated. Historical research suggests perhaps that the final push for ideological hegemony and changes in welfare coincide within the early twentieth century.

THE SOCIAL MODEL OF DISABILITY

When teaching, Mike Oliver sought a way of conveying the social interpretation of disability as a model, in the first instance, to his students. His aim was to convey the fact that too frequently the target for professional intervention and practice was the perceived individual's 'problems' stemming from their functional limitations or psychological losses.

What is often underplayed is the fact that he developed two models which would be used in a binary way to illustrate the need to re-situate the 'problem' of disability. He employed the individual model to explain the basis of 'the personal tragedy theory of disability', which portrays disability as some terrible chance event which occurs at random to unfortunate individuals. Oliver used the elaboration of the social model to provide a way of applying the idea that it was society and not people with impairments that should be the focus of problem solving – that is, changing social relations and the environment rather than change people or shoehorn them into the status quo.[53]

From the classroom into the Disabled People's Movement, the development and articulation of the social model of disability was undertaken by disabled people who were ready to reject the dominant explanation of disability and instead, not to deny the problem of disability but locate it squarely within society. Through the design and delivery of disability equality training, it was argued that it is not individual limitations, of whatever kind, which are the cause of the problem but

> ... society's failure to provide appropriate services and adequately ensure the needs of disabled people are fully taken into account in its social organisation. Further, the consequences of this failure does not simply and randomly fall on individuals but systematically upon disabled people as a group who experience this failure as discrimination institutionalised throughout society.[54]

To what extent this idea is understood by disabled and nondisabled people alike is open to question. Often what is ignored is that the social model has as its sole focus the unnecessary social restrictions imposed on top of impairment reality. The nature of this treatment viewed as disabling barriers is experienced in a myriad of ways. People with physical impairments and mental health service-users, for example, can encounter very different disabling barriers due to how, historically, society has determined the social relations of, and with, the membership of these groups. This includes the use of pejorative labels. At a micro level of society, disabling barriers can be viewed as the failure to introduce inclusive practice but this fails to tell the whole story. It is necessary to recognise that at a macro level, disablement gave rise to disablism which exists within the structures, systems, values and cultures of society and takes on the character of institutional discrimination – for example, the labour market, legal system, government policy, etc.

The emphasis within all social approaches to disability is simple: look at ways of changing the social organisation of society in order to accommodate people with impairments. It must be acknowledged that social models, not just Oliver's, have been extended to include all people who identify as disabled people. Oliver's three-fold criteria for identifying as a disabled person and the diversity within the encountered oppression was outlined earlier.[55]

There are now an array of 'interpretations' of the social oppression approach to disability ranging from reformist to revolutionary. Gleeson, however, argues:

> The 'materialist' or 'radical' social model understands disability to be a logical outcome of the capitalist mode of production … This version of the social model insists that 'the fundamental relationships of capitalist society are implicated in the social oppression of disabled people'. Logically, 'the elimination of disablement … requires a radical transformation, rather than a reform of capitalism.[56]

Whilst agreeing with Gleeson that this is the logic of the radical social model, I believe, as I will argue in a later chapter, this is not the version ultimately adopted by the British Disabled People's Movement. The crucial point is that the materialist social approach does focus upon the consequences of the failure to address how to accommodate people with impairments. Oliver, as we saw, states their experience is of systematic discrimination which has been institutionalised throughout society.[57] There is a specific focus within this radical social approach towards disability: the addressing of the imposed social restrictions which emerge from the existing structures, systems, cultures, attitudes and practices. The imposition stems from the failure to factor disabled people into the social organisation of society; however, for society to undertake such a task, it would require a transformation of social relations and the adoption of a completely different way of approaching the issue of impairment. It is for this reason I share Paul Abberley's criticism that neither UPIAS nor Oliver adequately drilled down far enough into the nature of disabled people's oppression. The absence of a social model of impairment has had, in my opinion, a profound impact upon disability politics, because its absence has provided areas of ambiguity over the relations between impairment realities and encountered social environments.

Having bodies and minds that are judged to be non-conforming, the nature of impairment 'production', and the material realities associated, need to be factored into our understanding of disabled people's experience of social oppression. The social interpretation and model of disability both correctly break the causal link between impairment and disadvantage, but I support the view that the relational nature of the social interpretation of disability has not been theorised adequately.[58]

Despite the flaws of some of the ideas and practice that has flowed from the fundamental principles of disability, they did establish the first cornerstone of disability politics which has influenced scholars, activists and ordinary disabled people alike. Over the years, countless numbers of disabled people have recalled how their first encounter with either the social interpretation or social model of disability transformed their lives. For some, this was a lightbulb moment, whereas for others, it confirmed those gut feelings they had held in silence for years.

By assisting disabled people to free themselves from accepting the yoke of oppression, these ideas lay the foundations not only for individual emancipation, but a collective one. The transformation of ideas around the nature of disablement and its impact upon the lives of oppressed people, lay the seeds for a new politics, a new social movement and a collective identity based upon solidarity and the belief that a better future was possible.

3

The Second Cornerstone:
The Self-organisation of
Disabled People

The task of constructing a socio-political challenge to what constitutes disability via a new set of ideas laid the headstone cornerstone of disability politics and initiated disabled people's emancipation struggle. To see how the self-organisation of disabled people became the second cornerstone, it is important to explore the rationale behind the development of disabled people's organisations, including contradictions and tensions that arose as disabled people sought to self-organise after the Second World War. This chapter will conclude with a discussion on the role of disabled people's organisations in twenty-first century disability politics.

HISTORICAL BACKGROUND

In November 2010, the Greater Manchester Coalition of Disabled People (GMCDP) produced a booklet, *A Brief History Of Disabled People's Self-Organisation*, in which they wrote:

> Disabled people have been organising since the late 19th century, when the British Deaf Association and National League of the Blind were the first two recorded organisations 'of' disabled people to form.
>
> 'Of' means a group or organisation that is run and controlled by disabled people. This is different to organisations 'for' disabled people, which are run by non-disabled people to 'provide for' disabled people.[1]

What do we know about these organisations?

The British Deaf Association (BDA) was formed in Leeds as The British Deaf and Dumb Association (BDDA) on 24 July 1890. It followed six months on from the organising of the 'National Conference of Adult Deaf and Dumb Missions and Associations' by four men including the BDA's founder, Francis Maginn. The conference's purpose was to consider the formation of a national society to 'elevate the education and social status of the Deaf and Dumb in the United Kingdom'. It was also a belated response to an international congress held in Milan ten years earlier which passed a resolution banning the use of sign languages throughout the world.[2]

There is an ongoing debate as to what the relationship is between Deaf and disabled people because many within the Deaf community reject the idea that they are impaired or can be classed as 'disabled', despite being judged as such within the British legal system.[3] I have included the BDA in this section as I see the oppression and discriminatory Deaf people face as having common ground with disabled people.[4]

The other organisation mentioned in the GMCDP booklet was the National League of the Blind (NLB). Towards the end of the nineteenth century, increasing numbers of blind people were joining the labour force. As a result of exploitation, within both private industry and in the charity sector, a group formed a trade union specifically for blind workers – the National League of the Blind (NLB). The League affiliated to the TUC in 1902, and to the Labour Party in 1909. The TUC informs us:

> In 1912, blind workers went on strike in Bristol, staying out for six months … In 1920, a Labour MP Ben Tillett introduced a Private Member's Bill, entitled 'The Blind (Education, Employment and Maintenance) Bill'. His aim was to raise awareness of the demands of blind workers. Although few MPs opposed it, the government wouldn't offer its support, instead promising to introduce their own bill.[5]

History was to repeat itself in the 1990s.[6] In the spring of 1920, the League organised a march to London from three cities to press their demands and build public awareness of their campaign. This culminated in a mass meeting at Trafalgar Square. Their central slogan was 'We demand justice not charity.' The TUC reported:

> When the march arrived in London, the League's leaders had to wait five days before being permitted to meet with Prime Minister Lloyd George. And while the Blind Act did pass into law in September 1920, it wasn't as far-reaching as the League had hoped. But for the first time, the particular needs of blind people were recognised in law … While it's often forgotten today, the 1920 march was the first of its kind and provided the inspira-

tion for many other similar efforts – most famously the Jarrow March of 1936.[7]

In 1968, the League expanded to become the 'National League of the Blind and Disabled', which later merged with the Iron and Steel Trades Confederation to become part of the union, Community.

No matter which period of history one is interested in, it is difficult to unearth documentary evidence about disabled people's self-organisation within mainstream accounts. Searches suggest that many local self-help groups did exist between the 1880s and 1960s; however, one particular group stood out as it was formed by former servicemen. The existence of the 'Disabled' Society was short-lived, but it is nonetheless of interest in relation to understanding disabled people's emancipation struggle. I discovered this limited information on its history:

> Poppies went on sale on the first ever Poppy Day, which was the eleventh of November 1921. Major George Howson served on the Western Front in the Great War. After the war ended, Howson founded the Disabled Society and, with a grant of £2000 from the Unity Relief Fund, set up a small poppy factory in London with five ex-servicemen. The Disabled Society and its poppy making factory, became part of the British Legion.[8]

The Disabled Society's first president, Arthur Stanley, had an interesting life. Son of the 16th Earl of Derby, he entered the diplomatic service before becoming private secretary to Mr Balfour (Britain's Prime Minister 1902–05). Stanley entered Parliament in 1898, but in 1918 he resigned to devote all his time working with the sick and wounded from the War. As president of the Disabled Society, he wrote a letter to *The Times* which appeared on 23 May 1924, in which he called for support for a Bill going through Parliament that would compel employers to take a certain percentage of disabled ex-servicemen as employees. Stanley spoke about 'reserved occupations', such as lift attendants and other jobs considered suitable for men with only one arm. Why did the Disabled Society disappear? General Haig, due to fears arising from the Russian Revolution, worked with Lister of the Federation of Discharged and Demobilised Sailors and Soldiers to bring together the amalgamation of four associations to become part of the British Legion.[9] This was off the back of the Bolsheviks' effective mobilisation of disabled ex-servicemen.

Members of the Disabled Society objected to the 'useless cripple' [sic] label; however, they found themselves caught up in narratives around disability being viewed as 'a personal tragedy'. This in turn was not challenged until after the Second World War. Judy Hunt in her book *No Limits* outlines a radical history of the British Disabled People's Movement from a social interpretative analysis.[10] Each chapter builds up a picture of how disablement developed and the eventual birth of a movement to counteract its impact. She speaks of the post-Second World War period where there was growing discontent with unnecessary hospitalisation, authoritarian regimes within segregated residential homes and workshops, and frustration with other exclusionary practices. What developed were single-issue campaigns around housing, transport, access and finance. These campaigns had corresponding organisations such as the Invalid Tricycle Association (ITA), which became the Disabled Drivers Association (DDA), the Joint Committee on Mobility for the Disabled (JCMD), and the Disablement Income Group (DIG). In 1966, Hunt's partner Paul edited a book of essays by disabled individuals which illuminated their lives.[11] This is taken from the National Disability Arts Collection and Archive: 'Through his experiences at Le Court, Paul began to reflect upon important questions relating to the position of disabled people within society; the oppression they faced, the barriers they encountered, and the rights they should have to exact control over their own lives.'[12] A significant point Judy makes is that

... it can be seen how the campaigns of the 1960s were beginning to link up. Within institutions, important questions had been raised about the nature and provision of care services and about the rights of disabled people to some self-determination. Within the community, pressure had mounted to improve disabled mobility and access to public facilities and for all adults to have some income support in their own right.[13]

The self-organisation of disabled people in Britain cannot, however, be viewed in isolation from the growth of an international movement. In *The Last Civil Rights Movement*, Diane Driedger wrote:

Even in places where some groups of disabled people organized relatively early, such as in Sweden in the late nineteenth century, other oppressed groups have organized before them. As of the 1980s, disabled people all over the world have taken up the struggle for equality and participation on an equal footing with other citizens.[14]

There are many reasons why disabled people were late to embark on a struggle for human rights, but the primary reasons are the nature of their oppression and the systematic ways in which they have been excluded from, or marginalised within, society. It is important however not to confuse the emancipation struggle (incorporating fighting for civil and human rights) of the late 1960s onwards, with the earlier activities of Deaf and disabled people to self-organise in order to protect their interests. Driedger explains:

> Disabled people have come to a realization that their societies were built without their input and participation. One of the results of this recognition was a gathering … in 1981 to form Disabled Peoples' International (DPI). DPI's mandate is to be the voice of disabled people and it believes that disabled people should be integrated into society and participate with the same rights as everyone else.[15]

The emerging Disabled People's Movement in Britain and worldwide needs to be situated within the context of a growing political consciousness. The 1960s and '70s saw an upsurge of radicalism with the revitalising of the women's movement, and the emergence of other movements such as those for Civil Rights, against the war in Vietnam, and the Gay and Lesbian Movement, all of which provided examples for how disabled people could self-organise. Many young disabled people and ex-servicemen in Britain were influenced by these events and started to question their location within society. What was, and remains, disabled people's shared interest? Many would focus on two things: challenging how society sees disability and treats disabled people, and seeking to overthrow the conditions whereby disabled people find themselves excluded from, or marginalised within, mainstream society. Groups of disabled people in the 1960s began to understand that only by coming together would they be in a position to identify and promote their collective interests. For many disabled people across the world, their struggle was focused on achieving social improvement, not simply about fighting for civil and human rights. To achieve these things required the second cornerstone of disability politics: the self-organisation of disabled people.

The social restrictions encountered by disabled people have played a major role in holding them back from developing a political consciousness and therefore mounting an emancipation struggle. These oppressive conditions have existed throughout the history of disabled people's social oppression. Since the nineteenth century, the label 'the disabled' [*sic*] has been employed not to signify a social group of people, but instead to describe individuals deemed as 'Other' and therefore diminished in worth and status. The self-organisation of disabled people must be viewed against this backdrop.[16]

THE ROLE OF DISABLED PEOPLE'S ORGANISATIONS (DPOS)

The majority of self-organised groups are referred to as DPOs; however, in Britain these should not be confused with the user-led organisations (ULOs) initiated by New Labour in their *Improving Life Chances of Disabled People* report, which recommended that by 2010 there should be a ULO in each locality (defined as a local authority) and modelled on a Centre for Independent Living.[17]

To explore the role of DPOs, we can look to a discussion paper written by Henry Enns who helped found the Disabled People's International (DPI) and in the 1990s served as its executive director. In 'The Role of Organizations of Disabled People: A Disabled Peoples' International Discussion Paper', it is suggested that the central unifying feature of DPOs is their underlying philosophy which promotes 'self-representation', and their core orientation towards the protection and promotion of 'rights'.[18]

At the heart of this philosophy is the belief that if disabled people unite in broad organisations, this provides a stronger voice for change compared to operating via separate impairment-specific groups. The paper breaks down the role of an organisation into various functions. Primarily, self-representation, in an organisational sense, is viewed as creating 'a voice of our own', sending out the key message that DPOs promoted self-determination. DPI's motto 'VOX NOSTRA' means 'Our Voice'. Enns writes, 'In the words of Ed Roberts, a disabled American, "… when others speak for you, you lose."'[19] As a consequence, the slogan, 'Nothing About Us, Without Us', was adopted because the young movement believed disabled people knew best their own needs and aspirations. At both international and national levels, DPOs were formed to represent the interests of disabled people 'to governments, service providers, the United Nations and the public'.[20]

In both a material and an ideological sense, DPOs were asserting a direct challenge to the status quo whereby disabled people were redefining 'themselves as citizens with rights, not as patients and clients of professionals, nor as beggars asking for hand-outs'.[21]

DPOs tend to share the common understanding that barriers to participation exist for disabled people and their role is to address them by identifying disabled people's needs and aspirations developed via grassroots communities. A telling point Enns makes is that 'The disabled people who start such organisations are usually educated and are better off financially than the majority of disabled persons in their countries.'[22]

Class position, financial status and lived experience are real issues for any social movement to negotiate; however, they have a particular purchase when it comes to understanding disabled people's oppression. In his 1996 book, *Understanding Disability*, Oliver acknowledges Gramsci's distinction between structural/positional and organic intellectuals as useful, as it is difficult to represent, identify needs, or develop praxis if there is no connection with the people directly experiencing oppression. Often tensions exist between intellectuals who create theory and political activists who enact social change. These can be mediated when praxis involves theorising from the experience of those who are oppressed rather than marginal intellectuals. Organic intellectuals are individuals who can connect their ideas with the collective experiences of social movements.[23] Oliver explains, 'social movements have less to fear from organic intellectuals than they do from positional ones. Organic intellectuals are less likely to distort the collective experience of oppression and are less likely to sell out ... '.[24]

This, as I have indicated, relates to disability praxis, because self-organisation is concerned with furthering collective interests. Hence, disability praxis is about providing the means whereby disabled people can identify their own needs and how to meet them. Enns rightly states that Paulo Freire explains in *Pedagogy of the Oppressed*:

> ... those who recognize, or begin to recognize themselves as oppressed must be among the developers of the pedagogy. No pedagogy that is truly liberating can remain distant from the oppressed by treating them as unfortunates and by presenting for their emulation models from among the oppressors. The oppressed must be their own example in the struggle for their redemption.[25]

Enns' discussion paper suggests three ways in which this can be accomplished – firstly, by promoting the organising of local groups affiliated to national bodies. Members were urged 'not only to build the infrastructures of their organisations, but [also] to solicit and represent the views of all disabled people in a country'.[26] The British Council of Organisations of Disabled People had this infrastructure and approach. Secondly, DPI encouraged open forums. The idea was for disabled people's organisations to hold open forums to discuss issues of concern to disabled persons. Whilst

I do not recall many open forums being organised by BCODP, some national conferences, however, were held.*

The third way of furthering the interests of disabled people was identified as being through democratic representation. This involves electing people to speak on behalf of the collective interest of the organisation, and reporting back to the group ensures accountability. Thus a major role of international, national and local DPOs is to make representations to various bodies, such as United Nations bodies, governments and service-providers. In this way, organisations of disabled people can fulfil their role as a vehicle to represent the needs of disabled people to decision-makers and service-providers at local, national and international levels.

Having DPOs that can exercise a collective voice is extremely important because without such a mechanism, decision-makers argue that it is difficult to know which group to give priority to in the consultation process. Later in the book, I will raise the issue of co-production as being a more progressive mechanism for self-determination and democratic representation. Enns states that across the globe, 'Too often priorities are set in social services that have little to do with the actual needs of disabled people. It, thus, is good economic and policy planning to include disabled persons in the planning process because they are the ones that best know the needs of disabled people.'[27]

DPOs are often associated with evaluating and monitoring services as well. In Britain, all the features of developing and running a disabled people's organisation have existed; however, there is another crucial role I believe ought to be present. Organisations of disabled people will fail, and did fail, where they neglected developing disabled people's skills in negotiation processes, organisational management, and other activities such as proposal-writing and public speaking. The most successful organisations are those who give disabled people the opportunity to be volunteer committee members or salaried employees.

Since the 1980s, I have viewed organisations of disabled people, at all levels, as vehicles for social change. As someone instrumental in setting up and running the Birmingham Disability Rights Group, I recognised that at its heart was the development of mutual support and solidarity. I therefore endorse what Enns wrote: 'Disabled people who belong to these groups find that they have a common purpose, that of promoting their right to live

---

* In October 1986, the British Council of Organisations of Disabled People held a weekend conference on Centres for Integrated/Independent Living.

as citizens in society. This common purpose engenders feelings of mutual support and solidarity in a common cause.'[28]

This is why I see self-organisation as the second cornerstone of disability politics. Through creating DPOs, internationally and in Britain, disabled people were able to not only forge a new collective socio-political identity, but at the same time establish the grounds for common purpose. In their book, *Disability Politics*, Oliver and Campbell cite Ann MacFarlane: 'Well I do see the BCODP as the focus and I think the BCODP's good points are that it's certainly got the debate going when there was no debate before. It's brought many disabled people together and given them a sense of identity and a sense of belonging, however tenuous that is.'[29]

Across the globe, DPOs have initiated self-help projects aimed at integrating disabled people into the mainstream of society. Enns' discussion paper refers to two main areas where self-help projects have been initiated: independent living and employment.[30] In Britain, there was a government-funded project, the National Disability Information Project, which clearly illustrated how DPOs provided the opportunity for disabled people to share ideas and information, but at the same time it revealed the huge barriers encountered.[31] A crucial function identified by Enns is how DPOs promoted public awareness. He wrote, 'This awareness is promoted through many of the activities of disabled people's organisations: lobbying government, monitoring service agencies, publishing a newsletter, speaking in the national media, conferences, etc.'[32]

If these can be identified as the key aspects of the self-organisation of disabled people, how should they be viewed? Did the 1980s witness the emergence of new social movements led by disabled people? The debate as to whether or not the Disabled People's Movement was a social movement should not detract from recognising the self-organisation of disabled people as the second cornerstone of disability politics. By considering the Disabled People's Movement as a social movement provides insights into the way it both developed and declined. These insights may also assist disabled people to avoid or address similar mistakes in the future.

THE DISABLED PEOPLE'S MOVEMENT AS A SOCIAL MOVEMENT

A commonly held view is that social movements display four main distinctive features: the collective character of the political action; a purpose or an issue whose importance and need for support are recognised and shared by those involved in the action; an opponent against which the action is directed

and the claim is made, and the contentious interaction with political institutions.[33] Tom Shakespeare notes that none of the major social movement
theorists include disability politics in their thinking.[34] I believe the British
Disabled People's Movement had the characteristics of a social movement,
but the crucial issue to be appraised is to what extent the need for disabled
people to self-organise was catered for by disabled people's organisations
and the Movement generally.

A detailed description of a social movement has been adapted from definitions by Batliwala[35] by BRIDGE, UK: Institute of Development Studies,
who describe them as:

1. Pursuit of a common political agenda or 'common cause'
2. Has a visible constituency or membership base
3. Involves members collectivised in either formal or informal
   organisations
4. Engages in collective actions and activities in pursuit of the
   movement's political goals
5. Uses a variety of actions and strategies
6. Engages clear internal or external targets in the change process
7. Retains some continuity over time.[36]

This raises the issue of 'collective power' within disability politics.

Batliwala explains how the processes that build the collective power
around a change agenda enables oppressed groups 'to access the full body of
human rights, challenge the distribution of wealth and control of resources,
challenge dominant ideologies, and transform social power relations in their
favour'.[37]

Oliver and Barnes suggest the British movement did engage in challenges
of this nature; however, towards the end of a section on social movements in
their book, they write:

> Overall, the disabled people's movement has utilized both radical and
> conventional politics. The balance between the two has varied historically
> … Of course, there is no 'royal road' to 'independent living' or 'empow-
> erment', and no user's manual, overarching set of political tactics or
> universally applicable form of self-organisation; nor can there be.[38]

Disability politics cannot be totally 'universal' in their nature because they
must relate to material conditions and situations. Differing factors inter-

play with each other and articulating perceived 'shared agendas' can prove problematic. There are tensions between the way Western disabled activists engage in political struggles and those from other parts of the globe. One of the fundamental issues that must be discussed is the extent to which disability politics operates from an anti-capitalist stance. Alison Sheldon wrote, 'It is acknowledged that disability is very much a development issue shared by north and south ... However, an idealist focus on cultural differences separates disabled people one from another, suggesting that we are *not* one people, and are *not* involved in the same struggle.'[39]

Whilst Oliver and Barnes are correct to say there is 'considerable variation in their political analysis and strategies', it must be clearly stated that differing political and ideological positions are held by disabled people and this fact has had significant implications for the development of their social movements. Cloke, in 'Conflict and Movements for Social Change: The Politics of Mediation and the Mediation of Politics', writes:

> Internal conflicts are endemic and natural to progressive political and social movements, in part because it is difficult to agree on how to define and change highly complex, volatile and evolving social problems. As a result, over time, different definitions of the problem and perceptions about the nature of those who defend and represent it result in radically different notions about what needs to be done to change it.[40]

Of course, political and theoretical differences did surface. As someone who witnessed the development of the British Movement from the early 1980s, this resonates with me, as does the view that:

> ... debates over means vs. ends and goals vs. process are a part of the history of all social movements, which are simultaneously fixed on achieving specific goals or demands, and at the same time searching for principled ways of achieving them that do not replicate the worst of what unjust and alienated social practices have created.[41]

This became a major issue as the Movement shifted its focus from the late 1980s onwards, but specifically after the passing of the 1995 Disability Discrimination Act.[42] This in turn feeds into another feature of social movements and was discussed earlier in terms of self-organisation: who is chosen to speak on behalf of movements agendas? This played out within the debates around the 1990s in British disability politics. There were issues raised around the language used and tensions surfaced in relation to how the Movement interacted with what BRIDGE UK refer to as more institution-based or mainstream activist spaces: 'Class and educational differences as well as grades of radicalism in movement politics come into play as movements negotiate how their demands are presented and who is supported as messenger.'[43]

The issue of grades of radicalism in movement politics returns us to the formation and nature of the Disabled People's Movement. Oliver's characterisation of disability politics in the early 1980s underpins to a large extent his claim that the Movement can be viewed as a social movement; however, by 2012 Oliver and Barnes appear to retreat from this position.[44] They state that a 'key feature of the disabled people's movement has been its focus on social exclusion and oppression.'[45]

Groups that adhered to social approaches towards disability became the backbone of the Disabled People's Movement and therefore it makes sense that self-organisation and self-determination were pivotal to their praxis. This said, these characteristics are not static over time, because the 'commitment to radical political action to promote change' has been questioned, as we shall see.

One person who has written on how new social movements theory relates to disability politics is Tom Shakespeare. His paper, 'Disabled People's Self-Organisation: A New Social Movement?' engages with numerous themes running through this book – themes such as self-organisation, political identity, discrimination and praxis – among others. Shakespeare's arguments contain elements we have in common, but also reveal differences in positions held by Oliver and myself. It can also be viewed as a critique of Oliver's approach.

Shakespeare acknowledges that disabled people became a coherent political force from the 1970s onwards, and asks if this means they also became a new social movement as described by Oliver. He makes comparisons with other oppressed groups and concludes that social movement theory fails to grasp liberation politics. His interpretation of what 'liberation politics' are can be called into question; nonetheless, we agree that the development of the Movement, debates around the social interpretation of disability, and political interventions by disabled people need to be viewed as:

> ... examples of praxis, the unity of theory and practice within struggle. But because of the priority afforded to achieving change, there has been little space for considering the nature of the movement itself, historically

and politically, and the significance of new definitions of disability for the self-identity of disabled people.[46]

Shakespeare compares and contrasts the US and British Movements. He acknowledges the former is deeply rooted in the civil rights traditions and consumerism, whereas he sees the British focus was on rejecting what he called 'social normality' and changing the system that produces disability. It is nonetheless noted that both movements saw direct action as part of their liberation struggle and he links this to various historical civil rights struggles. Interestingly, Shakespeare also links direct action with challenging passive stereotyping of disabled people. He sees a shared political identity and use of direct action as being in common with other social movements. Like Oliver, he speaks of disabled people being failed by conventional party politics and turning towards grassroots campaigning. He concludes that liberation struggles had to be led by the oppressed communities: 'So, identifying as a member of an oppressed group and organising to effect social change, are critical.'[47]

Shakespeare makes a link between disability identity and the empowering role of direct action. Whilst this is a valid connection, I would suggest that there is a need for a more critical appraisal of the role of direct action as employed by disabled activists. Direct action did make certain disabled people's issues visible, and built solidarity and a sense of identity, but nevertheless the Campaign for Accessible Transport, Campaign against Patronage, and Stop Telethon, were all single-issue campaigns around the theme of discrimination and denial of 'rights'. I also accept the tactics involved in direct action correspond with those of other civil rights and social movements, thus breaking the mould of stereotyping disabled people as 'victims'. In terms of consciousness raising, as implied earlier, did activists using direct action fail to ground the campaigns alongside grassroots community building, and has this had consequences for developing disability praxis further than what was done?[48] Shakespeare speaks of shifting 'from private woes to public wrongs'. Leaving aside this characterisation, I would argue the articulation of 'public wrong' was to a degree stunted where engagement in direct action became seen as an end in itself rather than a means to an end.[49]

Key narratives within the Movement were always around fostering social and political understandings of self-determination and therefore stood directly in opposition to the role of charities and those demonstrating paternalism. This said, I believe the Movement's ability to raise consciousness around the political identity of being 'disabled people' was badly restricted by the hegemonic power of dominant thinking and practice. In my opinion, Shakespeare's approach towards seeing identity formation as feeding into group consciousness, which resulted in creation of social movements and collective political action, is a distortion of what unfolded from the middle of the 1990s and raises questions about the relations between identity formation, group consciousness and disability praxis. Seeing identity formation as part of disability praxis enables us to see how recognising disability as a form of social oppression, rather than an individualised 'problem', allows individuals to not only reflect upon their own personal 'experience' but also to connect it with the experiences of others. Once acknowledged, this becomes the platform for both activity and embracing the political identity of being 'disabled by society'.

The Movement attracted people who, to various degrees, had become aware of disability as a political or social issue through self-awareness or having contact with its ideas. Shakespeare is right to say people are socialised into how they view disability; however, he underplays the pervasive nature of societal approaches towards disability. Due to the exclusionary practices of disablism, it has always been difficult for people with impairments to 'discover' alternatives to seeing disability as other than 'a personal tragedy'. Making parallels with the Marxist concept of 'false consciousness' and the feminist approach towards 'internalised oppression' in the manner he suggests is unhelpful. This said, I do believe there is a debate to be had in relation to 'internalised oppression', but not necessarily in terms of political consciousness raising in the first instance.[50]

In his article, Shakespeare discusses the issue of social movement theories and differences between traditional and new movement and acknowledges the absence of disabled people from the scholarly literature. He refers to the self-organisation of disabled people in a historical context as I have. The relevance to our discussion is that he makes a distinction between 'two types of contemporary popular struggle: the "post-materialist" tendency, on the one hand, and the "liberation" movements on the other'.[51]

Shakespeare argues: 'A simple opposition is drawn between the traditional claim for more resources, the materialist position, and the post-materialist value consensus ... '.[52] What does 'the post-materialist value consensus' mean? A slightly different take suggests 'Until the 1970s, it was nearly universal for individuals to prioritize so-called materialist values such as economic growth and maintaining order; on the other hand, postmaterialists give top priority to such goals as environmental protection, freedom of speech, and gender equality'.[53]

In terms of global values within the twentieth century, it is argued that these are now equally distributed. I would question Shakespeare's definition of materialist values because if we accept his interpretation, it completely changes the narrative he presents in relation to the Disabled People's Movement and other struggles, as well as the characterisations offered by Oliver.[54]

I cannot agree with his view that 'Most of the struggles mentioned above *are* about resource allocation: women, black people and disabled people are crucially concerned with their economic exploitation and poverty.'[55] In each case, the struggles against economic exploitation and poverty are factors in challenging oppression, but it would be reductionist and false to claim, as he implied, that liberation struggles are simply 'resource' led or driven. Shakespeare then goes on to say: 'The whole thrust of the British disability movement is for more resources to be channelled towards disabled people, and challenges the distributive logic of capitalism.'[56]

Shakespeare qualifies this by suggesting these social movements are often concerned with the interrelations of the market and the welfare state. He refers to groups marginal to the labour market. I view his position as being a political one and it is reflective of the social democratic position held both inside and outside the Disabled People's Movement. My reading of Shakespeare's position is that by using aspects of theorists' positions on social movements, he is able to present a clear division between 'liberation' movements and social movements. In my view, he constructs a straw argument which he proceeds to knock down. I believe the Disabled People's Movement was a social movement and its core values did originate from post-materialist values – that is, putting an emphasis on self-expression and quality of life over economic and physical security – but these were abandoned by an ascending liberal and social democratic tendency. Both Shakespeare and Oliver, from their differing political and theoretical positions, fail to acknowledge that as a social movement the Movement became a broad church around 'aspirations' [*sic*] rather than around the creation of a detailed programme of action. BRIDGE states:

> In understanding social movements it is vital to remember that they are dynamic, historical phenomena and as such 'are shaped by circumstance; they are contingent things, which grow or shrink in response to factors that enable or constrain them' … Movements may also end due to internal factors such as failure to adapt political agendas to changing contexts or concerns of movement members, or conflicts over politics and power

among movement members, which leads to a lack of consensus or desire to continue movement actions.[57]

This can be related to the tensions that developed within BCODP. As Barnes wrote, 'the 1980s BCODP and its member organisations produced a wealth of policy initiatives which, when implemented, will benefit not only them but the disabled population generally. Furthermore, these strategies owe as much to the political ideologies of the right as they do to those of the left.'[58]

Shakespeare's views assist us in part to reveal aspects of the ideological and political differences that emerged. According to him, the Movement's core values were autonomy, integration and independence. He refers to Scott's suggestion that 'a key feature of new social movements is the stress on autonomy, at the level of the personal (the focus on consciousness, personal power, etc.); in the challenge of restrictions on freedom, and in what he calls the "autonomy of struggle".'[59]

Scott views this as being 'the insistence that the movement and those it represents be allowed to fight their own corner without interference from other movements, and without subordinating their demands to other external priorities.'[60]

The generalised emphasis Shakespeare and Scott place on 'the stress on autonomy' raises issues around why disabled people saw self-organisation as such a central aspect of disability politics. The opening chapter of this book begins with a quotation from UPIAS which outlines the basis upon which they came together. The commonality was not their personhood, nor the issue of having impairments, but rather the social situation of being subjected to disablement. The social interpretation of disability focuses on disabled people's exclusion and disempowerment. A key slogan that emerged from the global Disabled People's Movement was 'Nothing About Us, Without Us'. Within disability praxis, there is a recognition that dominant ideologies and practice, as we have seen, treats 'disability' as an individualised problem. Self-organisation provides a challenge to this oppressive treatment by giving disabled people space to discover their own interpretation of the world, define the issues that matter to them, and transform the invisible into the visible. From this perspective, the autonomy that exists within self-organisation relates to how best to address the inequalities of power and social relations within society. Through collective engagement, disabled people empowered themselves not only to speak on their own behalf, but also to challenge disablement within mainstream society. Just like the question of how to employ civil and human rights; self-organisation ought to be viewed as a means to an end.

This perspective, however, is not shared by everyone and therefore, like so many concepts, autonomy means different things to different people. One example of this fact is the idea that 'the stress on autonomy' can be viewed as relating to the emergence of 'identity politics'.[61]

THE SELF-ORGANISATION OF DISABLED PEOPLE
AND IDENTITY POLITICS

By discussing whether or not the Disabled People's Movement was a social movement, invites consideration as to what extent the self-organisation of disabled people can be regarded as a form of identity politics. Going down this route means entering a minefield: the phrase 'identity politics' has not only come to signify a wide range of political activity and theorizing; it has also been contested in terms of its meaning and to which 'social groups within societies' it can attached. One of the ways in which identity politics is understood is that it refers to members of certain social groups who have a shared experiences of injustice. There are many other nuanced meanings also connected to the phrase – for example, it is also perceived to mean 'politics in which groups of people having a particular racial, religious, ethnic, social, or cultural identity tend to promote their own specific interests or concerns without regard to the interests or concerns of any larger political group.'[62]

It is the emphasis on promoting their own interests and concerns that has led to the association with the formation of new social movements. This association comes from the fact that within both social movements and identity politics there is a tendency which breaks with just organising traditional factors such as 'belief systems, programmatic manifestos, or party affiliation'.[63] Many social movements are also single-issue based; however, as we have seen, the British Disabled People's Movement emerged from a rejection of addressing disablement through the pursuit of single issues. Finkelstein also acknowledged that at specific times there may be a need to campaign around particular issues.[64]

Perhaps the central feature of most identity-political formations is their core aim of securing the political freedom for a specific constituency. It is this feature which is often seized upon when it is claimed that disability politics are identity politics. This is because the common ground is that both 'assert or reclaim ways of understanding their distinctiveness that challenge dominant characterizations, with the goal of greater self-determination.[65] Whilst acknowledging common ground does exist, this does not alone merit confirming disability politics as identity politics, because other factors need to be brought into play. Going beyond this central feature is what makes identity politics not only a minefield to navigate, but also a terrain which contains rabbit holes one can disappear into.

By exploring general aspects of identity politics, before specifically addressing how they might relate to the characterisations of disability politics, offers possible insights into some of the complexities involved. Identity politics as a mode of organizing is intimately connected to the idea that some social groups are oppressed and through one's identity members of specific groups are subjected to cultural imperialism, which can involve stereotyping, violence, exploitation, marginalisation, or powerlessness.[66]

Identity politics begins from analysing how social injustice is experienced, then moves on through various methods, to challenge and transform what are regarded to be previously stigmatised accounts of group membership. This is viewed in terms of overthrowing 'scripts offered by a dominant culture about one's own inferiority', and replacing them with ones that promote a sense of one's self and community.

Given this description, it follows that the scope of political movements described as identity politics is extremely broad and therefore there cannot be a 'straightforward criterion that makes a political struggle into an example of "identity politics"'. Partly, as a consequence of this fluidity, many of the critics of 'identity politics' struggle to pin down the exact focus of their critiques, and therefore result in using it as a blanket label when addressing a range of shortcomings. Whatever one's view of the development or validity of the arguments surrounding identity politics, it cannot be denied that 'the public rhetoric of identity politics served useful and empowering purposes for some, even while it sometimes belied the ... complexity of any claim to a shared experience or common group characteristics.'[67]

Interestingly, Tom Shakespeare in his book, *Disability Rights and Wrongs*, makes the same assertion about the social model of disability.[68] Separating the rhetoric from the theoretical grounding of identity politics is an arduous task in general terms; however, when we consider the claims around disability politics as identity politics, there are so many conflicting and contested areas involved, it almost becomes impossible to unpack them all.

The notion of 'identity politics' can be linked to historical texts, including, for example, the works of Frantz Fanon, Steve Biko and first-wave feminists.[69] Nonetheless, how it has been articulated and challenged within the later stages of the twentieth century has been identified as beginning in the 1970s.

No matter what position one takes on identity politics, there is an agreed recognition that 'the notion of identity has become indispensable to contemporary political discourse.'[70] In addition, what this also means is that the notion of identity has produced 'troubling implications for models of the self, political inclusiveness, and our possibilities for solidarity and resistance.'[71]

In the following chapter, the question of 'identity' is discussed in the context of how a disabled individual sees their 'self' and how others view them. The immediate focus is on why certain social groups organise collectively; however, as we can see, this is far from straightforward.

Discussions around identity politics do concern how 'identity' is addressed, but these discussions are further complicated by the fact that often the issues are intersected by the politics of difference. It is claimed that the politics of difference 'has appropriated the language of authenticity to describe ways of living that are true to the identities of marginalized social groups.'[72] In other words, the narratives or storytelling reflect or express what you and your group are, as distinct from others. As Sonia Kruks states, 'The demand is not for inclusion within the fold of "universal humankind" on the basis of shared human attributes; nor is it for respect "in spite of" one's differences. Rather, what is demanded is respect for oneself as different.'[73]

Some critics of identity politics argue that among the dangers is that 'it casts as authentic to the self or group a self-understanding that in fact is defined by its opposition to a dominant identity, which typically represents itself as neutral.'[74] Both Liggett and Shakespeare question the idea of the 'disabled identity' because it reinforces the dichotomy between 'disabled' and 'non-disabled'. Liggett draws from Foucauldian ideas to argue:

From an interpretative point of view the minority group approach is double edged because it means enlarging the discursive practices which participates in the constitution of disability ... [In] order to participate in their own management disabled people have had to participate as disabled. Even among the politically active, the price of being heard is understanding it is the disabled who are speaking.[75]

The charge here is that by reclaiming 'the disabled identity' for one's self simply reinforces the dependency on being viewed as 'Other' and, as a consequence, leads to increased internalisation and contributes to an oppressive hierarchy. As a counter-argument, it could be said that this charge is quite reductionist and ignores the dialectical nature of how disabled people mediate the imposed identity when forging and taking ownership of an alternative one (as discussed in the next chapter). Nevertheless, the tendency within identity politics and the politics of difference to foreground 'difference' assists us to acknowledge fundamental points of departure and conversely commonalities, within theories and praxis in relation to not only understanding approaches towards impairment and disability, but specifically, disability politics and culture. Navigating the complexities involved has played a major role in creating tensions, conflicts and disagreements, among disabled scholar activists and disabled communities in general. It forces those engaged in sites of struggle to question why we come together and organise; to question what it is that we are seeking to achieve.

It goes without saying that the meanings attached to 'difference' in relation to bodies are contested. This fact is very apparent when comparisons are made between 'minority group' politics and the politics associated with the British social interpretation. Goodley informs us:

> The minority model demanded cultural redefinition in opposition to 'cutthroat individualism' of the dominant North American and Canadian societies. The people-first language ... was coined to recognise humanity and diversity beyond the narrow confines of labour and consumption. [It] combined neo-Marxist critiques of capitalism with theories of race and racialisation, and adopted an eclectic understanding of the socio-cultural formations of disability.[76]

This approach is very different to the underpinning of the British Disabled People's Movement's early theorising. The description offered by Goodley assists to situate the 'minority group' approach within the frame of identity politics. It is important, however, not to give the impression that all theories or praxis coming out of North America or Canada should be discounted. Similarly, the fact that things are placed under the heading of 'identity politics' should not make them taboo or necessarily pigeonholed in that fashion. Some of the issues and areas are problematic, create conflict and indicate alternative perspectives, however, developing a new disability praxis requires dialogue around them.

A potential opportunity to explore areas of similarities and difference might begin by considering a specific approach towards humanism offered by Simone de Beauvoir as articulated by Sonia Kruks. Kruks refers to de Beauvoir's approach to humanism as a critical one, but specifically, it is an ambiguous one. Marso informs us that Kruks summarises this as being 'a humanism that acknowledges that contradictions and harm to others, that egregious failures in the pursuit of commendable goals, are inevitable'.[77]

Importantly, in terms of the arguments being presented in this book, Marso also points to how Kruks relates the way de Beauvoir approaches humanism to the importance 'of keeping both "macro" and "micro" politics in view: women's inferiority, for instance ... is produced both through location in "macro" social structures and through "micro" interpersonal encounters and "idiosyncratic experiences"'.[78]

What this means is that her humanism is characterised by the '"always already-situated, always material, always social" reality of the lived body, which emphasizes that to be human is to be a body that is both free yet constrained and vulnerable'.[79] Thus her humanism centres upon the relationship between subjective embodiment and contingent systems of power. Embodiment here refers to the bodily context of a particular individual. Adopting this approach towards humanism, it can be argued, connects not only with Abberley's thoughts on disabled people's oppression, but also connects with the ideas being developed around a materialist eco-social approach towards disability. Kruks believes de Beauvoir's embodiment and social context leads to the conclusion that what is required is political action 'to take up the ambiguities of existence, rather than a politics that addresses an abstract subject'.[80] The significance of de Beauvoir's thinking along these lines is that she recognised embodiment and location in the world as constituting the oppression of groups, as well as affecting individuals. This assists in helping us to understand how the body becomes a site of struggle under capitalism.

The issues being addressed have been described as a minefield because we have acknowledged not everyone defines 'disability', 'identity', or 'identity politics' in the same way. It can be argued that how one defines 'disability' impacts upon how you define or analyse the other two. Acknowledging disabled people as an oppressed group does not automatically establish this recognition as 'identity politics' because, I would argue, UPIAS saw the 'identity' as referring to the situation itself, not the individuals in that situation – that is, people disabled by society.

What is the basis of this assertion? From a sociological perspective, there is an emphasis placed on collective identity where an individual's identity is strongly associated with how group memberships define themselves or that group's activities. Within specific contexts, referring to 'disabled people' or 'disabled person' constitutes a political identity associated with the collective experience of being excluded from or marginalised within society as a consequence of disablement which, in turn, is maintained through disablism.

In 2010, Shakespeare argued that politically, 'the social model has generated a form of identity politics which has become inward looking and separatist.'[81] A stronger case could be made to suggest that rather than the radical social model laying the foundations for a rigid form of identity politics, it was in fact the people who focused upon obtaining legal rights and sought social acceptance, who opened that particular door. The mistake many made when treading the 'rights' path without a wider context, is that they saw the challenge to dominant ideologies and exclusionary practice as simply one of seeking to redefine who we are in terms of social acceptance and being individuals with citizenship. Problems arose when the broad objectives of the Disabled People's Movement became reduced to obtaining civil and human rights as 'personal freedoms', rather than as a collective push for a transformative agenda. This shift coincided with the shifting role of disabled people's organisations and their relationship with the state.

What became lost was an appreciation of the central purpose of self-organisation which put into practice the realisation that the radical roots of disability politics as stemming from the desire to end 'what we are' – subjected to social oppression; excluded or marginalised within mainstream social activities by disablement – and become part of a collective movement engaged in transforming society. This engagement requires both self-organisation and involvement in mainstream social and political activities. What lies between these two positions – seeking acceptance versus seeking transformation – is the tension that exists around how disabled people view their collective identity and the socio-political arguments behind it. Shakespeare illustrates this when he writes 'pride is about the assertion of a positive identity, personally and collectively, in the face of prejudice and discrimination.'[82]

It can be argued, however, that the focus on culture, pride, 'difference' and embodiment, as witnessed in certain geopolitical circles, can be likened to identity politics more than the politics underpinned by the radical social interpretation of disability and the objectives arising from it. In Britain, the social interpretation of disability was a unifying, not a separatist agenda, as Finkelstein explained time and time again.[83]

Perhaps, in the final analysis, recognition needs to be given to this view:

Given how many contexts these debates must generalize, it is hard to see how one can draw any conclusions about the merits of a thing called 'identity politics' over and above any other kind. At this historical juncture, then, asking whether one is for or against identity politics is to ask an impossible question.[84]

THE DEMISE OF THE DISABLED PEOPLE'S MOVEMENT AND THE SECOND CORNERSTONE

The Disabled People's Movement did from the outset have 'a change agenda', but we need to consider whether or not this became diluted by the mid-1990s. The central question is the extent to which the Movement, using disabled people's organisations as a spearhead, was about changing the social relations that existed between disabled and non-disabled people – that is, removing the restrictions that prevented disabled people from full and active participation within established structures of society. In other words, ending the social exclusion or marginalisation disabled people encountered.

With hindsight, I have begun to question the assumptions that were made by disabled academics and activists about the nature of the Movement, especially in terms of its the political depth. The focus was always on coming together to force social change and to challenge inequality. During the early 1990s, however, I would not characterise the Movement as 'anti-capitalist', although the internal logic of the social interpretation of disability goes in that direction. Disabled activists were nonetheless aware that traditional Labour Party values were more sympathetic to our cause than the values underpinning Conservatism. This situation ruptured when Tony Blair introduced his 'Third Way' neoliberalism.

The political shift further to the right within neoliberal policies caught the Disabled People's Movement off-guard and as a consequence, it was unable to address the ramifications that followed. In Chapter 8, consideration will be given to the extent the Movement had a commitment to radical political action to promote change. My general appraisal is that from the middle of the 1990s, the vast majority of disabled people's organisations simply sought to change how disabled people were seen and treated, whilst at the same time sought to fund their existence through being service-providers. When we consider the political task of challenging disabling barriers, it is necessary to recognise the role played by disabled people who called for civil and human rights. As previously stated, this call should have been seen as a means to an end rather than an end in itself. However, by focusing entirely on obtaining legal 'rights' – viewed in terms of human and civil rights – the Movement lost sight of the bigger picture and halted any critical evaluation of the nature of capitalist society. There was always a risk that by demanding legal protection against discrimination, the debate would not be about the oppressive and discriminatory *nature of society*, but the extent to which individuals encountered discriminatory attitudes and behaviours within specific areas of social life. The difference between the Civil Rights Bill and the Disability Discrimination Act was lost on the majority of the population. Twenty years after the passing of the DDA, I wrote an article entitled 'The Falsification of History: The Twenty Year Burial of the Civil Rights Bill', which outlines the events that took place.[85]

It seems highly questionable as to whether or not we can still speak of a Disabled People's Movement under these conditions, because the original arguments contained within the social interpretation of disability and the need for self-organisation have been 'lost' or placed upon a back burner. The demise of the Movement calls into question whether it was ever realistic to see it as being capable of functioning autonomously from the wider class struggle. While a negative note to end this chapter on, it can still be argued that the self-organisation of disabled people is still necessary and a cornerstone of disability politics. Whether the forms of self-organisation need changing or not, is an issue that requires consideration.

4

The Third Cornerstone:
Self-determination,
De-institutionalisation and
Promotion of Self-directed Living

The first two cornerstones of disability politics – a counter-hegemonic interpretation of disability and the need for self-organisation – began the process of laying the basis for the self-determination of disabled people. The third cornerstone concerns itself with the processes employed to achieve self-determination: de-institutionalisation and the promotion of independent living (IL). A crucial feature of the struggle for emancipation has been working towards de-institutionalisation and the promotion of IL; therefore within this chapter, I will introduce the history of the Independent Living Movement (ILM) which has its origins in the US civil and human rights movements of the late 1960s.[1]

THE FOUNDATIONS OF THE INDEPENDENT LIVING MOVEMENT

Judy Hunt, writing about the early days of the British welfare state in the 1960s, notes:

> The social policy of the Welfare State, regarding disabled people, was still ill-thought out, and so when the State began to intervene it jumped on a bandwagon started by the voluntary sector. It too accepted, without much question, the need for special institutions to house people and assisted this with an injection of funding and pressure on the respective authorities.[2]

This was the backdrop to the discontent that grew within these institutions spoken about in previous chapters. John Evans, a long-standing campaigner for disabled people's emancipation, perhaps qualifies why I see de-institutionalisation and the campaign for self-directed living as the third cornerstone of disability politics:

> Institutional life denies a person real citizenship and participation in the community ... For those disabled people who have already experienced institutional living and have tasted that reality and the loss of control over the basic decisions of their life, know too well, that it is a large price to pay, sacrificing one's own contribution and livelihood in the community.[3]

The right to real citizenship and participation in the community was always the goal of disability politics from the outset. However, this was coupled with an understanding that this would only occur through disabled people's control over the basic decisions affecting their lives. Paul Hunt, in a letter to *The Guardian* newspaper, framed British disability politics when he argued that:

> ... practically every sentence in her article [relating to the so-called mentally handicapped] could apply with equal force to the severely physically handicapped, many of whom also find themselves in isolated and unsuitable institutions, where their views are ignored and they are subject to authoritarian and often cruel regimes.
>
> I am proposing the formation of a consumer group to put forward nationally the views of actual and potential residents of these successors to the workhouse. We hope in particular to formulate and publicise plans for alternative kinds of care.[4]

It is interesting that Hunt wrote his letter in response to Ann Shearer's account of a Campaign for the Mentally Handicapped conference relating to learning disabled people. Historically, de-institutionalisation discussions are associated more with learning disabled people or survivors of the mental health system than with people with physical impairments. Paradoxically, both of these groups subsequently found themselves marginalised within the British Disabled People's Movement.[5] Peter Durrant provides us with some context when he recalled that:

> In the 1960s, Frank Field was the first Child Poverty Action Group director and Ann Shearer, Peter Moss and the rest of us began working on a 'campaign for people with a mental handicap'. The radical social worker journal *Case-Con* was being published regularly, the physically impaired,

mental health patients and unemployed workers unions were radical, and the Seebohm Report in 1968 argued for joint working, insisting that alternatives to the status quo were possible.[6]

Hunt's letter mentions the proposal to establish a consumer group; however, what resulted from bringing people together was the setting up of the Union of the Physically Impaired Against Segregation and this in turn laid the foundations in Britain for a new movement. When he spoke of a 'consumer group', was Hunt stressing the need for self-determination in defining alternative services? I am asking this because events across the Pond gave rise to what became the foundations of the Independent Living Movement and, as we shall see, the American ILM had to a certain extent roots in the consumer rights social movement.

Today it may seem strange that one or two individuals could massively influence the growth of movements, but this is precisely what occurred in the 1960s and 1970s. Our American story begins with Ed Roberts who contracted polio at the age of 14 in 1953, two years before the Salk vaccine ended the epidemic. He was initially taught via a telephone until his mother insisted that he attend school for a few hours a week: 'At school, he faced his deep fear of being stared at and transformed his sense of personal identity. He gave up thinking of himself as a "helpless cripple," and decided to think of himself as a "star." He credited his mother with teaching him by example how to fight for what he needed.'[7]

He had to fight against being denied a diploma from high school and subsequently in relation to his application to attend the University of California, Berkeley. Roberts' search for housing met resistance partly due to having to sleep in an 800-pound iron lung at night. The director of the campus health service offered him a room in an empty wing of the Cowell Hospital. In true Roberts style, he accepted on the condition that his living space be treated as dormitory space and not as a medical facility. By gaining admission to Berkeley, he paved the way for other disabled students to join him over the next few years in what evolved into the Cowell Residence Program.

In his article, 'Becoming the Rolling Quads: Disability Politics at the University of California, Berkeley, in the 1960s', Scot Danforth explains that historical analyses of 1960s university campus activism have usually focused on activities related to the civil rights movement, Free Speech Movement, and opposition to the Vietnam War. His study however supplemented the historiography of civil disobedience and political activity on college campuses during that tumultuous era by offering an account of the initiation of the disability rights movement with the Rolling Quads, a group of disabled student activists at the University of California, Berkeley. Danforth's study explores a small group with

> ... little political experience and limited connections to campus and community activists, organized to combat the paternalistic managerial practices of the university and the California Department of Rehabilitation. Drawing from the philosophy and strategies of the seething political culture of 1969 Berkeley, the Rolling Quads formed an activist cell that expanded within less than a decade into the most influential disability rights organization in the country.[8]

How did this happen? Building on their success on campus, the Rolling Quads began advocating for curb cuts, opening access to the wider community, and creating the Physically Disabled Students' Program (PDSP) – the first student-led disability services program in the country. Crucially, for our story, the PDSP provided services including attendant referral and wheelchair repair to students at the university, but soon they were being contacted by disabled people with the same concerns who were not students. Recognising there was a need to serve the wider community led activists to create the Berkeley Center for Independent Living (CIL), the first independent living service and advocacy programme run by and for disabled people. Whilst Roberts did not establish the Berkeley CIL nor was he its first executive director, he did give up a teaching post to return to Berkeley and assume leadership of the fledgling organisation. Under his guidance, the CIL provided a model for a new kind of community organisation designed to address the needs and concerns of disabled people. The development of the Independent Living Movement should not be viewed in isolation. Its relationship with the American Disability Rights Movement was forged with the foundation of the World Institute on Disability, by Roberts, Judith Heumann and Joan Leon. It was through their leadership that both movements established an international reputation and are rightly linked with disability politics activism.

Disability rights activists, including Roberts and Heumann, sought an end to discriminatory practices and for disabled people to have rights that were mandated and protected by the law. Roberts and other activists held a sit-in to enforce section 504 of the Rehabilitation Act of 1973, which stated that disabled people should not face exclusion from activities, be denied the right to receive benefits, or be discriminated against within programmes using federal financial assistance solely on the basis of their impairment. Activists occupied the offices of the Carter Secretary of Health, Education and Welfare building which was located in San Francisco for 28 days.[9]

Shirley Wilcher informs us that 'the Rehabilitation Act ushered in a new age of activism and accomplishment in the pursuit of rights for individuals with disabilities in higher education, government, and private industry.' Wilcher goes on to say that 'The Rehabilitation Act served as a watershed moment in disability rights history. Most of its protections were eventually expanded to all organizations serving the public, regardless of whether they receive federal funds, via the Americans with Disabilities Act of 1990.'[10]

How should we describe the philosophy and practice of Independent Living as developed in the US? Employing British terminology and drawing upon American and Canadian sources, I will outline the key features as I see them. In simplistic terms, independent living is viewed as a service delivery system designed to enable individuals with significant impairments to live as independently as possible. This notion has always been contested or open to interpretation, however, within the US Independent Living Movement (USILM) itself there is broad agreement that it means 'It is being able to control your life, advocating for yourself, or knowing how to get support from others to do what you want and/or need to do.'[11]

It is also acknowledged that many people with impairments live independently without ongoing support services. Independent living is seen as having a distinct philosophy which is made up of a collection of key values, principles, attitudes and behaviours. Perhaps not surprisingly, the independent living philosophy is built upon 'commonly understood definitions of civil rights, social justice, personal responsibility, and equality of opportunity and participation in society'.[12]

Gerben DeJong suggests the disability rights and independent living movement are a compilation of five social movements as they pertain to and are defined by disabled people. These can be characterised as being:

1. Demanding civil and human rights sounds like the civil rights movement led by African-Americans during the 1950s and 1960s.
2. The notion of 'self-determination' in terms of choice and control, echoes Consumerism, a movement led by well-known national figures such as Ralph Nader. Disabled people were, for the first time, stressing their role as consumers first and 'patients' last.
3. Self-help is nothing new in the United States, but organized self-help programs were relatively new.

4. De-medicalization and de-institutionalization share certain common characteristics ... When disabled consumers established the right to buy the services that they needed for daily survival from whomever they choose, they were viewed as having 'de-medicalized' the service.

5. De-institutionalization, which began in response to large mental health facilities for those with mental ill health or those who were learning disabled, shares common ground with the principles of de-medicalization. Most institutions are staffed by medical personnel, even if residents are not ill. It is argued therefore that placement in institutions is inappropriate and far more costly than providing those same residents with the support services they need to live in their chosen communities.[13]

As we can see, one of the primary principles of the independent living philosophy is 'consumer control'. The rationale behind this is straightforward: a disabled individual *must* have control over his or her life and all decision-making.

The basic paradigm used by the ILM in the US and then across the globe was that existing systems created:

... dependence upon professionals, family members and others; hostile attitudes and environments; lack of legal protection; lack of recognition of inherent worth of disabled people. The problem was viewed as being within 'the socio-economic, political, and cultural environment; in the physical environment; in the medical, rehabilitation, service delivery or charity processes which were deemed as dependency-creating'.[14]

The solution to the problem was seen to be:

1) advocacy; 2) barrier removal; 3) consumer-control over options and services; 4) peer role models and leaders; 5) self-help – all leading to equitable socio-economic, cultural and political options.

Through these five actions, independent living was and still is promoted as producing the desired outcomes of 'independence through control over *acceptable* options for living in an integrated community of choice; pride in unique talents and attributes of each individual; positive disability identity'.[15]

There are areas of this paradigm that have been called into question or challenged in a variety of ways. This book, in Chapters 8 and 9, will explore some of the tensions and contradictions in relation to disability politics and practice, particularly around the issues of barrier removal, consumer-control, and the notion of positive disability identity. Ravi Malhotra in an article entitled 'Empowering People with Disabilities' explains how the politics of the independent living movement can be viewed as complex and even somewhat contradictory. On the one hand, it shares common ground with what he calls the social model of disablement, yet on the other it can have within it a market-oriented and conservative individualist strain. This he sees as having implications for all issues that it seeks to analyse.[16]

This fundamental contradiction of promoting both social change and market-oriented and conservative individualism has to be seen as a major thorn in the side of developing a radical emancipation struggle. In straightforward terms, the disability praxis of independent living via its centres can be summed up as:

- consumer control of the centre regarding decision-making, service delivery, management, and establishment of the policy and direction of the centre;
- self-help and self-advocacy;
- development of peer relationships and peer role models, and
- equal access of significantly disabled individuals to society and to all services, programmes, activities, resources, and facilities, whether public or private, and regardless of the funding source.

The original intent of the Title VII amendments to the Rehabilitation Act in 1978 were to initiate centres and to provide services. It should be noted that an organisation is 'consumer-controlled' if a majority of its board of directors and a majority of its staff are disabled people. Unfortunately, across the globe, it is acknowledged there are many organisations which have a majority of disabled people on their board of directors and hired as staff who do not practice self-directed decision-making in their programmes or services.[17]

Centres for independent living were created with funds from the Federal Rehabilitation Act for the sole purpose of providing services for people with significant impairments. The 1978 amendments to the Rehabilitation Act were written not solely for the purpose of providing services to individuals but also to act as catalysts for social and systems change. The USILM activists, as indicated above, view the mission and purpose of a CIL as assisting to eliminate attitudinal, architectural and communication barriers to full integration of disabled people and promotion of full integration.

The global interpretation of the independent living philosophy is that it is rooted in the principle of self-determination, namely, 'choice and control'. In the US, given the ILM's history and culture, the notion of self-determination is articulated as 'consumer choice'. We are told that this means 'providing assistance and support to individuals making choices, even if it means moving into a nursing home'.[18] Whilst this principle can be seen as empowerment, it nonetheless needs to be understood and practiced in terms of the socio-economic, cultural and political realities facing disabled people. As Maggie Shreve has stated:

> The problem is that in America today, most options available are not acceptable. Whenever a person 'chooses' to live in an environment where s/he has *less control*, this is not independent living. Centres should be highly visible agents of social change which do not accept institutionalisation as 'a natural or obvious' option.
>
> Independent living means having control over your own life and being able to make decisions about life, work and play in the same ways that nondisabled people do. This is exactly what 'independent living' means.[19]

Once again, this returns us to the identified contradiction inherent in Independent Living philosophy. It is acknowledged that IL would not be possible without federal funding support; however, the Rehabilitation Act stipulates that 'In order to be eligible for independent living services, a person must be able to prove that s/he has a severe disability which limits her/his ability to function independently in the family or community or to gain, maintain or advance in employment.[20]

This promotes dominant thinking and interests, and therefore contradicts not only the social interpretation of disability, but as Shreve reminds us, that these centres 'were created to be different from traditional service providers'.[21] Another factor to consider is that independent living is supposed to be a campaign cry for equal rights and integration. Shreve points out that a major barrier to promoting 'systems or social change' has been identified as being the fact that if 'the independent living movement has struggled or failed to make its philosophy known and understood, it may be because centers, leaders and advocates have not known how to educate others about it.'[22]

This however is only part of the problem. The nature of our oppression and the deep-rooted hegemonic power of dominant ideologies are extremely difficult to combat. Have disabled activists ever been in a position to deliver what disabled people want and need?

Despite the critical edge I have constructed, I believe the American Independent Living Movement did assist us to forge the third cornerstone of disability politics. Colin Barnes captures this when he writes:

> The concept [independent living] evolved out of the groundswell of initiatives from within the disabled community during the 1960s and 1970s; the impetus for which stemmed from a widespread disillusionment with existing provision and its tendency to focus on people's impairments rather than on the factors which disable them. Much of the inspiration for this development came from abroad – particularly the United States.[23]

What inspired British disabled activists was the fact that American disabled people could be seen to be engaging in self-determination. Barnes notes:

> Severely critical of existing services and the way they were managed, disabled Americans established a more appropriate alternative controlled and run by disabled people themselves. 'Independent living', therefore, is not simply a philosophy but a practical solution to the problems faced by disabled people. It is a metaphor for a range of services designed to give disabled people the same rights and opportunities as non-disabled peers. Inevitably, the American 'Independent Living Movement' (ILM) had a profound influence on disabled people worldwide. Subsequently, organisations controlled and run by disabled people providing similar services proliferated in both developed and undeveloped countries.[24]

THE FOUNDATIONS OF THE BRITISH INDEPENDENT LIVING MOVEMENT

The roots of the British Independent Living Movement lie in the creation of an alternative solution to institutional care by disabled people who formed the Project 81 group. The late rock singer Ian Dury named this group the 'escape committee'. John Evans, a leading IL activist in Britain and Europe, explains how leading disabled activists raised funds to explore Independent Living possibilities in the US during 1980 and 1981. These included Vic Finkelstein, a founder of UPIAS; Rosalie Wilkins, presenter of a television programme focusing on disability, and John Evans, one of the founders of Project 81.[25]

The Project 81 group was able to live in the community because of their ability to successfully negotiate with their Local Authorities to receive a grant which would be used to pay for their support in the community. Due to the National Assistance Act 1948, local Social Services could only provide 'care' and were not permitted to give money to disabled people directly. Project 81 and the Local Authorities resolved this problem by using a third party, for example, a charity, housing association, or voluntary organisation. These bodies would then transfer the grant into the individual's bank account. Enabling disabled people to manage their own support through grants or direct payments has always been a key feature of the British ILM due to the nature of the welfare state. The arrangement of using third parties would remain until the Direct Payments Act of 1996.

Independent Living activists were often uncomfortable about this for a variety of reasons. Disabled people who lived in areas where Local Authorities did not see the benefits of developing schemes to enhance independent lifestyles were forced to accept traditional service delivery. A watershed moment came in 1986 when the county treasurer and solicitor of Hampshire County Council got cold feet about the scheme and decided that it was illegal. Ironically, this coincided with the Audit Commission, a national body monitoring the services of local authorities, publishing the report, 'Making a Reality of Community Care',[26] where Hampshire's approach was held up as a model of good practice. This led the council to allow the scheme to continue. The precarious nature of these arrangements were further tested in 1992, when the Department of Health issued a circular which instructed councils to halt all direct payments. Many councils complied, but others held their nerves. It is acknowledged by Independent Living activists that by keeping their nerves, the local authorities ensured the survival of independent living in Britain during these years of uncertainty.[27]

Being able to manage their own support is a key feature of the British ILM, but there are also other key areas which are fundamental to its development. The emergence and founding of the first Centres for Independent Living should be viewed as a vital component of disability politics. John Evans explains that:

These organisations were able to provide an infrastructure of support, advice and information which could promote further independent living initiatives. They were endowed with an invaluable expertise, which was essential in supporting a sustainable framework to enable the movement to flourish. It was a collective approach which soon developed a dynamic network of different models of exchange, ideas and practices throughout the country.[28]

The Derbyshire and Hampshire CILs were the first to be set up in 1984. These CILs were founded on similar lines to those in the US, incorporating the basic 'Independent Living Principles'. During the early years, disabled people in Britain gained much encouragement from their disabled colleagues in the US. It is documented that regular meetings took place between the Derbyshire and Hampshire CILs and other disabled people interested in developing projects in other areas. Evans writes, 'This collaboration enabled both groups to prosper and develop a cross-fertilization of ideas. This helped them support each other in strengthening their will and determination to secure a firm platform for their infrastructural development and to look at creating a national network and movement.'[29]

The political debate around how the British Movement approached the differences between the two concepts of independence and integration, over time found itself pushed into the background. Finkelstein and I agree that the failure to make this debate central to the development of disability politics played a major part in the demise of both wings of the Disabled People's Movement.[30] What makes this debate so important?

SELF-DETERMINATION: THE HISTORICAL DEBATE BETWEEN INDEPENDENCE AND INTEGRATION

Conceptual differences existed among British activists with regards to how independence and integration were viewed. The first two CILs were different from each other in terms of the models they established for themselves; however, together they created the basis of a framework that other CILs were able to use when setting up their own. One of the earliest disabled people's organisations, Derbyshire Coalition of Disabled People (DCDP), gained the support of the County Council for the establishment of a Centre for Integrated Living in the county. Ken Davis informs us that this set the scene for a collaborative approach to the development of practical services and facilities.[31]

This was similar to what occurred in Birmingham three years later, when the Birmingham Disability Rights Group approached the City Council about establishing a Disability Resource Centre.[32] The Derbyshire Coalition was conscious of the need to review the philosophy and practices of the independent living movement as it had developed throughout the 1970s in the US, in order to relate it to the work undertaken by the Disabled People's Movement in Britain over the same period. Within his paper on the development of the Derbyshire Centre for Integrated Living, Davis makes a crucial point that, due to the existence of our welfare state, the newly created movement took a different form to that of their counterparts in the US:

> The call was not for control of their own services through 'independent living centres' or their equivalent, but rather for the State to provide better benefits or other services. The assumption was that more money or better organisation of existing resources would solve the problem of our exclusion from mainstream social activity. Some disabled people, however argued strongly that such an administrative approach would be quite wrong and as the movement developed the issue of control over our own lives became paramount.[33]

The Coalition in line with the thinking of UPIAS fully accepted that disabled people need help to overcome disability (i.e., social restriction), but in addition, held the view that appropriate aspects of professional practice can be potent and productive elements in this process. This recognition has become lost over time and there is an unhelpful 'anti-professional' tendency among some disabled activists. There is a tendency to collapse together the management of professional theory and practice with the knowledge and activities in the field, thereby throwing the baby out with the bathwater. What this does is undermine disabled people's ability to gain allies, build alliances, and create progressive forms of co-production.

A significant observation was made by Davis and DCIL when they argued that the removal of barriers, per se, is not particularly progressive and may even generate oppressive practices in the process. DCIL therefore maintained that 'the ILM will become a genuinely radical current within the wider movement when it inquires more searchingly into the causes of the barriers it seeks to remove. This requires development of an historical perspective and a more searching analysis of the social relations between disabled and non-disabled people.'[34]

The logic behind this is that unless we analyse the nature of the society that exists, it will be impossible to address the root causes of disabled people's social oppression. The failure to undertake disability praxis in this way has contributed to the divisions which appeared within the British ILM.

How integration was viewed in the early 1980s compared to today must be placed within the context of how disabled people see their social positioning within society.

The questioning of the use of the term 'independent living' has always existed because there are problems with what 'independence' means. DCDP acknowledged that mainstream interpretations of 'independent' differed significantly from definitions put out by those *who identify with the ILM*; they nonetheless believed that because the *raison d'être* of the movement crystallised around the issue of 'independence', this would itself eventually prove to be a barrier to making progress. Ken explains that 'the ILM has had no option but to choose its own definitions since the world in which the ILM seeks to participate is often confused as to the purpose of the movement.'[35]

DCDP also place the word 'independence' within the socio-political and cultural context of American society's commitment to promoting 'rugged individualism and untrammelled personal freedom as the epitome of human development'. Years later, Finkelstein made a similar point when he argued that the USILM corresponded to 'a basic commitment to the American capitalist system with its free market, pluralist ideology'.[36]

It is important to try and understand how the difference in approach from a political stance impacts working towards social change. Davis argues that both terms – 'independent' and 'integrated' – inevitably carry deeper, symbolic messages and given their historical usage, he identified the fundamental difference between them. He saw 'Integrated Living' as implying a commitment to society whereas 'Independent Living' signalled a commitment to self. Davis, however, acknowledged that talking of 'independence' had a certain attraction because it worked against the material and psychological damage experienced by 'disabled people whose personal development has been controlled by others'. In addition, it also acts as 'a potent motivator to hold up the idea of independence before those who are denied it'. Nevertheless, he believed 'the more one attempts to explain what "independent living" is, paradoxically, the closer one comes to discussing the concept in terms of integration.'[37]

Davis also highlights a tension that surfaces when arguments around personal and collective rights and freedoms are forwarded. He explains how 'independent living' is presented as a process of 'identifying choices and creating personal solutions', and at the same time providing, a 'quality of life attained with help'.[38] However, he goes on to explain that: 'In other words, personal choices for disabled people can be sterile in the absence of the help necessary to make them a reality. *Introducing help is to introduce the reali-*

ties of dependence and interdependence which are the very building blocks of integration.'[39]

Whilst acknowledging the importance of the point Davis makes, especially with the addition of knowledge about the marketisation of personal support, it must be placed in a wider political context. Having choice and control over lifestyles is conditioned in most instances by the social relations that exist for individuals and distinct groups within society. To negate this reality prevents us from understanding how oppressions manifest. It is a core aspect of the social interpretation of disability – that, unless we break the causal link between impairment and encountered social restrictions (disability), then we negate the existence of social oppression. We end up 'blaming' the individual's body for their social situation, rather than arguing for the creation of new social relations that would accommodate diverse bodies and lifestyles. This is the challenge and at the same time, the tension: how do we create new social relations within a society reliant on inequalities and exploitative relations?

Davis's article proceeds to consider potentially destructive connotations that can lie behind certain perspectives on 'independent living'. The question of having choice and control must be considered within the context of power. He suggests that to 'seek the ability to decide and choose what one personally wants, to seek to assume and establish self-control and self-determination are potent mental constructs which can have devastating effects in the real world.'[40] The first example he gives is where disabled people can resort to using human and other resources simply to achieve personal ends, thereby only caring about their own needs and interests. Exercising power over choice and control without considering interpersonal relationships can lead to nondisabled people being employed merely as 'mechanical extensions of our own physical inability to translate thought into action'.[41] Unfortunately, some of us have witnessed behaviour of this kind.

These examples are also an extremely chilling reminder of how current practices around self-directed living have turned disabled people into employers with staff to manage inside a capitalist marketplace, and this situation corresponds to the politics that underpins those practice. A lot of water has passed under the bridge since DCDP published Davis's paper; however I still see a need to question aspects of the culture within the ILM, where it seems to collude with dominant ideologies and practice. If the focus is indeed on 'self', then implicit within this prioritisation is the possibility of a lack of true commitment to all things outside oneself, except those which serve immediate ends. The psychological, social and ecological consequences of this mode of thought are all too obvious in today's world.

It is important to understand how DCDP viewed the term 'integrated living', and how it shaped the work of the Derbyshire Centre for Integrated Living (DCIL). Davis wrote, 'The use of the term "integrated living" is an attempt to make clear and get in context both the end and the means of the DCIL. It aims for the full social integration of disabled people and it seeks to achieve it by disabled and non-disabled people working together ... '.[42] The DCIL worked with the local authorities and the NHS to plan a strategy aimed at the integration of disabled people into the social, economic and political life of the County.

What is striking about the approach advocated by DCDP and DCIL in Davis's article is that I could quite simply substitute 'inclusive' for 'integration' and leave the rest of the text unaltered and it would sit quite comfortably with the vision developed by Act 4 Inclusion discussed later in this book in Chapter 9. It is important, I believe, not to view the change of terminology as simply a matter of semantics, or to explore the approach advocated by DCDP and DCIL in isolation. It is important to link it with the work undertaken by Vic Finkelstein and others.[43]

The attraction of Finkelstein's work is its emphasis on meeting the challenge of developing appropriate mainstream community services and winning over service-users, providers and policymakers to new ways of providing services and training.[44]

Equally striking, in my opinion, is that he views the new ways of providing services and training as adopting a lifestyle orientation which 'would be geared towards assisting people attain their personal goals and aspirations. The focus of any identification or assessment procedure would not be on the origin and meaning of an individual's deficits but making resources available for future goals.'[45]

While I would question certain aspects of his proposals, I am broadly supportive of what he sought to achieve. Unfortunately to date, the remnants of the old British ILM have not considered Finkelstein's approach seriously enough – probably because it marks a radical departure from what currently exists – and thus it sits as a bridge too far. Perhaps through the work begun by Act 4 Inclusion, Finkelstein's thinking can be introduced into the dialogue around transforming Social Care and Independent Living.

There is one further issue raised by Davis's paper that relates to the way disabled people need to develop our thinking. Within DCIL's approach towards 'integrated living', which I personally view as a form of 'co-production, there is a vital operational consideration that outlines the Centre's relationship with the Coalition. DCDP and the DCIL recognised that having a mixture of 'consumer advocacy' and service provision within one organisation can be counter-productive, which is why they were legally separate, autonomous bodies. This meant they could pursue separate roles, but with the same overarching aim. Thus DCIL did not have to worry about 'biting the hand that feeds' it.[46]

In the late 1980s, Birmingham Disability Rights Group held a similar position in relation to the Birmingham Disability Resource Centre. Operating on a division in purpose however does not mean there should be no relationship between the two bodies. The right to representation from BDRG on the BDRC management board was in the constitution.

The third cornerstone concerns itself with three interlocking issues: self-determination, de-institutionalisation and promotion of self-directed living. Throughout the development of ideas around these issues, there has always been a need to address what we want by addressing at the same time the things which prevent us from achieving our goal. To overcome disability, which is the removal of the social restrictions that cause disabled people's exclusion from, and marginalisation within, mainstream social activities, one must address existing social relations. For disabled people to be 'included' requires removing the causes behind the exclusion and that means dealing with *the nature of society itself* and its significance for those with impairments. This in turn returns us to the question of what we understand by self-determination.

Withers reaches the heart of the problem when they write, 'When folks approach self-determination from a Western perspective, we define it as individualistic self-management. Here, it is synonymous with independence and self-reliance.'[47] This has been a thread throughout this chapter. What are the issues that arise if the emphasis is upon individualistic self-management? We need to consider this question from two angles: firstly, the internalising of dominant discourses which articulate existing social policy, and secondly, how various sections of the Disabled People's Movement have approached self-determination. Oliver in part addressed this point when he spoke of conflicts between disabled people and professionals within policy and practice due to the operation of differing definitions:

At first glance it would seem that the big idea of independent living is one that ... disabled people, professionals and even Governments would agree on. However, this is appearance rather than reality ... The professions see independence as the ability to undertake the full range of self-care activities. Disabled people see independence in terms of personal autonomy and the ability to take control of all aspects of our own lives.[48]

Both Finkelstein and Withers state the emphasis on self-management leads to the severance of community from self-determination. Finkelstein wrote:

> Independent living is a lie. Human beings are by nature dependent ... In fact, life in modern society is inconceivable without being dependent on others for assistance. Disabled people, of all human beings, should know this and to pretend otherwise is to accede to a humiliating deception propagated by USA cultural imperialism.[49]

The European Network for Independent Living acknowledges that there is a continuous debate on whether we speak of independence or interdependence. Their considered view is that 'all human beings are interdependent and that the concept of IL does not contravene this. IL does not mean being independent from other persons, but having the freedom of choice and control over one's own life and lifestyle.'[50]

Whilst I view self-determination and processes of de-institutionalisation and promotion of self-directed living as the third cornerstone of disability politics, I believe there remains a need to frame these debates via a new radical disability praxis.

5

The Fourth Cornerstone:
Disability Culture and Identity

Disability politics are essentially to do with developing a praxis to advance social change, to emancipate disabled people from social exclusion and marginalisation. To do disability politics, it is necessary to come to terms with disability; to understand our collective experience of coming up against it, and to see its oppressive impact upon disabled people's lives. The struggle for emancipation therefore involves theory and action developed through exploring and expressing common experiences as disabled people. The self-organisation of disabled people requires acknowledgement of shared social and political objectives alongside the development of disability culture and a collective identity. As discussed in a previous chapter, the relationship between self-organisation and developing a socio-political identity has been called into question from a number of viewpoints. The fourth cornerstone of disability politics is therefore perhaps the most contentious.

The term 'disability culture' is made up of two words where both have a host of meanings and, as a result, makes it difficult to define. My starting point, as I am primarily talking about the British Disabled People's Movement, is a question posed by Vic Finkelstein at the first annual meeting of the London Disability Arts Forum:

> So why now, when there is much greater awareness of our desire to be fully integrated into society, do we suddenly want to go off at a tangent and start trying to promote our differences, our separate identity? [Even] if we do want to promote our own identity, our own culture, there has been precious little opportunity for us to develop such a cultural life.[1]

In this chapter, I want to drill down into some of the issues raised by the creation of a disability culture, and what others have written about culture and identity. Some may question my decision to identify these two elements as the fourth cornerstone of the movement; however, Finkelstein provides a compelling reason for this decision. He writes:

> ... we are still in very early days and culture cannot be imposed by an individual from the top down. It must develop spontaneously and creatively out of the collective experiences of disabled people. Nevertheless, we can say, in my view, that the willingness of disabled people to present a clear and unashamed self-identity and our ability to organise our own effective organisations for social change will greatly help the development of a disability culture.[2]

It is important to recognise that the denial of access to standard mainstream social activities will result in many disabled people not only having different experiences to those of their non-disabled peers, but it will mean they are likely 'to interpret the world differently ... see it, think about it, have feelings about it and talk about it differently'.[3]

This, I would argue, is the bedrock of disability culture. Before exploring issues around the notion of disability culture, it is necessary to consider them in relation to identity formation.

THE MEANING OF IDENTITY

The notion of identity has many meanings. It can mean the condition of being a certain person or thing, or the fact or condition of being associated or affiliated with something else. Weinreich and Saunderson put forward the view that:

> ... the formation of one's identity occurs through one's identifications with significant others ... These others may be benign such that one aspires to their characteristics, values and beliefs (a process of idealistic-identification), or malign when one wishes to dissociate from their characteristics (a process of defensive contra-identification).[4]

A crucial factor in identity formation for individuals born with significant impairments is how they negotiate how they see themselves and how significant others view them. This is both a psychological and a social issue; the nature of one's identity is influenced by the social environment in which someone operates, including the people they encounter. Self-identity can be viewed as 'the perception or recognition of one's characteristics as a particular individual, especially in relation to social context', and as 'personhood', or 'the quality or condition of being an individual person'.[5] Both definitions are used in this chapter.

Disabled people fighting against exclusion and marginalisation, and for their right to self-determination and liberation, are the bedrock of disability politics and the essence of our collective identity. However, Nancy Whittier informs us that a collective identity is not a simple reflection of a group's structural location, for example, its race or gender. It is an interpretation of that structural location or status that emerges from activism, conversation, experience and reflection.[6]

Disabled people's structural location is not a shared personal characteristic, but a socio-political one – that is, our exclusion and marginalisation within society, due to society's framing of impairment/disability.

Finkelstein identifies two aspects of forming a cultural identity. The first aspect involves creating a public image which he sees as the 'free acceptance of our distinctive group identity'. Establishing a distinctive group identity provides a platform for participation in what he calls the 'multicultural world'. Finkelstein saw creating a cultural identity as having a vital role in developing the confidence necessary to form organisations capable of promoting the social change. The second aspect of forming a cultural identity he saw as being the essential task of bringing together disabled people who are involved with the politics of disability and disabled people involved in the arts, in order to forge a creative interaction that would spearhead the initiative of developing a new disability culture.[7] In his opinion, the development of a culture is a central task of the movement.

There is often confusion as to the relationship between self and identity. Chayko views it thus: 'Your self is your personhood – literally, the person that you are, physically, psychologically, and socially. Your identity comprises your personal qualities and characteristics – what you are like? This includes your internal self-definition – preferences, values, beliefs, interests.'[8]

When a person or group is marginalised or threatened in some way, it is common to see this action being supported by an imposed 'identity' which is often undertaken via negative stereotyping.[9] A crucial aspect of both disability politics and culture, in general and specifically, is addressing the duality of having a 'disabled identity'. The duality stems from the struggle to overthrow the oppressive imposed identity at the same time as forging a collective new one.

Central to Murugami's understanding of identity in relation to disabled people, whether individually or collectively, is to what extent they are 'knowing oneself, accepting oneself with one's limitations, not being ashamed of the limitations but simply seeing them as part of the reality one is in, and perhaps as a boundary one is challenged to expand'.[10]

Thus, it is possible to recognise one's limitations without having a negative appraisal of them. Self-management of impairment has been subject to debate within the arena of disability politics over many years.[11]

Cherry informs us that self-concept is composed of two key parts: personal identity and social identity. In this way, 'Our personal identity includes such things as personality traits and other characteristics that make each person unique. Social identity includes the groups we belong to including our community, religion, college, and other groups.'[12]

As I have argued elsewhere, the interactions between the two identities – personal and social – are often very problematic for many disabled people. Disabled people's sense of self is often distorted by an array of factors stemming from dominant ideologies and practice, which can result in psychological and material disadvantages – leading to experiences of underachievement and, for many, a sense of inadequate fulfilment. To a certain extent, this can legitimise well-established stereotypes of disabled people.

Lack of knowledge and experience in confronting obstacles, meeting challenges, and engaging in activities that develop problem-solving strategies commonly stem from the failure to gain access to peer-group support and positive role models. Being isolated from other disabled people and subjected to normative values instilled by professionals, family and society can hinder a disabled person's ability to develop impairment-based strategies for addressing disabling barriers.[13]

The psychological or emotional experience of trying to negotiate the mainstream varies greatly from individual to individual and is itself very fluid. In many instances, being viewed as 'disabled' equates with negative appraisals, ranging from being viewed as abnormal through to being classed as non-human. Knowing that, in certain social contexts, you are not even considered 'human' can hit someone extremely hard. Thus, when a person internalises social oppression, it is likely they will have low self-esteem. How does this occur? Voigt suggests, 'Our society places emphasis on looks, speed, and being the same as everyone else. Thus, people with disabilities might place additional pressure on themselves to try to meet society's impossible standards.'[14]

Understanding these common and dominant responses is important because if we are constantly reminded that we are lacking in social worth, then it becomes increasingly likely that individuals will internalise these 'woundings'. Being 'acted upon' as if one is lacking in social worth can take many particular forms, but treating someone as invisible or as a non-person means that psychologically their very existence as a social being is denied. In a psychological sense, this type of denial, according to Ikäheimo, is another form of social exclusion – in other words, being prevented from full engagement in social life.[15] What if significant others, who play a crucial role in identity formation and determine how disabled people experience psychological social exclusion, are unable to view a disabled person's personhood because their life experiences and lifestyles are completely alien to them?

They may want to accept a disabled person's 'humanity', but only through making you a token 'normal person' [sic], not really understanding or wanting to be bothered to deal with you as a disabled person. Often this can result in inappropriate responses which compound one's 'Otherness' and social exclusion.[16]

DISABLEMENT, DISABLISM AND INTERNALISED OPPRESSION

More recently, the oppressive treatment of disabled people has been called 'disablism'. Carol Thomas writes, 'Disablism is a form of social oppression involving the social imposition of restrictions of activity on people with impairments and the socially engendered undermining of their psycho-emotional well-being.'[17]

It is necessary to cover how disablism, psychologically as well as socially, impacts upon disabled people in relation to disability culture and identity. Historically, for many disabled people, managing the transition period from segregation to mainstreaming was not easy, not just in terms of the realities of day-to-day living, but also in terms of dealing with disablism and personal interactions with the public, or those one relies on for support.

Campbell discusses the harm that can be done by living in cultures where 'disability' is relentlessly and inherently viewed as negative. She argues that it can produce self-loathing because the negativity surrounding how bodily difference is viewed can become internalised by those subjected to societal responses.[18]

Paulo Freire, when working with the oppressed poor in Latin America, noted that a characteristic of those who are oppressed is self-deprecation. Micheline Mason explains this observation well:

It would not exist without the real external oppression that forms the social climate in which we exist ... Once oppression has been internalised, little force is needed to keep us submissive. We harbour inside ourselves the pain and the memories, the fears and the confusions, the negative self-images and the low expectations, turning them into weapons with which to re-injure ourselves.[19]

UPIAS expressed concern over the notion of internalised oppression because of the risk that discussions could return to the focusing on individualised experiences rather than the social causes of oppression.[20] However, many escapees from institutional living believe they must both learn and unlearn how to relate to themselves as disabled people when transferring from a seg-regated impairment-focused environment into a primarily non-disabled culture, which at the time was alien to them. For example:

> There was of course no rehabilitation scheme to assist me to make the transition into the alien world of 'normal persons' or offer me advice on living within a disabling society. On reflection then, it's necessary to ask: how did I internalise the fact that at any given moment I could be sub-jected to an accepting or rejecting public gaze?[21]

The learning and unlearning process can be part of disability praxis. Those who acknowledge they have an impairment, but who reject seeing disabil-ity as a personal characteristic, often go on a journey of self-discovery and acceptance. This relates to Oliver's definition of being a politically conscious disabled person. Seeing oneself as a disabled person can, and often does, involve the conscious decision to embrace what I consider to be a collec-tive political identity. By speaking about ourselves as disabled people, we signify that (whether individually or as a social group) our disabled iden-tity is forged around the impact of disablement rather than using 'disability' as part of a personalised identity. The fact that the terms 'disabled people' and 'disabled person' are used in different ways, depending upon whether they adhere to the Equality Act 2010 definition or social model definition of disability, perhaps offers an indication as to where much of the confusion around the duality of the identity as a 'disabled person' comes from.

In Britain, the benefits system is said to operate from the bio-psycho-social approach. Personal Independence Payments has two components – daily living and mobility – and to be eligible to claim both, it is necessary to demonstrate one's ability to carry out twelve activities, including eating and drinking, washing, going to the toilet, communicating and getting around. In reality, the criteria focuses on functional capacity, which means demonstrating what a person is 'unable to do' [*sic*]). There is no scope for introducing social contexts, for example, identifying external disabling barriers. To receive the benefit, one must negatively describe one's self, rather than describe encountered disabling environments which are the root cause of additional cost. This often results in conflicts in terms of how a disabled person would want to present themselves and the support they require, and what the State wants them to comply with in order to qualify as being seen as 'disabled enough' to make a claim.

For many disabled people, this becomes a need to manage a dual 'disabled identity'. The dual identity consists of the imposed identity arising from dominant ideas that equate 'disability' with personal incapacity, and the self-defined political identity many disabled people struggle to establish – that is, the political and social recognition of being 'disabled by the social organisation of society'.

Thus, issues around identity and disability politics are intertwined.

THE DUALITY OF THE 'DISABLED' IDENTITY

The duality contained within the identity of 'disabled' people can be challenged and, in many cases, overthrown by speaking about who we believe we are and validating our own self and lifestyles. I would go beyond the argument Murugami makes and say that our ability to sustain our stories, which take us beyond being 'acceptable Crips' or 'token non-disabled people', is often influenced by our ability to connect with the knowledge and experiences of other disabled people and this, in turn, supports us to maintain our sense of self. I have argued that in many instances 'disabled lives' are invisible. Therefore, without transforming this situation, so that our lives are both visible and meaningful, it is extremely difficult to challenge – let alone overthrow – the oppressive experiences associated with society's treatment of disabled people.

The individual either accepts and embraces external identities, or seeks out alternatives which coincide with their own self-concept. It is common to hear disabled people talk about the 'lightbulb' moment when they discover the collective disabled identity of being among others who are 'disabled by society'. Colin Cameron advocates an affirmative model of disability where:

> Disability is a role imposed on people with impairments which leaves us unable to relate positively to impairment. So, we are always expected to be too busy trying to prove how well we've overcome impairment. Or too

busy with feeling sorry about our own tragedy … And this has a role in reinforcing and validating the idea of normality being a good thing.[22]

While this is a different approach to disability to the one I advocate, Cameron's use of the word 'role' corresponds to the notion of imposed identity that I use here. He links his model to the development of disability arts and culture. There is a fly in the ointment in that a major barrier to developing both individual and collective identities has been and continues to be the actual nature of both our oppression and the world disabled people inhabit. Paradoxically, what unites us also keeps us apart. Paul Abberley captured this when he wrote:

> … we need to develop theoretical perspectives which express the standpoint of disabled people, whose interests are not necessarily served by the standpoints of other social groups, dominant or themselves oppressed, of which disabled people are also members … Disabled people have inhabited a cultural, political and intellectual world from whose making they have been excluded and in which they have been relevant only as problems.[23]

Disabled people's oppression comes from being either excluded or marginalised, and denied identities which do not ascribe them as 'incomplete individuals'. The oppressive experiences we encounter make it difficult for disabled people to come together not simply as a social group but also as a socio-political community with a collective identity. When it comes to understanding this collective identity, we need to be mindful not to neglect how disablism intersects with other forms of oppression.[24]

In terms of having some form of socio-cultural-political awareness, self-identity as a disabled person has been recognised as important. For most disabled people, however, this 'identity' is not the first they encounter; if they ever do. For most people with impairments, irrespective of when they acquire it, their first encounter with 'disabled identities' tends to be through interaction with medical professionals, and the externally imposed identities that are part of any assessment.[25]

People who acquire an impairment, for example, in later life, are more likely to deny or reject an identity of being a 'disabled person' because they both accept and reject, at the same time, the oppressive meanings attached to seeing 'disability as a personal tragedy'. Often this sees members of this group applying the identity to others but not themselves.

Watson encountered people with impairments who seek to 'pass as normal', thus rejecting any 'disabled identity'; however, how they see themselves may not match up with the 'public gaze' that falls upon them.[26] The exact opposite may occur where people with impairments who accept that they have a 'disabled identity', then discover that this is denied either through the definitions used by the state, or the public not accepting their particular 'disabled identity'. I would argue that ultimately imposed 'disabled identities' are not static; people can slip in and out of them depending upon the social situations they find themselves in. Often the person with the impairment has no control over or involvement with the processes involved.

IS THERE A DISABILITY CULTURE?

Gramsci, however, outlined how the interests of ruling classes can be furthered more efficiently without the direct use of force, but rather through the dominance of their culture.[27] The discussion so far has focused upon how various social groups exist in relation to dominant culture and the development of sub-cultures; this, however, in itself does not take into account the positioning of disabled people within society. As we have previously noted, Oliver defines disabled people by appealing to three elements: the presence of impairment, the experience of externally imposed restrictions, and self-identification as a disabled person.[28]

Disabled people's positioning within society, it is argued, has been cemented by dominant ideologies and cultural representations which present 'disability' as an individual's nonconformity and inability to perform 'normal' social roles.

Abberley states that, for 'disabled people, the body is the site of oppression, both in form, and in what is done with it.'[29] This statement must be considered against the backdrop of the socio-political way in which a 'disabled person' is defined by those who see disability as a form of social oppression and their approach towards impairment reality. It should be noted that the separation of the presence of an impairment and the social situation or experience of disability remains one of the major contested areas within disability politics, culture and studies.[30]

When considering the cases for and against disability culture, the issue of impairment cannot be ignored; however, I argue it should be contextualised as something that is struggled over. The place of the 'impaired body' has particular significance when considering how 'the body' is viewed in mainstream art and culture. This in turn intersects with dominant ideologies and practices associated with disability. As Hevey points out, 'the tragedy principle uses the impairment as a metaphor and a symbol for a socially unacceptable person and it is the tragedy principle which is the bone-cage surrounding historical and current representation.'[31]

Disabled people are generally absent or invisible in dominant culture, except as stereotyped images which generally reinforce negative and oppressive attitudes towards impairment and disabled people.[32] As we have seen, the argument suggests that the self-organisation of disabled people and the development of the social model of disability gave rise to new cultural forms among sections of radicalised disabled people.[33] Does this add up to being a distinct disability culture and the fourth cornerstone of disability politics?

There is a strong tendency among those who see disabled people as socially oppressed to also claim there is an emerging disability culture sitting alongside the collective identity. There are also forces that oppose this view for a number of reasons. Peters informs us that:

> Bragg contended that in order for disabled people to claim a disability culture and therefore, a cultural identity, several requirements must be satisfied: 1) a common language; 2) a historical lineage that can be traced textually (through archives, memorials and distinctive media/ press publications); 3) evidence of a cohesive social community; 4) political solidarity; 5) acculturation within the family at an early age (and/or in segregated residential schools and clubs); 6) generational or genetic links; and 7) pride and identity in segregation from Others.*[34]

Peters herself offers an alternative view.

The dissenting voices raise questions as to how culture and disability are 'understood' and defined. Addressing these questions is complicated by the fact that often the language used in these discussions is not shared between participants in different countries, political and theoretical traditions, or activist sub-cultures. While there are conflicting concepts at play, it is still possible to argue that the self-organisation of the disabled led to forms of cultural and social solidarity being expressed, which is an essential feature of forging a specific culture. Peters, drawing upon McLean, argues, 'solidarity does not mean consensus, but recognises multiple antagonisms and struggles that characterise both the notion of self and the wider social reality.'[35]

---

* At the Society for Disability Studies Annual Conference in Washington, DC in May 1999, Lois Bragg, the keynote speaker from Gallaudet University who is Deaf, addressed the conference participants regarding the issue of disability culture.

With this in mind, one can consider Paulo Freire's description of a 'culture of silence' that he saw as perpetuating the oppression of disadvantaged minority groups.[36] The various critiques of disabled people's social oppression would support the idea that historically they have been encouraged to be passive, subjected to external pressures to conform to the norms and values of others, and denied the opportunity and resources for self-appraisal, both as individuals and as a social group.[37]

Under these conditions, the ability of disabled people to both reveal and develop their culture has been prevented by the nature of their oppression. Returning to a point made earlier, in a politico-cultural sense, disabled people were experiencing a 'dual identity', one imposed from the outside through attitudes, practices and imagery associated with 'the disabled' [sic] and an emerging new identity that they are forging through their own cultural expression and politics.[38]

A ROUTE TOWARDS EMPOWERMENT AND EMANCIPATION?

Central to the development of disability culture is the idea of a new social and collective identity. Historically, because of institutionalisation disabled people often were 'forced' to live and socialise together; therefore, it is common for disabled people to 'distance' themselves from others once free from institutions.[39] Many, however, have spoken about how their politicisation around the 'rights agenda' led to them seeing other disabled people in a new light where 'A developing disability culture can not only increase insight into the progress of disabled people becoming active in the area of civil rights, but can provide important opportunities for individuals to gain confidence by forming a new and independent social identity'.[40]

The idea of a new social identity raises a number of questions. It is not uncommon, as we have already witnessed, that in the US, disability culture is incorporated into a minority-group perspective where disability is analysed 'as a sociopolitical construction occasioned by the impact on ... disabled people of an environment shaped by and for the dominant majority'.[41]

One criticism of this perspective might be that it opens up the idea that disabled people can be accommodated within the existing political and cultural framework where they would be viewed as one more special-interest group or sub-culture. This is based on the view that 'The minority model normalizes the experience of disability as a minority experience no more or less aberrant or deviant than other minority groups' experiences (sex, race, sexual orientation, etc.)'.[42]

This perspective also misses out on the opportunity to build on the anti-hegemonic nature of disability culture. Disabled people have differing views as to what 'disability pride' means. Those critical and supportive of disability culture and the social model, have suggested some ambiguity remains. In the US, Steven Brown argues, 'Disability culture is about visibility and self-value. As with many groups in society, recognition by others only comes with self-awareness within the group of the groups' differences and strengths.'[43]

This reminds me of UPIAS's statement: 'The Union unashamedly identifies itself as an organisation of physically impaired people, and encourages its members to seek pride in ourselves, in all aspects of what we are.'[44]

There is a tension here between addressing the imposed oppressive identity of being 'disabled', and the struggle for social acceptance within the framework of being 'disabled by society'. Swain and French sought to address some of these issues by advocating for an affirmation model of disability; nevertheless, their argument remains at the margins of the debate.[45] I will return to the debates around 'disability pride' and the affirmation model of disability elsewhere in this book.

In the previous chapter, it was noted that many postmodernists question the wisdom of not only the minority-group perspective, but any attempt to construct a 'disabled' social identity. Liggett argues, 'the price of becoming politically active on their own behalf is accepting the consequences of defining disability within new perspectives, which have their own priorities and needs.'[46]

While recognising that within the postmodernist arguments there are useful insights into the limitations and pitfalls in terms of attempting to build disability culture based on identity politics, none of them adequately address the power relationships that exist within the struggle against the cultural hegemony of dominant ideologies and culture. Shakespeare, on the other hand, appears to want to rehabilitate aspects of dominant ideologies rather than combat them.[47] As stated previously, without a meaningful alternative pole of attraction, it is not difficult to understand why disabled people have adopted the strategies they have in relation to identity politics and disability culture.

DISABILITY CULTURE AS AN EMPOWERING FORCE

The general argument that has been put forward is that the relationship between the Movement's political and cultural identities underpins its uniqueness because they stem from the *nature* of disabled people's oppression. The dual identity emerges from the social, political and cultural challenges to dominant ideologies and practice, imposing what Goffman termed a 'spoiled identity', which referred to an identity that causes a person to experience stigma due to an attribute that is deeply discrediting. Thus, the existence of impairment is viewed as an attribute which divides people into 'those-who-are-normal' and 'those-who-are-not', thereby making those-who-are-not less worthy. Throwing off this appraisal of 'the impaired' body, within disability politics, re-situated what it means to be a disabled person.[48] Pratt says identity politics is 'a concept that refers to social movements organised around the politicisation of particular cultural identities'; however, I believe the collective identity of disabled people is in the first instance a political rather than a cultural one.[49] I would argue that the British Disabled People's Movement was first and foremost concerned with finding:

... ways of changing the physical and social environment so that we are no longer prevented from realising our human potential, rather than thinking of what care is needed in the able bodied world when a cure has failed to materialise ... This growing awareness amongst ourselves has already resulted in setting up our own organisations, and even our own services, all over the country, all over the world. We need now to speed up this shift in thinking from an individualistic, 'cure or care' approach to a social interpretation of disability.[50]

Thus, Finkelstein goes on to say, 'Given the long history of disability our developing self-awareness still needs to be cultivated with care and understanding. No doubt both greater study and the development of a disability culture will be needed before our impact on society will become irresistible.'[51]

My reading of this is the development of a disability culture is viewed as being transformative; acknowledging living with impairments in a disabling world, whilst at the same time striving to have choice and control of lifestyles shaped by the interactions between people with impairments and social environments. Disability politics and culture interact to challenge the status quo. In this sense, the forging of a political and cultural collective identity is transitional because it becomes a means to an end, with the end being the acceptance of diversity within humanity.

An interesting argument put forward is that 'There is no real identity – individual or group-based – that is separable from its conditions of possibility, and any political appeal to identity formations must engage with the paradox of acting from the very subject-positions it must also oppose.'[52] This is why I speak of the duality of the 'disabled identity'. Connolly argues:

> An identity is established in relation to a series of differences that have become socially recognized. These differences are essential to its being. If they did not coexist as differences, it would not exist in its distinctness and solidity ... Identity requires differences in order to be, and it converts difference into otherness in order to secure its own self-certainty.[53]

This assertion leads to claims that:

> The danger of identity politics, then, is that it casts as authentic to the self or group a self-understanding that in fact is defined by its opposition to a dominant identity, which typically represents itself as neutral. Reclaiming such an identity as one's own merely reinforces its dependence on this Other, and further internalizes and reinforces an oppressive hierarchy. This danger is frequently obscured by claims that particular identities are essential or natural ... .[54]

This is contrary to what I believe lies behind forging a collective identity and developing disability culture which is a rejection of the dual identity as *natural*. I believe Shakespeare follows a similar line of argument to the one above in his chapter, 'Labels and Badges – The Politics of Disability Identity'. He writes:

> However, there is potentially a higher price to adopting the disabled label than to highlight separateness and difference. A more serious problem, within disability context, is that building an identity around oppression leads the minority group into taking up a victim position. In this sense, a social model of disability can be as negative as a medical model ... In both versions, the agency of disabled people is denied and the scope for positive engagement with either impairment or society is diminished.[55]

Is acknowledging and combating oppression adopting a 'victim position'? I would argue the exact opposite is true: the forging of a collective identity and developing disability culture is overthrowing the identity and associated labels with define disabled people as 'victims' and oppressively seeing them as 'Other'.

My own view shares much with those offered by Gurminder K. Bhambra and Victoria Margree in their paper 'Identity Politics and the Need for a "Tomorrow"'. They argue for a rethinking of '"politicised identities" in terms of a commitment to a desired future, as a corrective to the conservative effects that frequently accompany "identity" (here identified as "exclusionary politics" and "reification of identities")'.[56] Their emphasis on the future, however, does not negate the need to make a commitment to addressing traumatic pasts.

A particularly strong and important aspect of their argument is that they see a productive identity politics as one 'which understands the identity of the political grouping as provisional, since it is based on the need to respond to an existing injustice, and therefore, oriented to a future in which that injustice, and hence, the need for the identity claim, is no longer present.'[57]

Gill expresses the view that 'we could oppose our social devaluation through developing a strong disability community-family and elaborating a proud disability culture.'[58] Undertaking such a task would not simply confront non-disabled people, it would also challenge some disabled people as well. Simon Brisenden perhaps puts this in the sharpest of terms when he wrote, 'Some disabled people avoid the issues of disability culture simply because it touches areas of their lives that they would rather not think about. If you have carved out a life against all the odds as an alien in a non-disabled world, you do not want to think too hard about the price you have had to pay.'[59]

I have touched upon this when discussing the issue of self-identity. Brisenden suggests there is a struggle between those who seek acceptance and buy into non-disabled people's views of how disabled people should think, feel, and behave, and those who 'no longer need to build our lives on a denial and dis-valuing of our background and the experiences of pain and triumph, sadness and joy, which form the reality of our upbringing.'[60]

Brisenden stresses the fact that disability culture is built upon disabled people being 'ruthlessly honest' about 'who we are' and 'our role within society'. It could be argued that this is a core element in making disability culture challenging and potentially empowering not only for individuals, but for groups of disabled people. Finkelstein and Morrison elaborate upon this when they write, 'In order to participate meaningfully within the community, members of this group must actively engage in the issues that confront them. In doing this they provide the material for their own cultural development that is self-determining and self-governing.'[61]

In other words, disabled people need to 'interpret' the world through their own eyes – not just those of non-disabled people. This means looking afresh at perceptions of the world, how it is constructed and whose interests it serves. This creates the possibility of transforming 'interpretation' into 'active participation' which, in turn, not only acts as a challenge to the status quo, but also brings disabled people together 'on their own terms' and has the potential of being a platform for political action. Does disability culture have other functions?

Another example of disability culture's empowering force, it is argued, is its ability to reach out to disabled people who might not immediately identify with disability politics or being 'disabled'; however, by being exposed to disabled people's stories or their 'take on the world', they can begin to engage with it 'on their own terms'. Disability culture becomes a recruitment officer and organiser.

Given the nature of disabled people's oppression, many have been disempowered by mainstream culture(s); disability culture on the other hand recruits, educates and equips disabled people to explore their own identities, differences and values within environments they control and in which they feel valued. The exclusion and marginalisation of disabled people within cultural production means that few role models exist or are known about; therefore many disabled artists are breaking new ground.

Disability culture intersects with personal and collective identity formation and to various degrees of self-awareness of the significance of impairment reality at personal, social, political and cultural levels of engagement. Disability culture can be viewed as contributing to the creation of social solidarity and the forging of a new social collective identity through the production of cultural activities.

Galvin speaks of 'a sense of connectedness that can break down the feelings of isolation and alienation.'[62] This takes place, according to Gill, by giving 'definition and expression of our value as a community', which 'charges us up and enriches our lives, giving us energy and endurance against oppression'. Gill recognises diversity among disabled people, but she is also aware of how society actively separates disabled people from one another.[63]

In 2014, I questioned whether or not the direction of disability art and culture was capable of maintaining its radicalism – that is, acting as a subversive edge against the oppressive nature of dominant culture, whilst giving disabled people progressive cultural forms to identify with.[64] Disabled people did become increasingly engaged in the production and distribution of a myriad of cultural and artistic forms; however, an ambiguity nonetheless existed. Tony Heaton states, 'The widely held definition of Disability Arts is: *Art made by Disabled artists that is informed by or reflects the personal experience of disability.*' How should we interpret what this means? Allan Sutherland writes: 'Disability arts is art informed by a personal experience of disability, by which I mean both physical, sensory or neurological impairment and the discriminatory barriers which limit the lives of disabled people.'[65]

Art, of course, is only an aspect of culture, but the way Allan presents 'disability art' as being informed by 'personal experience of disability' meaning both impairment and disabling barriers, raises questions in terms of how 'disability' is perceived by disabled artists. In part, this returns us to a previous discussion about 'the personal is political', but it also touches upon the problematic area of where impairment reality and living with impairment in a disablist society, fits into disability politics and culture.

Perhaps drawing upon an interchange that took place between Linda Rocco and Tony in 2019, we can gain some insight into how disability art is, or at least was, viewed. Linda asked, 'Nowadays, do you think there is still the same drive to make art political and politics through art, as it was during the golden age of the Disability Arts Movement? Are the current generations still involved in the debate or do they somehow remain fairly passive towards societal change?'[66]

What is evident is that, from the 1980s onwards, there have been growing numbers of disabled people engaging in counter-cultural activities. There is evidence of disabled people worldwide expressing themselves in cultural as well as political terms. The decline in self-organisation and disability politics has had a negative impact on developing disability culture; however, I would still argue that for disabled people who do identify as individuals belonging to an oppressed social group, the impact of disability culture upon many of their lives is empowering.

Despite the unanswered questions and differing takes that exist, I retain the view that both disability art and culture contribute towards forging a collective social identity, aiding both resistance and emancipatory struggles; which is why I see disability culture as the fourth cornerstone of disability politics. It is vital nonetheless to have absolute clarity as to what 'sociopolitical identity' means for disabled people and how this relates to questions around self and collective identities.

PART II

Towards a New Disability Praxis?

6

Impairment and Oppression:
The Battleground Reviewed

To begin an exploration of what a radical disability praxis might look like, it is necessary to address an issue that has divided disabled activist and scholar opinion for decades: where does the question of impairment fit within disability politics? At the heart of the matter is the role played by impairment within disabled people's oppression. Within the boundaries of disability politics and scholarship, the relationship between impairment and disability is a contentious area of debate. Indeed, even to suggest that 'impairment' exists as a material reality has been contested by postmodernist theorists.

Within this and the following chapter justice cannot be done to the myriad of debates that exist around impairment and disability. My primary aim is to challenge the misrepresentation of the positioning of impairment within the social interpretation of disability and Oliver's social model. Without addressing this thorny question, it will remain difficult to articulate the view that within disabled people's emancipation struggle, it must be acknowledged that 'the body is the site of oppression, both in form, and in what is done with it.'[1] I have referred to disabled people's oppression as being subjected to *unequal and differential treatment* in terms of people with impairments' social relations; however, these are shaped by economic, ideological, social and cultural factors. The battleground has always been concerned with the ways certain bodies have been seen and treated. Often, impairment is viewed as an entity in its own right; at other times, it is an abstract concept, but what is inescapable irrespective of how it is understood, is the fact that it has become employed as an instrument of oppression.

PREPARING THE BATTLEGROUND

Too often debates around impairment and disability fail to situate them within their historical or cultural contexts, thereby underplaying the social factors involved. It is important to acknowledge that the central issue running through most debates revolves around the variations of the 'body' as determined by those who gaze upon it. The ways in which bodily differences have been viewed are historically specific. Wasserman informs us that 'The lack of attention to "disability" or "impairment" in general may have a simple explanation: there were no such concepts to attend to until 19th century scientific thinking put variations in human function and form into categories of abnormality and deviance.'[2]

The introduction of concepts were around specific lines of enquiry; this fact should not be confused with the much older practice of distinguishing between those seen to have the ability to labour and those who were viewed as 'impotent'.[3]

Pratt informs us that 'The Industrial Revolution, embodying the shift from an agrarian to industrial economy and the massive shifts in population and social structures it induced, was shortly to usher in a set of political changes that would establish a framework for modern Western states that has survived up to the present day.'[4]

Russell and Malhotra also argue that industrial capitalism 'created not only a class of proletarians but also a new class of "disabled" who did not conform to the standard worker's body and whose labour-power was effectively erased, excluded from paid work.'[5]

For almost a hundred years, the prevailing attitude towards people deemed 'defective' remained unaltered. Morton notes that in 1930, Julian Huxley, secretary of the London Zoological Society and chairman of the Eugenics Society wrote: 'What are we going to do? Every defective man, woman and child is a burden. Every defective is an extra body for the nation to feed and clothe, but produces little or nothing in return.'[6]

Until the 1960s, the language and concepts used in relation to disease and injury were imprecise. Dixon and colleagues state that 'Philip [Wood] said that this set him thinking about the concepts of impairment, handicap, and disability, words often used interchangeably but relevant at that time to the Amelia Harris survey of disability in relation to the chronic sick and disabled legislation.'[7] Given this lack of clarity, I want to suggest that Oliver presents us with a watershed moment when he writes:

> Starting from the work of Harris (1971) and her national survey of disabled people, a threefold distinction of impairment, disability and handicap was developed. Following various discussions and refinements, a more sophisticated scheme was advanced by Wood (1981) and this was accepted by the World Health Organization as the basis for classifying illness, disease and disability. However, these definitions have not

received universal acceptance, particularly amongst disabled people and their organisations.[8]

The significance of Harris and colleagues' work can be seen in the words of Alf Morris MP, when he spoke in Parliament a decade later:

> ... the survey carried out in the late 1970s by Amelia Harris for the OPCS on 'The Handicapped and Impaired in Great Britain' has been a standard work of reference on the characteristics and requirements of disabled people.
> This monumental work of international renown was the first attempt to draw together information pertaining to all aspects of handicap: employment, housing, health and leisure. It is a detailed and comprehensive guide for planners to the accurate and economic allocation of resources. It has, in fact, been the foundation for the development of benefits and services for the disabled over the past decade.[9]

The triad definition of disability established the global hegemonic view that 'disease led to the impairment of bodily functions which in turn restricted what people could do (disability) and as a consequence limited their participation in society (handicap)'.[10]

It is therefore against this backdrop that broader dialogue began to take place among people with physical impairments, who came together in the Union of the Physically Impaired Against Segregation (UPIAS). As noted, during the 1970s and early 1980s, the Office of Population Censuses and Surveys (OPCS) Survey,[11] and later the International Classification of Impairment, Disability and Handicap (ICIDH), set out the framework for defining how 'disability' was to be seen. The few disabled scholar activists that existed at the time not only saw these definitions as representing the oppressive ways disabled people were viewed, but they also saw the political necessity to construct an alternative way of seeing disability. The path they chose initially was to subvert the official definitions, because very little else existed in terms of supporting the view that disability should be seen as a social problem and not a medicalised one.[12] In 1975, Vic Finkelstein wrote an article in which he transformed the triad definition of disability based upon those of Amelia Harris. He suggested impairment be defined as 'lacking part of or all of a limb, or having a defective limb, organ or mechanism of the body'. He then switched handicap and disability around so that handicap was viewed as 'the loss or reduction of functional ability', and disability regarded as 'the disadvantage or restriction of activity caused by social relationships which take no or little account of people who have physical impairments'.[13] I consider this exercise as being extremely important for a number of reasons. Firstly, the roots of the social approach to disability are to be found within the outlined definitions. However, it is necessary to grasp that Finkelstein limits his focus at this stage to people with physical impairments. Neither Finkelstein nor UPIAS were concerned with the nature of differing types of impairment, but simply sought to take their existence as a given, in order to centre specifically upon how those with physical impairments were denied participation within society. UPIAS believed that in the material reality of 'lacking all or part of a limb, or having a defective limb, organ or mechanism of the body' lay the basis for their social oppression.

Withers argues the acceptance of the definition of impairment de facto means that the social approach acknowledged the notion of 'normality'.[14] In discussions during UPIAS's formation, the meaning of impairment as 'flawed' and 'abnormal' were raised. It was argued that a distinction was being made between the altered physiology of an individual which was viewed as a material reality and the overlaid ideologically driven pathologising of the individual's body. ICIDH viewed bodily deviation as an 'abnormality'.

Finkelstein's decision to flip the handicap and disability from Harris' triad definition is an important shift. In common usage, the word 'handicap' refers to 'a circumstance that makes progress or success difficult'.[15] The swap was no mere whim. It was a conscious decision to acknowledge that a loss of bodily functioning can be 'restrictive' to various degrees; however, this needs to be placed not only within social contexts, but also within an understanding of specific relations that take place. The focus is on interaction between individuals involving collective groups of people with physical impairments and the socialised environments they encounter. Barnett and Casper suggest that human 'social environments encompass the immediate physical surroundings, social relationships, and cultural milieus within which defined groups of people function and interact.'[16] Hence, Finkelstein saw disability as arising from *negative social interaction* between people who were considered physically impaired and the lived-in or desired environments that only primarily catered for people without significant impairments. He nevertheless argued that within dominant thinking, the negative aspects of the interaction, were always blamed on the impaired body:

If it is recognised that it is the interaction between a person's particular and permanent physical or mental characterisations … and the environment in which the person functions that makes a person disabled, then clearly the actual nature, status and degree of the disability will be determined by the precise characteristics of one or both sides of the interaction … Despite the fact the degree of disability arises out of an interaction, disability still seems to be wholly located in the human being![17]

It is important to note that Finkelstein is speaking here about the micro level of society and in relation to the barriers to community life. The final sentence relates to the causal link within dominant thinking. Returning to the articulation of the definition of disability developed by Finkelstein and UPIAS, there is a lack of clarity. They state 'disability [is viewed] as the disadvantage or restriction of activity caused by a contemporary social organisation *which takes no or little account of people who have physical impairments* and thus excludes them from participation in the mainstream of social activities.'[18]

While agreeing that in the final analysis, it is the *nature* of capitalist society's contemporary social organisation that causes disabled people to be excluded from, or marginalised within, mainstream social activities; nevertheless, there is a limitation to this view. The social oppression stems from precisely *how* disabled people are, in the first instance, 'taken into account' via negative appraisals of their bodies, which ultimately results in blaming them *directly* for being unable to participate.

The medicalised appraisals of the body legitimated giving social value to some bodies; those deemed healthy, fit and 'normal' [sic], and viewing others as burdens on society because they were unable to conform to the accepted and expected body types and fulfil the social roles deemed 'normal' [sic].[19] The removal of 'undesirable bodies' took place both materially and ideologically via institutionalisation, promoting eugenics, and charity.[20] It is not simply a case of paying little or no attention to the reality of impairment; it is a question of understanding who benefits from how disabled people were historically seen and treated. This point connects not only with Abberley's assertion that the impaired body itself is the site of oppression, but also why breaking the causal link between impairment and disability was an important aspect of the social interpretation of disability.

COMING TO TERMS WITH DISABILITY

When outlining the ICIDH, Philip Wood argued that there was no such thing as a 'disabled person', but instead he claimed a person 'had a disability'.[21] His premise was based upon seeing 'disability' as the measurable impact of the loss of functional capacity within a precise bodily performed 'activity' – for example, seeing, hearing, speaking, walking, etc. Very few people, he argued, were totally incapacitated and therefore to view them as 'disabled' would be imprecise. Although there is a logic to this argument, it also plays down or ignores many crucial factors, among them being how 'measuring functional loss' relates to the differing social, economic and cultural environments that people with impairments inhabit or find themselves excluded from.

A major criticism of the ICIDH's framework was that it was individualistic and offered a functional-limitations perspective which grounded all social restrictions within the context of the causal nature and degree of an individual's impairment.[22] Imrie sums up the approach taken in the ICIDH:

Foremost, Western bio-medical discourses have been highly influential in contributing to explanations about the nature of disability. They stem from the medical profession and reflect its interest in the impaired, or functionally limited, body as an object of scientific interest, classification and medical intervention. A bio-medical understanding of disability reduces impairment to categories of the diseased body and 'focuses on the patient not the person'. Disability, then, is understood to be a consequence of the biological malfunctioning of bodily organisms. Such discourses encourage the study of how chronic and acute conditions affect bodily functions, and the implications for a person's movement, mobility and independence.[23]

The history of social policies with regards to disabled people has been largely determined by bio-medical discourses, which is why many critics still refer to this process as the 'medical model of disability'. However, I agree with Oliver that the 'medicalisation' of what is viewed as disablement is not the whole account for the dominant ways in which disabled people are both seen and treated. Dominant thinking employs the medicalisation of individual bodies to legitimate seeing people-with-impairments' social disadvantage as stemming from the functional limitations or psychological losses which are then assumed to arise from 'disability'. It was not simply the medical professions who socially constructed 'disability as a personal tragedy', as I have demonstrated elsewhere.

It is often implied that Wood sought to develop a non-medical conception of disability; however, many critics of the ICIDH argue that it nevertheless maintained the reductionist understanding of seeing handicap as the social disadvantages stemming from the presence of 'impairments and disabilities'. In passing, it should be noted that the use of the word 'handicap' in Britain took on particular negative connotations due to cultural interpretations and mythology among disabled people.[24] Within bio-medical discourses, it is argued that while certain impairments do not produce functional loss – for example, a facial disfigurement – nonetheless they are still viewed as the *direct cause of* social disadvantage. The word 'handicap' was phased out of official language in Britain, with only 'impairment' and 'disability' being employed within official definitions. Among British activists, the middle aspect of the original triad definition – functionality of body/mind – has over time been assumed into the notion of impairment.[25] This definitional change has had consequences for British scholar activists because not only has the definition of impairment remained unaltered, thus making acknowledgement of 'impairment reality' invisible, but it has also contributed to crude articulations of the processes through which people with impairments are 'disabled by society'.

At a theoretical level, the debate around the imposition of social restrictions cannot take place without addressing the relationship between impairment and social environments. Both Wood and Finkelstein acknowledged that social disadvantage arose from interactions between people viewed as having significantly impaired bodies and their social environments. Taking as a given, the causal link between impairment and social disadvantage is legitimated by, but also legitimates in turn, professional practice. Finkelstein refers to this as being the administrative model in which both cure and care approaches towards disabled people can be found. These approaches derive from the view that 'disability means social death necessitating interventions by able-bodied professional and lay workers who then "administer" the cure or care solutions.'[26]

The notion of disability as 'social death' has filtered down into societal *common sense* in relation to how disabled people are viewed. Common sense arrives as a result of the hegemonic power that is contained within the dominant ideologies that underpinned professional practice around the lives of disabled people. For Gramsci, 'hegemony is a power which saturates, influences, and permeates all aspects of one's life: the economic, cultural, social, ethical, political, and so on. In doing so, it shapes and moulds consciousness, conceptions of common sense and world-views.'[27]

It is possible to go as far back as 1951 and Talcott Parsons' 'sick role' where people 'who are sick break the rules of society because they are viewed as non-productive members. Yet, unlike other "deviants," people who are sick or disabled are not setting out to be deviant. They are forced into that role.'[28]

Smith explores the term 'sanctioned deviance', often used 'based on the idea that society tolerates this divergence from social norms and expectations because of the understanding that there are extenuating circumstances which must be weighed when evaluating the situation.'[29]

This is a historical theme within social policy down the ages. In 1388, the Statute of Cambridge insisted on Letters Testimonial for all able-bodied beggars;* whereas the statute reiterated that 'the needy who were incapable of labouring, were permitted to beg for alms, but only in their own communities.' This distinction found its way into the Poor Laws with the idea of 'deserving' and 'undeserving' poor. It has also had resonance in recent British austerity policies. Powell, for example, says about New Labour's Third Way as appearing to be 'neither distinctive nor new, leaning to the right rather than the centre or centre-left, and having some roots in the New Poor Law and the mixed economy of welfare of Beveridge.'[30]

Although impairment might be seen as a 'neutral' dimension in the first instance, it is quickly consumed into 'negative associations'.[31] Thus the professional and societal gaze focuses upon the loss of functionality and the attached social consequences that are read into the interaction between the impaired body and social environments established by people without significant impairment. The idea of 'sanctioned deviance' and the recognition of 'extenuating circumstances' feeds into what is considered acceptable or expected of people with chronic illnesses and significant impairments, and therefore connects with common-sense views on who is and who is not 'deserving' of support.

These views are not static, but like other forms of common sense, they are historically specific.**[32] These are the ideas, values and practice that UPIAS and Finkelstein saw embedded within the ICIDH and why they considered it to be not only a vehicle for reinforcing how disabled people were both seen and treated, but also as a major barrier to finding meaningful solutions to disabled people's social situation. The language employed within the ICIDH triad definition reflects the bias that existed.

Maria Barile cites a literature survey reviewing the definition of disability conducted by Solomon in 1993, stating:

---

* Statutes of the Realm, v. 2, p. 58: 12 Rich. II, c. 7.
** Just as Hall speaks of 'racisms' and that they are historically specific, I would argue how the 'body' is viewed, socially constructed and treated, creates specific social relations for impaired/ disabled people.

In the community at large, the ICIDH terminology reinforces the fear of impairment and the medical perception of disability. Opposition to the ICIDH steadily increased among disabled people's organisations and disquiet had been mounting from professional circles as well. Much of this criticism came from how the classification system was being employed.[33]

A number of disabled scholar activists, led by David Pfeiffer, rounded upon the WHO's ICIDH and early drafts of what was known as 'ICIDH-2'.[34] Feeling under increased pressure, the WHO in 2001 adopted the International Classification of Functioning, Disability and Health (ICF). Within the World Health Organization's ICF, the word 'disabilities' is used as an umbrella term to cover impairments, activity limitations and participation restrictions. Hence, 'an activity limitation is a difficulty encountered by an individual in executing a task or action; while a restriction is a problem experienced by an individual (due to having an impairment) in involvement in life situations.'[35]

Interestingly, Marks argues that the ICF 'seeks to develop the conception that "mind, body, and environment are not easily separable but rather mutually constitute each other in complex ways."'[36] The upshot of this shift is that whereas within the ICIDH 'social barriers' were reduced to simply being the consequence of the impact of an impairment, including the loss or reduction of functionality, what the ICF does is to conceive 'disability' as 'a compound phenomenon' where the individual and social elements are viewed as integral.

Over the last 25 years, disabled activists in Britain and worldwide have criticised how the ICF and approaches based upon it have been used by governments to construct bio-psycho-social models to determine neoliberal welfare policies.[37]

The introduction of the ICF therefore needs to be understood from within the context of its impact upon socio-economic policies. When the welfare state entered into 'crisis', governments attempted to narrow the definition of disablement and to cut entitlement levels.[38] In Britain, the lives of many disabled people are dependent on the welfare state and social policies that underpin it. Despite the claim in 2013 that the new Personal Independent Payment's assessment process would employ a bio-psycho-social approach, the Department of Works and Pension's use of the UNUM Company's model focused entirely on measuring functionality.[39]

Dominant ways of appraising impairment, disability and handicap have been a central feature of disabled people's encountered oppression. Given this, the idea of impairment reality as a site of struggle necessitates exploring the relationship between impairment and oppression further. Paul Abberley and Carol Thomas both raise issues concerning this relationship which have implications for how we view or employ the social interpretation or model of disability.

THE CONCEPT OF OPPRESSION AND THE 'IMPAIRED BODY' AS A SITE OF STRUGGLE

Abberley's paper 'The Concept of Oppression and the Development of a Social Theory of Disability' is a product of its time, yet in other ways, it was in advance of current thinking. Abberley writes, for example:

> ... to usefully apply the notion of oppression to the complex of impairment, disability and handicap involves the development of a theory which connects together the common features of economic, social and psychological disadvantage with an understanding of the material basis of these disadvantages and the ideologies which propagate and reproduce them.[40]

Despite appearing to 'use' the OPCS definitions, he nevertheless does provide a useful way to consider impairment from within a social interpretation of disability and assists us to address questions about impairment in relation to Oliver's model.[41] Abberley suggests in his early work at least, Oliver used oppression interchangeably with exploitation, and as a consequence, it is not defined but rather seen as an 'obvious' but difficult to substantiate characteristic of 'social relations under capitalism'.[42] The lack of clarity surrounding the meaning of oppression in his work is demonstrated when Oliver writes 'the social model of disability, as articulated by disabled people themselves, which sees disability as social restriction or oppression'.[43]

Oliver's use of the word 'or' is problematic; is he suggesting that they are one and the same or elements of disability? Abberley provides an insight into his understanding of the impairment–oppression relationship when he writes, 'A crucial feature of oppression and the way it operates is its specificity, of form, content and location; so to analyse the oppression of disabled people in part involves pointing to the essential differences between their lives and those of other sections of society, including those who are, in other ways, oppressed.'[44]

Among the essential differences, for Abberley, are the significant dimensions which place disabled people in an inferior position to other members of society. He speaks of how the disadvantages experienced by disabled people dialectically relate to what I refer to as the 'individual tragedy approach' towards disability which justifies and perpetuates their situation. Another important point he raises is how class analysis per se has been shown to have limitations for the analysis of racial and sexual disadvantage. The historical materialist approach must therefore go beyond just viewing disability as being simply caused by the economic interests within capitalist societies, and incorporate other dimensions which has led to disabled people's social exclusion. Abberley states, 'While in the cases of sexual and racial oppression, biological difference serves only as a qualificatory condition of a wholly ideological oppression, for disabled people the biological difference, albeit as I shall argue itself a consequence of social practices, is itself a part of the oppression.'[45]

Several points emerge from distinguishing between different oppressions. Firstly, we need to place Abberley's work within its historical context, where 'disabled people' were primarily viewed as having physical impairments and therefore issues specifically relating to what is often termed 'hidden impairment' are not discussed.* Secondly, there is a need for caution with regards to how 'biological difference' is being employed within the text.[46] Lastly, the notion of 'social practices' needs context as well. Reckwitz views social practices as everyday practices which are typically and habitually performed in (much of) a society. These practices are seen as meaningful parts of their everyday life activities, for example, going to work, cooking, showering.[47] I see Abberley's usage linking to the view that disabled people's oppression stems from their differential and unequal treatment due to how their loss of functionality is viewed in terms of fulfilling social practices.

Here lies the fundamental basis for seeing disabled people's oppression as a specific form. Abberley writes:

> It is crucial that a theory of disability as oppression comes to grips with this 'real' inferiority, since it forms a bedrock upon which justificatory oppressive theories are based and, psychologically, an immense impediment to the development of political consciousness amongst disabled people. Such a development is systematically blocked through the naturalisation of impairment.[48]

---

* The term, 'hidden impairment' usually refers to differences that are neither obvious nor visible.

At this point, we should perhaps remind ourselves of what Finkelstein writes: 'The universal instinct of disabled people to separate their experience of discrimination (which should be opposed) from the experience of living with a body impairment (which has to be managed) may explain the general reservation about identifying oneself with a term which confuses both states.'[49]

In essence, what is being described here is the distinction between accepting impairment reality – that is, managing the impact of functional loss or any other body/mind consequence of having an impairment – and rejecting how that impairment reality is subjected to oppressive societal appraisals which subsequently leads to discriminatory treatment.* Within dominant ways of seeing disability as we have seen, no such distinction exists. Impairment reality is seen and operationalised as the direct cause of an individual's social disadvantage. The process however is two-fold: the oppressive appraisals stem from both the impairment reality and the ideological construction of nonconformity, thereby 'explaining' the absence of significantly impaired bodies from mainstream social activity.

Key here is the emphasis that Abberley places upon the 'naturalisation of impairment'. His argument is that impairments are not per se naturally occurring, but are social products, is supported by a detailed look at how impairments are socially produced by various aspects of social relations which involve socio-economic and geographical contexts. There are a number of acute ramifications behind this argument for our understanding of the relationship between impairment and oppression.

Within Western disability politics, this relationship is often framed solely within the terms of disabled people's treatment vis-à-vis social activity, whereas in the Global South, scholar activists acknowledge the social production of impairment as a crucial aspect of disabled people's oppression. Soldatic informs us that 'Within the realm of disability theory and politics, a growing number of papers have articulated an elaboration of a disability theoretical praxis that critically engages with issues of impairment production with the enduring relations of (neo-)colonization, global neoliberal capitalism, and imperialism.'[50]

This theoretical work needs undertaking, but there are unresolved differences in play. I am sympathetic to the notion of developing an understanding of the politics of impairment, as it relates to Abberley's view that a social theory of impairment is required. The failure to address impairment

---

* Impairment reality as a concept is discussed in the following chapter.

as a social product has undermined the development of a radical disability praxis involving theoretical and political consideration. Soldatic notes that:

> Writers such as Abberley (1987), Berghs (2010) and Stone (1999) have clearly articulated the ways in which impairment is not always natural. However, within the global hegemonic consensus of justice claims on the grounds of disability within the [Convention on the Rights of Persons with Disabilities – CRPD], it is an 'interaction between persons with impairments and attitudinal and environmental barriers that hinders their full and effective participation in society on an equal basis with others'.[51]

Soldatic points out that the focus of the Convention is concerned with the impaired body and the socio-political implications; 'the production of impairment is outside its referential frame'.[52]

As I suggested earlier with reference to Barile, the issue of how the ICF is employed within the Convention, and for what purpose, is an important consideration in how 'impairment' is viewed in the current period. This links back to Abberley's view that:

> At a political level, focusing upon kinds and rates of impairment, posing as they do in an explicit and graphic form the contradictions between the potentially beneficial nature of medical science and its restrictions and deformations in the capitalist mode of production, can be seen as forming a materialist basis for a theory of disability as oppression.[53]

In 2013, the International Labour Organisation reported that the nature of occupational diseases is altering rapidly due to technological and social changes, along with global economic conditions. These factors were seen as aggravating existing health hazards and creating new ones.[54]

Abberley contentiously suggests the development of 'an attitude of ambivalence towards impairment'. This leads him to argue that 'Impairment must be identified as a bad thing, insofar as it is an undesirable consequence of a distorted social development, at the same time as it is held to be a positive attribute of the individual who is impaired'.[55]

On the face of it, the key distinction being made by Abberley is between the need to prevent socially produced impairments, on the one hand, and challenging the negative attitudes towards and treatment of people who become or are already impaired on the other. This has huge ramifications, because for such an approach towards impairment to exist, then all social actors would need to see the benefits of such an approach. Currently, I see neither the oppressors nor those who are oppressed being inclined to adopt such a dualist approach towards addressing 'impairment'.

A further ramification of how the naturalisation of impairment impacts is the question of age. Abberley suggests that when impairments are taken as a given 'natural' property, rather than a social product, the 'explanation' for discrimination and social disadvantage are found wanting. He proceeds to argue that many research studies assist in producing and propagating a misidentification of who disabled people are. An example being that the presence of impairment is predominately found within people over 50 years of age, yet this situation is 'explained' predominantly as 'wear and tear'.[56] Abberley sees the misrepresentation of who disabled people are as connected to the misidentification of causes of impairment as well. Drawing them together leads him to conclude that this misidentification leads to false stereotyping of who is considered 'disabled' and why.

In Britain, the boundaries of disability politics have been limited to addressing 'post-impairment' reality – that is, focusing on the social consequences of being, or perceived as, 'impaired'. UPIAS argued that 'disability' is *imposed* on top of our impairments by the way we are 'unnecessarily isolated and excluded from full participation in society'. Within UPIAS's approach towards disability, impairment – which is how it is viewed and responded to – becomes central to the development of any theory or intervention around disabled people's oppression. To understand this as an aspect of the disability dialectic, it is therefore necessary, I wish to stress once again, to see the 'impaired body' as a site of struggle. How this body is socially produced, evaluated and policed within social relations underpins disabled people's social oppression. If their demand for social acceptance and entry into mainstream society is to be realised, then society needs to address impairment reality as a dialectical issue involving both acceptance and prevention at the same time.

It is understandable that disabled activists have focused upon ending social exclusion and discrimination in terms of disabled people's lives; nonetheless, the lack of attention paid to issues surrounding the social production of impairment has held back the development of a better understanding of disablement and disablism as oppressive agents of capitalism and colonialism. As Soldatic notes:

> The growing claims for transnational justice on the grounds of impairment production emerging from the South are inadmissible within the current zone of disability justice. While the CRPD is about the impaired

body and its socio-political reproduction into disability and disablement, the production of impairment is outside its referential frame.[57]

Abberley, like Russell and Malhotra, views the 'disability category' as performing certain tasks in the current social system. Firstly, it maintains stereotypes assisting in 'directing attention away from impairment associated with ageing', thereby constructing 'the ageing process' as a naturalised phenomenon, and thus reducing 'the amount of perceived disability in society, so that disability appears as "exceptional"'.[58] Secondly, it has historically served to police the labour force by 'explaining' who is and who is not fit for work. Any theory of disability as oppression needs to also address the question of who benefits from that oppression. The 'disability category' works within what Antonio Gramsci calls 'cultural hegemony'. Cole explains: 'Cultural hegemony refers to domination or rule maintained through ideological or cultural means. It is usually achieved through social institutions, which allow those in power to strongly influence the values, norms, ideas, expectations, worldview, and behavior of the rest of society.'[59]

Abberley offers us a way of understanding how 'impairment' becomes a site of struggle in relation to the impact of oppression upon disabled people's lives. As previously noted, the 'disability category' has been employed to discourage individuals from trying to exploit the 'disability status' which exempts them from the work process. Secondly, the production of negative stereotypes and maintenance of material disadvantages connected to impairment/disability, 'encourages people, where possible, to normalise suffering and disease so as not to include themselves in a despised and disadvantaged sub-group'.[60]

The third general effect of oppression is that it helps at specific historical conjunctures within capitalism to constitute particular groups of disabled people to be 'part of a passive "sub-class" of welfare recipients ... which serves as a powerful warning against falling off the achievement ladder'.[61] At other times, this oppressive treatment results in these groups being targeted as being 'burdens' and 'benefit cheats'.[62]

In order to combat these general effects, Abberley advocates the view that a theory of disability as oppression must address the social origins of impairment alongside opposing the social, financial, environmental and psychological disadvantages inflicted on impaired people. This requires addressing both of these points as historical products, not the result of nature, human or otherwise. A theory of disability as oppression would also need to assert 'the value of disabled modes of living', whilst at the same time condemning the social production of impairment. I want to query what Abberley means here by 'asserts the value of disabled modes of living'. Does this mean the right of disabled people to establish their specific lifestyles and have them valued? Is this, in the first instance, a transitional demand in relation to an acceptance of living with impairments within capitalist societies?

Abberley sees this theory as having an inevitable political perspective which 'involves the defence and transformation, both material and ideological, of state health and welfare provision as an essential condition of transforming the lives of the vast majority of disabled people'.[63] Whilst agreeing entirely with his final point where he speaks about the centrality of the need to conduct the defence and transformation of state health and welfare provision, perhaps the political perspective we need today requires us to situate health and welfare provision in a wider context. This is the subject of Chapter 8.

Abberley counsels against conflating oppression and discrimination by articulating the view that capitalism's modes of production and living frequently produce impairment. Disabled people's oppression therefore is not just about the social construction of 'impairment', but also flows from the material conditions found within capitalism. A theory of disability as oppression and development of disability praxis requires the repositioning of 'impairment' within disability politics. Such a repositioning involves critically engaging with issues of impairment production as well as continuing the struggle for de-institutionalisation, alongside combating exclusion and marginalisation within mainstream social activities. Disability praxis therefore involves politicising how living with impairments within a capitalist society not only creates social oppression, discrimination and social disadvantage, but also how disabled people's modes of living are negated. The elephant in the room, however, within disability politics has always been the lack of attention given to the significant dimensions which place disabled people in an inferior position to other members of society. The following two chapters will seek to address them.

Location of Impairment Within Disability Politics: Impairment Effects and Impairment Reality

The previous chapter situated the debates around impairment and disability within specific historical contexts and argued that the 'impaired body' became a site of struggle. Building on that assertion, there is need to explore aspects of the contested view that impairment needs locating within disability politics. Just as the relations between impairment and disability are contested, so too are the relations between Disability Studies, disability praxis and disability politics. While the historical relationship between disability politics and Disability Studies is not explored in this book, specific theoretical positions relevant to the debates on the positioning of impairment within disability politics have been introduced.

In *Disability*, Barnes and Mercer include a chapter entitled 'Impairment, Disability and the Body', which outlines many of the debates that exist.[1] What is striking about this particular chapter in their book is the degree to which it reinforces some of the misrepresentations and confusion that exist around the relationship between impairment and disability debates. To develop a disability praxis that serves the twenty-first century, scholar activists and disabled communities need to understand the relevance of these debates to the emancipation struggle. Opening up a dialogue around these contested areas of debate will no doubt throw up more questions than answers; yet, at the same time, it provides an opportunity to examine why many of these misrepresentations exist and in so doing, assist in dispelling the confusion. A major contributor to the existing situation is the misrepresentation of the reasoning behind 'breaking the causal link' between impairment and disability.

HOW IS 'BREAKING A CAUSAL LINK' BETWEEN IMPAIRMENT AND DISABILITY VIEWED?

The starting point must be how the social interpretation of disability has made sense, as developed by UPIAS. Fundamental to understanding this interpretation, as explained previously, is the crucial act of breaking the causal link between impairment (impairment reality) and disability (the imposed social restrictions that cause marginalisation and exclusion). There is an important distinction to be made between 'breaking the causal link' and the articulation of 'the separation of impairment and disability' which is often used instead. How can you 'separate' something that was never 'a whole' in the first place except in a conceptual sense within an oppressive set of ideologies? It also leads to claims of this nature:

> Thus when feminism distinguishes sex and gender, disability studies separates impairment and disability, the former physical and the latter social and cultural (Shakespeare and Watson). There is, however, a key distinction to be made between the sex/gender and impairment/ disablement analysis. The former does not assume oppression instead gender is a social role or identity.[2]

Anyone viewing impairment and disability in this fashion has no connection with the work of UPIAS, Finkelstein, Oliver, and many others, as this is a false distinction. The real issue is that 'the link' exists through agency created by dominant appraisals of functional capacity which places the blame on individual bodies for the presence of social disadvantage. Barnes and Mercer state that Oliver saw the separation of impairment and disability as primarily a 'pragmatic attempt to identify and address issues that can be changed through collective action rather than medical or other professional treatment'.[3] If that is true, then it can be argued that Oliver undersells the argument put forward by UPIAS. Breaking the causal link challenges the reductionist arguments that not only legitimises social oppression but in so doing it also legitimates eugenics.[4]

A certain degree of confusion has arisen from how the purpose of the social model has been viewed. This is further compounded by the unfamiliarity with the notion of 'model'.[5] Barnes and Mercer, for example, claim that 'most early (male) interpreters of the social model dismissed "what it feels like" knowledge as a "discredited and sterile approach to understanding and changing the world", precisely because it rest on individual issues'.[6]

Feminist theorists such as Carol Thomas have questioned how and why disabled men ignore the personal as being political in the application of the social model. It is therefore claimed that this absence denies a role for impairment in exploring disablement. This has given rise to a number of tensions regarding feminist critiques of the positioning of impairment in relation to disability and relate to, among other things; the question of the personal experience of impairment, and the relationship between impairment and disablism, as well the question of viewing 'the personal as political'. The latter is seen as part of the broader aim amongst feminists to break down the traditional dichotomy between the public sphere and the private sphere. This is based on the understanding that gender expectations can both reflect and reinforce the power imbalance between men and women. Feminists argue that by demanding the private sphere should warrant the same degree of attention as other more conventional considerations, conditions can be created whereby females can escape the stifling confines of behaviour which are expected of them.

The issue of public sphere and private sphere is viewed as problematic in terms of Oliver's explanations of his social model and Finkelstein's criticism within the 'inside out' and 'outside in' debate.[7] Jenny Morris, for example, says that feminist analyses of women's oppression are themselves a way of asserting resistance, of struggling against oppression, and the studies, when showing the difficulties women face, rarely present them as passive victims.[8] The debates which took place in the 1990s saw little understanding of why each side took the stance they did, but many male disabled scholar activists were rightly criticised for their lack of awareness of the way sexism and disablism intersect.[9] Notwithstanding, there are also issues around how 'the personal is political' is articulated. American feminist Carol Hanisch put forward the argument that many personal experiences (particularly those of women) can be traced to one's location within a system of power relationships. Hanisch wrote an essay which focused on men's power and women's oppression. She suggested that personal experiences are the result of social structures or inequality, as in the case where a particular woman is being abused by a male partner, then societal oppression of women is an important factor in explaining this abuse. It is important to acknowledge that the original usage of the phrase is often misinterpreted as saying the opposite; namely, it is women's or disabled people's personal behaviour that is of political significance.[10]

Carol Thomas suggests the points raised by Jenny Morris, Sally French and others within Disability Studies, might not have arisen if disability were understood in a social relational sense, because it would then be entirely permissible to acknowledge that there are also impairment effects that restrict activity and impact in important ways upon the lives of impaired people.[11] This, however, fails to address how female scholars like Morris view personal politics in relation to the social interpretation of disability. Morris writes:

... they [some male advocates of the social model of disability] have been making the personal political in the sense that they have insisted that what appears to be personal experience of disability is in fact socially constructed. However, we also need to hang on to the other sense of making the personal political and that is owning, taking control of, and representation of the personal experience of disability – including the negative parts of the experience.[12]

What Morris says is considered questionable within the UPIAS definition of disability for three reasons. Firstly, what does Morris mean by 'experience of disability'? The final sentence appears to suggest a conflation of impairment and disability. However, from a social model perspective, how can there be anything other than negative appraisals of the experience of disability? Secondly, is it even possible for disability culture to collectively assist in facilitating the 'owning, taking control of, and representation of the personal experience of disability'; if it were, to what ends? Taking control of impairment management, and our own identities and lifestyles, are outside the original remit of the social model; these actions are, however, part of disability politics because our personal space is often invaded by disablist ideologies and practice. The problem therefore has not been the 'distancing' of ourselves from the *personal tragedy model*, but rather the failure to explore and utilise the model's insights. Similarly, Sally French says she believed that 'some of the most profound problems experienced by people with certain impairments are difficult, if not impossible, to solve by social manipulation.'[13]

The charge of not taking account of the personal experience of impairment or the psychological and emotional trauma of disablism, shares space with many other criticisms of the social model which I have argued distort its purpose. The criticism levelled by Thomas and Morris also implies there is some gendered determined reason as to why 'men' [sic] interpret the model as they do. The critiques of the social model also misrepresent the positions held by Finkelstein and UPIAS. Finkelstein, for instance, writes:

... we had engaged in a vigorous debate to take control over the way 'disability' was interpreted and understood. This involved encouraging disabled people (more so than 'the public' or professionals) to focus our attention on changing the disabling barriers 'outside there' rather than focusing our attention on the attitudes and emotions we held 'inside ourselves' about our experiences of discrimination.[14]

The issues around how disabled people address personal or collective experience of oppression and discrimination will be discussed in Chapter 9; however, in terms of the application of the social model, Finkelstein makes a link with praxis:

> This was an attempt to encourage an objective, practical and 'hands on' approach towards the struggle for social change ... the focus of attention was 'outside in' rather than 'inside out'. Since those exciting early years in advancing the movement of disabled people there has been a creeping re-interpretation of this radical concept of disability.[15]

Here are the roots of disability politics: it is an 'outside in' approach. Retaining the position that 'the social model is not an attempt to deal with the personal restrictions of impairment but the social barriers of disability' is of crucial importance; but there is also the need to acknowledge that other models or approaches can be applied within the furtherance of disability politics.[16] Consideration therefore must also be given to Finkelstein's assertion that:

> There is, of course, a profound difference between struggles based upon an analysis concerned with the processes leading to the creation of disability (the social construction of disability as a socio-economic relationship) and struggles based on reflections of the experience of disablement (or our conscious reflections on living with an impairment in a disabling world and interpreting the state of disability as a psycho-social experience).[17]

The difference in approach is reflected in how scholar activists such as Morris, Crow, and French, along with Thomas, spoke of impairment and disability in terms of experience.[18] Crow, for example, writes:

> The social model works well on a large scale – it is succeeding in tackling discriminatory social structures and demonstrating our need for civil rights legislation. Where it currently lets us down is at the personal level – its capacity to include and represent fully the range of disabled individuals.[19]

This illustrates how the purpose of 'the social model' was misunderstood, but it also highlights how important it is for some disabled people to reflect on living with an impairment in a disabling world.[20] Two issues need addressing here. Firstly, Oliver made it clear that the application of the social model sought to 'start from the ways oppression differentially impacts on different groups of people rather than with differences in experience among individuals with different impairments.'[21]

Within context Oliver's application makes sense, however, a contentious area of debate that exists surrounds the next stage of development. If social models, including Oliver's, become articulated as utilising the 'dismantling disabling barriers' approach, how do we ensure the application is employed along these lines?

The second issue, highlighted by the quotation from Crow, is how the question of impairment and disability are addressed at a personal level within disability politics. It is not just in relation to the social model of disability that there is confusion, but also within the debates around the prospect of a social model of impairment. Disabled People Against Cuts write, in relation to the book by Ellen Clifford, that it:

> ... suggests that alongside a social model of disability, we should also have a social model of impairment. According to this, 'impairment' would not be understood as something that is wrong with a person's body or brain. Instead, 'impairment' would refer to the disadvantage that a person faces because of how their particular condition is viewed within society. This would enable a wider range of people to identify as disabled – including Deaf people, autistic people, and people living with mental distress – to unite to fight against shared injustice.[22]

This confuses not only the purpose of developing a social model of impairment, but also reduces 'impairment' to being about addressing negative appraisals of bodies – a question of consciousness raising.

What is often ignored or glossed over is the fact that disability politics and praxis involve differing sites of struggle and not all of these can rely on the social model; nonetheless, different struggles or projects can utilise the social interpretation of disability. Finkelstein offered some insights into developing other models:

> Building a model which covers 'diverse interactive' human behaviour, therefore, must also include diverse illnesses alongside the 'diverse lifestyles' with its broader social concerns.
>
> Strictly speaking, this 'diverse interactive' model, and all of its sub-divisions, does not exclusively concern 'disability'. The focus is on the mosaic of human behaviour. This includes disabled people's varied lifestyles.[23]

Acknowledging the existence and possibility of diverse lifestyles enables us to consider the nature of differing sites of struggle, such as the collective fight against disablement and disability, the socio-political aspects of living with impairments in a disablist society, and the tensions surrounding the management of impairment reality. Carol Thomas's ideas and concepts touch upon all of these areas. She also sees her work contributing to developing a social model of impairment.

THE RELATIONS BETWEEN IMPAIRMENT AND DISABLISM: A CONTESTED AREA OF DEBATE

In 2004, Carol Thomas made a contribution to the book *Implementing the Social Model of Disability: Theory and Research*, in her chapter 'Developing the Social Relational in the Social Model of Disability: A Theoretical Agenda.'[24] While the chapter was aimed at assisting researchers to reflect upon existing theoretical ideas around implementing the social model, and an agenda for further work within Disability Studies, a number of her themes and arguments are relevant to disability politics outside of the academic environment.

Underlining the core observations she makes in her chapter and other writings, is a 'conviction that the social relational kernel of the early UPIAS formulation of a social understanding of disability holds the key to unlocking both the questions and answers concerning the nature of disability'.[25] Thomas refers to UPIAS's definition of disability which was critiqued earlier in this book.[26] She proceeds to outline the purpose of the social interpretation/model of disability in relation to praxis in the following manner:

> The new challenge was to: i) describe this nexus of social relationships, that is, to make clear the manifestations of disability in the social world (in organisations, systems, policies, practices, ideologies and discourses), and ii) to explain it, by employing theoretical paradigms that generate ways of understanding what gives form to and sustains these relationships.[27]

This view of disability praxis was criticised by Finkelstein in particular, who said that the social interpretation/model of disability was not developed to 'describe' or 'explain' the oppressive social relationships, or manifestations that followed from them, but instead to provide insights that would assist in analysing and addressing social restrictions and disabling barriers. This is not a question of splitting hairs over particular words and their meaning;

it concerns how we make sense of the material conditions which underpin social relations within society. Misunderstanding the fluidity of the relations between the two often results in harmful over-determined arguments about the nature of oppression.

Thomas refers to the emergence of a research literature on the 'social barriers' and exposing disablism, and how the exposure of barriers led to highlighting key features of the landscape of social exclusion. Her follow-up point connects to the different interpretations of the purpose of the social model. She writes, 'Less attention has been paid to barriers in more "intimate" life domains in which disablist social relationships operate, for example, familial and sexual attachments as well as in areas of reproduction, parenting and childrearing.'[28]

A number of issues come to the fore here. It is important to recognise that these issues often become sites of struggle for disabled people, due to both disablement and disablism. While the social interpretation of disability provides insights into oppressive social relationships that operate, the social model can only have application in terms of the structured areas that Thomas mentions. How we, as disabled and non-disabled people, address issues around more 'intimate' life domains where disablist social relationships operate, requires different social and political interventions which relate to living with impairment in a disablist society and does remain a problematical area of debate as it is interpersonal.[29] The elephant in the room appears to be how oppression and disablism are viewed.

As already noted, Abberley was critical of the ambiguity within Mike Oliver's writing with regards to oppression. It is important therefore to consider how both Oliver and Thomas define disablism. For Oliver: 'Disablism is the consequence of disability as oppression, whereby negative attitudes, disablist policies, discriminatory practices and environmental barriers prevent the full participation and inclusion of people with impairments in everyday society.'[30]

Carol Thomas, on the other hand, refers to disablism as:

… the social imposition of avoidable restrictions on the life activities, aspirations and psycho-emotional well-being of people categorised as 'impaired' by those deemed 'normal'. Disablism is social-relational in character and constitutes a form of social oppression in contemporary society – alongside sexism, racism, ageism, and homophobia. As well as enacted in person-to-person interactions, disablism may manifest itself in institutional and other socio-structural forms.[31]

Thomas's first sentence speaks of 'avoidable restrictions', which can be argued, calls into question the nature of disabled people's social relations with capitalist society. Do we make a distinction between unnecessary or avoidable social restrictions and those inherent within the system itself? This question goes to the heart of disability politics as raised earlier in Chapter 5; is the emancipatory struggle simply about 'barrier removal' in order to achieve integration or inclusion into society, or is it also concerned with a transformative agenda which will completely change the existing social structures of societies? Thomas goes on to assert that disablism as a concept allows a distance from 'disability', which has been 'invested with a rather confusing mix of imprecise and varying meanings both within disability studies and in society more broadly'.[32] Thomas believed introducing the notion of 'impairment effects' would aid our understanding of the relationship between disablism and impairment.

There are differences in how Thomas and Oliver define disablism, with implications for how the relations between disablement, disablism and impairment are articulated and understood. Thomas reveals her stance in relation to Oliver's social model by discussing the definitions of impairment and disability offered by Wendell, which retains the ICIDH's idea that 'disability is about the restriction of activity', but adds 'She refers to her analysis of disability as "social constructionist", but goes on to say that disability has biological, social and experiential components: "I call the interaction of the biological and the social to create (or prevent) disability 'the construction of disability'."'[33]

It could be argued that Wendell's definition could be 'interpreted' as a forerunner for the WHO's ICF. What does Wendell see 'the biological component' as being – functionality of the human body or something else? In an earlier article, Wendell states that 'However, by trying to define "impairment" and "disability" in physical terms and "handicap" in cultural, physical and social terms, the U.N. document appears to be making a shaky distinction between the physical and the social aspects of disability.'[34]

If the document referred to applies the ICIDH definition of disability, then it does see a direct causal link between the loss of functionality and 'handicap' in cultural, physical and social terms, however, Wendell states there is no acknowledgement of any bio-social aspects of functionality. The British social interpretation of disability's distinction between a person with an impairment and their interaction with specific social environments is purely on the basis of rejecting the reductionist view that it is the individual's impairment that causes the social 'handicap' (disability). This is what

UPIAS meant by imposed social restriction being placed 'on top of' impairment and why Finkelstein saw these interactions as 'relational' in nature, which means both sides – impairment and social environment – have an influence on the outcome. What maintains social oppression is the ideological purchase of maintaining the direct causal link thus drawing contours around functionality as a measurement of what is considered 'normal'. Wendell acknowledges this:

> Not only the 'normal' roles for one's age, sex, society, and culture, but also 'normal' structure and function, and 'normal' ability to perform an activity, depend on the society in which the standards of normality are generated. Paradigms of health and ideas about appropriate kinds and levels of performance are culturally-dependent. In addition, within each society there is much variation from the norm of any ability; at what point does this variation become disability?[35]

Having posed the question about what constitutes 'disability', she does not follow through and reach the same conclusion found within the British interpretation where disability is socially constructed and created. Instead, she argues, 'The idea that there is some universal, perhaps biologically or medically-describable paradigm of human physical ability is an illusion. Therefore, I prefer to use a single term, "disability," and to emphasize that disability is socially constructed from biological reality.'[36]

Thomas explains that Wendell sees restrictions of activity as being caused by the interaction of social, biological and other factors, but the social factors have a key role in disabled people's oppression. This leads Thomas to state that 'Wendell outlines a range of ways in which social factors, cultural processes and impairment cause disability', and concludes that this results in her taking 'account of the "causative" role play by a range of social factors which most British social modellists would ignore because they would be seen to be causes of impairment rather than disability'.[37]

This argument can be contested. Wendell argues that a wide range of social factors and cultural processes produce both impairment and encountered social restrictions. What is meant by 'disability is socially constructed from biological reality'? This links back to Abberley's assertion about disabled people's oppression being rooted in how their bodies are viewed and responded to within capitalist societies.

While Abberley's assertion mirrors the underpinning of the social interpretation and social model of disability, it is crucial to note the original social model developed by Oliver was based upon viewing disability as the outcome of societal responses towards disabled people, therefore it was not a 'theory' of oppression, or an analysis of disablement, but a practical tool to challenge the causes of disabled people's exclusion from mainstream society. The production of impairment is therefore irrelevant to the exploration of the nature of encountered disabling barriers and addressing them. The issue of impairment is neither absent nor ignored in Oliver's model; if there were no perceived notion of impairment, then disablism would simply not exist.[38] While arguing that neither the production of impairment nor individual experience of impairment reality are considerations within the application of the radical social model because of its socio-political focus, this does not mean the issue of impairment creation should not be part of disability politics or praxis. The social production of impairment and individual experience of impairment are implicit parts of disability as a form of social oppression. We must discontinue this absurd idea that disability politics or praxis can be reduced to using the social model. Oliver never claimed his model addressed everything to do with disability or disabled people.[39]

Thomas refers to Barnes and Mercer, who are credited with saying that 'the restriction of activity experienced by people with impairment – is wholly and exclusively socially caused', which leads to her stating 'I could think of plenty of instances where physical, sensory and intellectual states (impairment, illness) could directly cause restrictions of activity irrespective of any social arrangements and so be "disabling".'[40]

This sets up an unhelpful and unnecessary riddle: if 'disability' is presented as wholly and exclusively socially caused 'restrictions of activity', yet, as Thomas states, some 'restrictions of activity' are the result of an impairment or illness itself, how does anyone distinguish between differing types? Talking of 'restrictions of activity' without any contextual framing, leads down a rabbit hole à la Alice in Wonderland. In 1997, Gradwell and colleagues offered this view of impairment from a social interpretative perspective:

IMPAIRMENT is a characteristic, feature or attribute within an individual which is long term and may, or may not, be the result of disease, genetics or injury and may:

1. Affect that individual's appearance in a way which is not acceptable to society,
And / or

2. Affect the function of that individual's mind or body, either because of or regardless of society,
And / or
3. Cause pain, fatigue, affect communication and / reduce consciousness.[41]

It is the second part of the definition that is key to unpacking the differing meanings attached to 'restrictions of activity', because it acknowledges personal restriction arising from impaired functioning, and the imposed social restriction from society. There is also the acknowledgement of different possible causes of restriction.

It is equally as important to consider and unpack the meanings associated with 'activity'. An activity in a general sense means 'what is or can be done'; therefore it can refer to a functional performance such as seeing, speaking, walking, lifting, etc. At times, using one's senses or body movement such as walking on legs, are referred to as 'activity'. Within this framework, attached are normative values. This is distinct from the meaning associated with 'the restrictions of activity' contained within the social interpretation of disability. Within the socio-political approach towards disabled people's oppression and social disadvantage, 'the restrictions of activity' refers to the structural and organisational barriers and practices which are viewed as being imposed, therefore unnecessarily preventing people-with-impairment's participation within mainstream social engagement.[42]

Part of the confusion around how impairment and disability are viewed can be located within the assumed relationship between the two. This is clearly evident in the application of the WHO's ICF and calls into question their claims about abandoning 'the causal link':

The ICF provides a standard language for classifying body function and structure, activity, participation levels, and conditions in the world around us that influence health. According to the ICF:

Activity is the execution of a task or action by an individual.
Participation is a person's involvement in a life situation.

The ICF acknowledges that the distinction between these two categories is somewhat unclear and combines them [–] although basically, activities take place at a personal level and participation involves engagement in life roles, such as employment, education, or relationships. Activity limitations and participation restrictions have to do with difficulties an individual experiences in performing tasks and engaging in social roles.

Activities and participation can be made easier or more difficult as a result of environmental factors, such as technology, support and relationships, services, policies, or the beliefs of others.[43]

Thomas states the distinction between disability and impairment [effects] should not be mapped out as social/biological or cultural/natural dualism.[44] While rightly stating the word 'disability' has become ambiguous in its usage, she nevertheless still referred to the restriction of functioning within an individual as 'disabling'. Within the context of UPIAS's social interpretation of disability and the writing of Finkelstein, it is right to recognise that the nature and degree of an individual's impairment can cause restrictions of functional activity within the body.

Activity also refers to what people engage in, therefore social participation is understood to be made up of a series of activities such as taking part in family life, work and leisure. This is the context in which the social interpretation of disability was developed. Thomas argues that primarily UPIAS was trying to 'reflect theoretically upon the nature of the social treatment of disabled people in the 1970s, particularly in its welfarist form: residential care, minimal benefits, exclusion from employment and the educational mainstream and blocks on access to the built environment.'[45]

Finkelstein, in his work for the Open University, acknowledged that the significance of the impairment is not a given, because much depends upon how negative interaction between disabled people and their social environments are negotiated.[46] In terms of taking functional limitations into account, UPIAS made the distinction between managing the consequences of having an impairment and societal intervention. Someone without legs, for example, lacks the capacity to climb a mountain; however, if the 'impairment' is accepted – if the social context is also understood and accepted – then neither the individual nor society should regard this as a disabling situation, because the inability to climb the mountain was not caused by the organisation of society. The inability to climb a mountain in this instance results from what I call 'impairment reality'.

Thomas argues that Finkelstein's notion of disability – social relational in character – makes it 'a new form of social oppression associated with the relationships, at both macro and micro social scales, between impaired and non-impaired'.[47] Identifying differing relationships or interactions at both macro and micro levels of society is often lost in the application of social models. Viewing disability as social relational in character does not necessarily mean there is a shared approach to the 'relational' features involved.

Leaving aside consideration as to whether or not Finkelstein's disabling barriers model is a useful tool, what is of importance here is the approach found within it. Finkelstein writes:

[An] adoption of the disabling barriers model with its emphasis on citizenship rights leads to a separate consideration of health rights. This is especially significant for people who are restricted by disabling barriers because it increasingly divides social interpretations of dysfunction from explanations of personal dysfunction (welfare and health concerns).[48]

What the approach does is make a clear separation between two types of dysfunction: social and personal. When exploring Thomas's concept of 'impairment effects', it is important to do so within the context that Finkelstein believed:

Some disabled people have also been promoting a rectified social model of disability in which 'impairment' is once again included in the meaning of 'disability'. This return to a close bond between social and personal dysfunction (maintained in the medical and administrative models of disability), however, cannot resolve the heightened tension between the social and personal raised in the barriers model of disability.[49]

IMPAIRMENT EFFECTS OR IMPAIRMENT REALITY?

As noted earlier, UPIAS acknowledged the more significantly a person's impairment is experienced in terms of functioning, the less likely the encountered unaltered social environments are going to cater for their needs or lifestyle. Carol Thomas attempts to address this issue, saying, 'My own view is that in any social setting, impairment effects and disablism are thoroughly intermeshed with social conditions that bring them both into being and give them meaning.'[50]

Thomas rightly sees the interaction between a person with an impairment and their immediate social environments is a relational one. However, what that means is that it is a two-way process: the nature and degree of the impairment does influence the interaction, but the other side is the social environment which may be changeable in ways that can alter the interaction. Given this, it is possible to question if 'any social setting, impairment effects and disablism are thoroughly intermeshed'.

However, Thomas conflates a number of issues. Firstly, her definition of disablism merges two aspects of disabled people's oppression. It was noted that Thomas spoke of the manifestations of disability existing in organisations, systems, policies, practices, ideologies and discourses. This returns us to the marked differences in how she and Oliver articulate what disablism means. Within this book, there is a distinction made between disablement – the creation of social restrictions within society (structures, systems, cultures, etc.) – and disablism which consists of the ideas and practices which result in discrimination and oppression. Taken together, disablement and disablism create the social conditions whereby people with impairment can at any time find themselves being subjected to unequal and differential treatment. But these conditions are not fixed or static. Not every social environment or social interaction is disabling.

A central issue is whether or not it is possible or meaningful to speak of 'impairment effects'. Within the Equality Act 2010, it is said that 'A person has a disability if they have a physical or mental impairment that has a "substantial and adverse long-term effect" on their ability to carry out normal day-to-day activities.'[51]

In other words, a question is posed: does the impairment impact negatively on a person's ability to see, hear, talk, walk, comprehend information, etc.? The context presented here is that the 'impairment effect" corresponds to the negative impact of an impairment on functional ability. This poses a second and third question: how do we measure the impact of an impairment? Is it possible outside of imposing normative values?

The starting point for unpacking these questions must be to seek clarity with regards to what 'impact' and 'effect' mean. The distinction is that 'impact' refers to the influence of an action or phenomenon on something or someone, whereas 'effect' refers to the consequence or outcome of an action or a phenomenon. Within dominant bio-medical discourses, 'effect' and 'impact' are often intertwined, as we have seen within both the ICIDH and ICF. In Britain, the benefit system has a tendency to focus on the ability of an individual to undertake functional tasks within a framework of measuring 'difficulty in performance'. More often than not, these functional tasks are assessed with no or little social context. A troubling feature about Thomas's notion of 'impairment effects' is the lack of clarity around its application. It is important to stress once more the fact that not all impairments manifest themselves in the same way, nor are static in nature. If they are to be understood in a relational context, then it needs to be recognised that other factors may have an impact as much or if not more than the nature of the impairment itself.

In certain circumstances, the implications of the nature and degree of specific impairment are beyond dispute, because it is generally accepted that someone without sight cannot see, and an individual without legs cannot walk. Thus, in specific cases, the inability to function around particular bodily activities can be established; however, this is not possible to know in all instances, because the ability or inability to function can be influenced by a myriad of factors contributing to how a person performs a task at a certain moment in time, location, or in relation to an external object. Thomas argues that personal restrictions stem from 'impairment effects', whereas I would argue these restrictions are the manifestation of what can be knowable about the lived experience of having an impairment within particular contexts. Talking about 'impairment effects' risks denying or overlooking agency, and opens up the possibility of making assumptions about the impairment and, as a result, acting in a judgmental manner.

Owens and colleagues, for example, say:

> More recently, others have tried to use the concept of impairment effects but struggled to identify where the boundaries of disability and impairment began and ended, and suggest that analysing the public and private dimensions of living with a chronic condition enabled them to better ascertain where the boundaries lay.[52]

To avoid such pitfalls, it may be more fruitful to speak in terms of 'impairment reality'. A straightforward definition of reality is that it is 'the sum or aggregate of all that is real or existent, as opposed to that which is only imaginary'.[53] Employing this definition permits 'impairment reality' to be understood as being the undisputable consequences of having an impairment. When speaking of 'impairment reality', it is referring to the facts that are known by the individual themselves, or can be identified externally by others.

An example of 'impairment reality' would be what can be acknowledged by 'knowing' about the body of an ageing man born with cerebral palsy. It can be established that all four of his limbs are affected, and as a result we can ascertain that his balance is also affected. In addition, through social interaction, it can be verified that his speech and dexterity are affected as well. From this knowledge base, it is possible to discuss all four identified areas of impairment reality in relation to particular functioning social interactions, but even then, it cannot be a given, because it is impossible to know whether or not social interactions can ever be repeated. One functional impairment reality identified was the issue of dexterity. It can be established that the man has limited fine motor skills, but the implications in terms of performance is unknown because the success or failure is dependent upon context – that is, the degree of dexterity required and the nature of the task to be undertaken. Knowing he has reduced dexterity does not provide adequate information.

The design, weight, or surface of objects often have a disabling influence upon functioning ability in terms of dexterity, bodily movement, emotional response, etc. In the example just given, the wisdom of speaking in terms of 'the direct and unavoidable effect' can be challenged because it is impossible to 'isolate' what that might be. What we might end up with is either a generalised description of what did occur or might occur. In terms of impairment reality, the 'knowing' accepts it is not always possible to know or understand the complexities involved in an individual's experience of living in a disabling society, but it considers 'the possibilities' based upon what is known. It is not possible to 'know' what impairment reality means for every individual, in every situation, as both objective and subjective factors need to be brought into consideration.

By introducing 'impairment reality' as representing what is knowable about a person's circumstances in relation to their functional abilities, it is then possible to relate this 'reality' to the encountered interactions that take place at a micro level. Talking of impairment reality also creates space whereby in a non-judgemental manner, we can acknowledge personal restrictions as distinct from the imposed social restrictions which arise due to how society responds to impairment reality. Acknowledging impairment reality therefore seeks to reveal what *is*, thus reducing the pitfalls mentioned earlier. As a non-judgemental concept, it can enter disability politics by being a counter-hegemonic influence in disabled people's struggle to have our bodies and minds accepted as they are – as reality – and not through imposed appraisals which serve the interests of disabled people's oppressors.

One charge that might be levelled against the notion of 'impairment reality' is that it is a form of 'idealism', as not all things are 'knowable'. The counter-argument is that the purpose of speaking of impairment reality is to give disabled people control over how their bodies and minds are addressed – to be in a position to be able to say 'this is me, warts and all' – free of comparison with other bodies and minds with different material realities. If disability politics are concerned with transforming the social world, then acknowledging impairment reality is part of understanding how the body remains a site of struggle and lends itself to the task of developing a new disability praxis.

IMPAIRMENT AND DISABILITY WITHIN DISABILITY STUDIES AND BEYOND

It is not possible to ignore the fact that any future development of disability praxis in relation to disability politics must involve engagement with Disability Studies. In *Disability Praxis*, this engagement has been sidestepped for both practical reasons and the fact that the focus has largely focused on disability politics from within the Disabled People's Movement. Ensuring dialogue around the location of impairment within disability politics requires the acknowledgement that the two dominant traditions within Disability Studies are the Marxist/materialist and post-structuralist/postmodernist. The Marxist/materialist accounts of the positioning of impairment and disability within theoretical and political discourse has been challenged.

Among these challenging scholars are Tremain, Corker and Shakespeare, Shiddrick, and Goodley and colleagues, to name but a few.[54] Many reject the 'Marxist focus on socio-structural determinants of disablism and turned instead to cultural and linguistic theory for answers'.[55] From post-structuralist/postmodernist perspectives has emerged Critical Disability Studies which is described as a 'diverse set of approaches that largely seek to theorize disability as a cultural, political, and social phenomenon, rather than an individualized, medical matter attached to the body'.[56]

According to Schalk, critical disability theory is a methodology, not a 'subject-oriented area of study'; therefore, as a methodology, it 'involves scrutinizing not bodily or mental impairments but the social norms that define particular attributes as impairments, as well as the social conditions that concentrate stigmatized attributes in particular populations'.[57] What is included or excluded within critical disability theory or post-structuralist/postmodernist approaches appears debatable. In terms of the location of impairment within disability politics, neither traditional Disability Studies nor Critical Disability Studies provide clear paths to follow. In both camps, there are concepts and practice which could enrich disability praxis and politics in ways which draw together the differing sites of struggle; however, there are also others that risk leading to arid debates within ivory towers.

8

Disability Praxis: Unanswered Questions

Building on the exploration of the identified four cornerstones of British disability politics and how they relate to the global movement, the final chapters will address specific questions and issues with the aim of assisting to connect ideas from the past with the development of a potentially new radical version for disability praxis. Here I raise questions and issues that impact on the future of disability politics in relation to existing contradictions, tensions and conflicts.

It has been acknowledged that major issues surrounding the concepts and language used in relation to disability and disabled people complicate the development of a new disability praxis. In unapologetically articulating the historical materialist approach towards disability, this book seeks to frame the concepts outlined in terms of a dialectical relationship between disability and politics, praxis, culture, rights, etc. A dialectical relationship refers to the standing of two objects in direct opposition to each other. Disability politics, for example, signifies politics that stand in opposition to the encountered social restrictions and oppression (disablement) faced by disabled people. These dialectical relationships stem from the desire of disabled people to free themselves from oppressive social relations. This desire is created by what is referred to as the 'dialectics of disability' – that is, the antagonistic interactions that exist within capitalist societies for disabled and non-disabled people.

Costello writes:

While the capitalist economy as such rejected disabled people as unproductive, the state institutions created and reinforced negative social attitudes towards disability. Capitalist society had relegated disabled people to the most negative status of poverty and isolation. These negative attitudes were used to justify disadvantageous social positions, which strengthened the attitudes themselves. Institutions and attitudes were and are in a constant interplay with one another, feeding back into and altering each other. In Marxist terms, they interact dialectically.[1]

The word 'dialectic' has a number of meanings, including a description of a method of argument that systematically weighs contradictory facts or ideas with a view to seeking a resolution in terms of their real or apparent contradictions. Within Marxist thinking, dialectics are seen as forging a process of change through the conflict of opposing forces, where the interplay between them can produce a transformed relationship. The issue of the dialectics of disability is of importance to disability politics because they reveal the antagonistic relations of various processes disabled people are forced to negotiate.

THE DIALECTICS OF DISABILITY

A number of disability-related scholars have applied the notion of 'dialectics' to 'disability'; however, either the meaning or context of their usage is not always obvious.[2] In my writing, I am taking Marx's approach, rather than Hegel's. Hence:

> Karl Marx brought together dialectics and materialism to understand the world as a totality – but as a totality driven by inherent change, conflict and contradictions rooted in the material world, where human activity, including the ideas generated by humans about the world, can also react back on and in turn transform the material underpinnings of society.[3]

For Marx, at the root of existing contradictions within the material world is the conflict between the main contending classes of capitalist society: the bourgeoisie and the proletariat. He believed this could only be resolved through social transformation, where a revolution would abolish the antagonistic and the mutually interdependent relation of capitalist and worker. Like other Marxist disabled scholars, I contend that disablement and disablism are products of this conflict.[4] Abberley, as previously acknowledged, argued disabled people are in an inferior position to other members of society because their impairments are used against them. However, the disadvantages they face 'are dialectically related to an ideology or group of ideologies which justify and perpetuate this situation'.[5]

The dialectics of disability are the contradictions, antagonisms and conflicts arising from existing social relations between disabled and non-disabled people. The central feature of these dialectics is the contradiction that sees disabled people wanting to create a path towards inclusion or integration into a society/system that by its very nature has rejected and excluded them. Contradictions can be viewed as opposites in which the two sides interfere with each other, struggle against each other, or hold each other back. Not every opposition, of course, is a contradiction. Within this context, where disabled individuals can be 'assimilated' into mainstream social activity because their impairment reality can be accommodated, often their 'disabled' status is negated or deliberately overlooked.

Abberley's arguments around developing a theory of disability as oppression employs a dialectical method and encourages disability praxis. He speaks of asserting the value of the modes of living of people with impairments, whilst at the same time condemning the social production of impairment. There is the need to engage in praxis which transforms theory into a political perspective; this involves both the defence and transformation of systems, and provision which can lay the basis for transforming the lives of the vast majority of disabled people.[6] Defending the NHS, for example, involves contradictions, antagonisms and conflicts, because the health service often perpetuates oppression while at the same time saving lives.[7]

It is possible to identify other areas where the dialectics of disability are at work. In developing a new disability praxis, I believe an important avenue to be explored is what is known as 'relational dialectics'. Relational dialectics is an interpersonal communication theory about close personal ties and relationships that highlights the tensions, struggles and interplay between contrary tendencies. Developing an interplay between relational and disability dialectics would open up dialogue around the personal-political issues in terms of encountered disablism, interdependency in support arrangements, and addressing the communication between disabled and non-disabled people in terms of expressing desires, needs and wants. Relational dialectics theory could also play a crucial role in developing meaningful co-production of services and lifestyles.[8]

The examples of dialectics identified here can be found in personal, collective and organisational social relationships. One of the ideas behind this theory is that conflicts of opinion or interests can produce exact opposites. Disability politics exist within these conditions. A major dialectical contradiction is the relations between connection and autonomy. An obvious example of this is the emancipation struggle itself. Politically conscious disabled people want to change their social relations with or within society, with the original trajectory being from institutionalisation to self-directed living.

Disabled people recognised that, in order to push for integration, they had to make connections with and obtain allies among non-disabled people; yet, to achieve 'integration' rather than assimilation, collectively and individually, they needed a degree of autonomy to self-determine their needs and interests. Autonomy and connectedness refers to the tensions that exist in wanting to have ties and connections with others versus the need to separate oneself off as a unique individual or a social movement for change. This integration versus separation dialectic is an issue within building social movements.[9]

Another obvious set of opposites is the struggle for equality against inequality. Disabled people's social oppression involves forms of discrimination and inequality; what are the opposites of these? Finkelstein in his work spoke of 'equal opportunities for all' as an agitational slogan; however, I believe Clear and Gleeson offer a clearer picture when they argue existing social conditions set disabled people up to fail, as it cannot be realised. They state, 'But rights alone will never suffice: the goal of substantive inclusion requires that we create a new material world that embodies – literally – the aspirations and values of every human being.'[10]

The ultimate aim of understanding the dialectics of disability must be the transition of society in order to end disablement, disablism and oppression. A new disability praxis must incorporate this understanding. As Finkelstein stated:

I believe the radical social model of disability can inspire initiatives to guide our struggle for emancipation in entirely new ways. The responsibility is on us to pursue such initiatives even when fiercely resisted by people with capabilities, or when the insight into the struggle ahead looks very daunting, or when the champions of 'rights' in the disability movement lead us astray into pressure group politics … In my view we can enter the class struggle in our own right only when our needs and views are legitimately reflected in a section of the working class.[11]

In the remainder of this book, we will explore some of the possibilities for developing new initiatives and insights that will help to stimulate dialogue and action. Part of this process of reflection on the historical path of the struggle, must be the value of our cornerstones in terms of their ability to serve their purpose. There are many unanswered questions surrounding disabled people's self-organisation, for example.

SELF-DETERMINATION, SELF-ORGANISATION AND COMMUNITY: THE BARRIERS TO SUCCESS

Chapter 3 explored why self-organisation was viewed as a cornerstone of disability politics and how central to these politics was the forming of disabled people's organisations. Over the years, we have witnessed a decline in international, regional and local DPOs with varied causes for this situation. It was suggested that from the middle of the 1990s, the vast majority of disabled people's organisations simply sought to change how disabled people were seen and treated, whilst at the same time sought to fund their existence through being service providers. Attempting to play this dual role had negative consequences, because it is extremely unwise to bite the hand that feeds you.

The outcome was that fewer DPOs seemed capable of developing disability politics of an emancipatory nature and instead took to implementing accommodationist policies favoured and encouraged by local authorities.

In Britain, the New Labour government encouraged a hybrid movement where DPOs worked alongside disability charities. An example of this development was the formation of the Disability LIB (Listen, Include, Build) alliance, which consisted of six DPOs and the charity, Scope. Disability Lib sought to build capacity among DPOs. In 'A Statement of Common Understanding', they said:

> The landscape in which DPOs are operating is changing rapidly. The DDA 2005 put a duty on public authorities to proactively promote disabled people's equality; the government has made a public commitment to achieve equality for disabled people by 2025 which includes establishing a user-led organisation in every locality by 2010; and the UN Convention on the Rights of Persons with Disabilities, signed by the UK in March 2007, provides a new framework for understanding and protecting disabled people's human rights.
>
> However, despite these advances many DPOs are struggling to survive. It is clear that for DPOs to thrive rather than just survive they need not only to work together but to work with allies outside the DPO sector.[12]

Disability Lib, as I argued previously, employed the language of the Movement but emptied them of their radical meanings and replaced them with watered-down versions which fitted into the neoliberal economic agenda for self-reliance and marketisation. The statement, for example, declares:

We believe that Disabled People's Organisations should be the vehicle for bringing together disabled people to define, organise and lead their own struggle for emancipation and full human rights, including revisioning and reorganising society's economic, political, social and cultural structures and attitudes.[13]

The alliance saw its task as exploring the changing role of DPOs, and suggested a range of ways to ensure DPOs continue to represent disabled people in an effective and sustainable way. In a report it produced, the alliance put forward five models DPOs could use; however, in the majority of these models, the priority was promoting service delivery and ensuring financial growth, which placed, in most cases, the interests of the DPOs above those of the communities they were established to serve. Whilst this tension between income generation and political advancement has always existed, from the late 1980s, it had become problematic.

The global financial crisis of 2007–09 ushered in an age of austerity where the majority of DPOs lost financial support through cutbacks within local authorities. Many DPOs had become party to the market economy by this time.[14]

Finkelstein ruefully wrote, 'I find it extraordinary that people who campaigned so vigorously for the USA style of independent living services to be created in the expanding UK competitive market are now complaining that they are losing the government support upon which they are dependent!'[15]

There are different political perspectives involved; however, irrespective of whichever perspective one follows, three particular unanswered questions remain. Did DPOs cease to be the platform for promoting disabled people's self-determination? To what extent did or do existing DPOs engage with and understand the nature of disabled communities? Finally, if disabled people's self-determination is to be realised, does this still require forms of self-organisation?

All three questions raise a further question: to what degree are these activities dependent on resources being available? As indicated by Enns, in their early years, many DPOs relied on voluntary support to survive, but the world has changed with new expectations, responsibilities and ways of working. Disabled people remain largely among the low-income groups; therefore, self-financing DPOs are not a realistic option. How do we resource self-organisation if this remains a core part of disability politics and praxis?

DID THE DPOS CEASE TO BE THE PLATFORM FOR
PROMOTING DISABLED PEOPLE'S SELF-DETERMINATION?

Perhaps a starting point for exploring this question is to ask a slightly different one. Should we be talking about a disabled community or disabled communities? As I noted elsewhere in this book, Oliver speaks about the need for an individual to self-define themselves as a disabled person; however, how does this correspond to seeking to be part of a disabled community?

Disabled people and various other agencies talk about a 'disabled community' from time to time, but it is not a term that is well defined. To what extent disabled people would choose to be, or are in a position whereby they could see themselves as, a community is debatable. What, after all, would be considered as constituting a disabled community? Historically, as we have seen, disabled people were placed in institutional settings and had to put up with forced communal living and working with little or no choice involved. Disabled people were 'forced' to socialise with one another and among those who escaped institutional settings were people who then disassociated with other disabled people. Others formed bonds around impairment-specific issues and others who embraced the political collective identity by joining the disabled people's movement. People First is a disabled people's organisation representing learning-disabled people, who are among the most oppressed social groups due to having specific social restrictions. While the Disabled People's Movement acknowledged this fact to a degree, there is evidence to suggest it was extremely poor in terms of trying to develop inclusive practice. For different reasons, people who identified as mental health system survivors, were also largely absent from 'the disabled community'.

Taken as a complete whole, this complexity makes it extremely difficult to identify the boundaries around what might constitute 'the disabled community'; subsequently, it might prove difficult to agree which individuals might be included or not. Why does it matter? It matters because the fluidity or ambiguity of who is involved, and on what basis, undermines disabled people's ability to develop a collective and shared understanding of our experience of social oppression in general and, more specifically, in relation to the ability to mount a meaningful resistance to the current attacks upon our lives. Deaf people have been excluded from this discussion because not only do they consider themselves to be a distinct community with a well-developed identity and specific culture; the majority do not regard themselves to be disabled.[16]

DPOS' ENGAGEMENT WITH THE NATURE OF
DISABLED COMMUNITIES

I want to put forward the argument that disabled activists neglected 'community building' among people who might not share the political identity of being disabled people. It has proved difficult to forge a collective identity when people have little understanding of the social interpretation of disability and its implications. We cannot ignore the fact that the phrase 'disabled people' is used in mainstream society to define 'the disabled' [*sic*] in a more 'politically correct' manner. The notion of the 'disabled community' is therefore subject to ambiguity as a result. Many people with impairments have argued they are part of the 'disabled community' but do not see themselves as represented by the politics of the Disabled People's Movement.

The diversity of opinion that exists among disabled people cannot be ignored or pushed to one side. Living disabled lives in the age of austerity means the political terrain within what might have been referred to at one time as the 'disabled community' has changed, with great division existing. The term 'disabled activist' has a far wider meaning to what it did have twenty or forty years ago. The spectrum of the 'politics of disability' within campaigning is evident, with bloggers discussing their own personal angst caused by benefit reforms for example. In the past, the Disabled People's Movement tended to share a broad common approach towards seeing disabled people and their issues; however, the language and politics existing today are far more fractured then they were, which means that as a result the collective identity we once had is less obvious. The Disabled People's Movement always had to deal with questions around 'Who does the Movement represent?' and 'With what authority does it speak?'

Disabling barriers did constrain disabled people's ability to self-organise; however, it must be acknowledged that activists often neglected grassroots working as a result of trying to 'influence' policymakers. Rather than develop a better understanding of what self-determination means for a 'transformative agenda' – involving our communities, the tendency was to simply demand 'rights' and 'social inclusion', both adopting an individualistic approach. This approach was not 'from below' or 'outside in'; thus it used our communities to engage in pressure politics rather than build firm foundations. This returns to the dialectical nature of our struggle and the need to have, as Finkelstein said, 'our needs and views ... legitimately reflected in a section of the working class'. This means being clearer on what disabled people want and need in terms of their participation within society.

DOES DISABLED PEOPLE'S SELF-DETERMINATION STILL REQUIRE FORMS OF SELF-ORGANISATION?

Developing a new disability praxis requires us to view disability politics as defending the interests of all 'disabled communities', no matter how these are defined. At the same time, we must seek to reinvigorate a consciousness around a collective political 'disabled identity' in relation to the experience of social oppression, even though some groups and individuals may have conflicting interests or perspectives. Any new social movement built on resistance must seek to unite as many disabled people as possible by offering a framework to work within, and disabled activists must have a clearer picture of relationships with others within disabled communities. Whether or not DPOs are sustainable without compromising principles or getting sucked into the market system is debatable. The role of service provision – by whom and for whom – must be addressed in terms of developing a transformative agenda. New forms of working and organisation exist; however, these can have a contradictory impact on disabled people by removing barriers for some and creating new ones for others. It is being suggested that disabled people's self-determination still requires forms of self-organisation, but alongside alliances with non-disabled allies and other sections of society's oppressed. However, how best to finance emancipation struggles remains one of the most important unanswered questions impacting upon developing a new disability praxis.

OPPRESSION, DIVERSITY AND INTERSECTIONALITY: NEGLECTED DISCUSSIONS

In previous chapters, the nature of social oppression was discussed in relation to how impairment and disability are defined. It was noted that oppression was often equated with discrimination. By inference, it was also suggested that how oppression impacted upon specific groups of disabled people has largely been marginalised within disability politics.

Within the fifty years I have been a disabled activist, I have seen the language and concepts associated with oppression, discrimination and diversity change. As a disabled white male activist, my involvement in addressing the relationships between them has been a peripheral one, acting as an instigator of discussions and policies, alongside being an ally. When reflecting on the British Disabled People's Movement in order to write this book, I recognised that I was guilty of making assumptions, failing to question deeply enough the implications behind the diversity of our communities, and as a consequence, the complexities surrounding encountered oppressions.

What is meant by intersectionality? Phoenix explains:

> Coined by Kimberlé Crenshaw in 1989, intersectionality draws analytic attention to the fact that no social identity category exists in isolation of others. Rather, we are all simultaneously positioned within multiple social categories including gender, social class, sexuality, (dis)ability and racialisation among others. These categories reciprocally construct each other when they intersect, forming qualitatively different meanings and experiences that are situated in different contexts, times and power relations.[17]

This originates in the US, and thus intersectionality is often associated with 'privilege theory'.[18] Whilst acknowledging the roots of this theory, just like the social model, it has been subjected to interpretation and problematised. The focus is on addressing the power relations within, as well as between, social categories. Intersectionality requires recognition of the fact that some groups, and therefore individuals within those groups, have advantages or disadvantages as a result of how capitalist society positions them. Oppression is conducted through power relations; therefore, white disabled men, for example, are not subjected to the unequal and differential treatment experienced by disabled women. How oppression is encountered is therefore a question of how differing forms can combine, intersect, or be absent in specific incidents. Impairment reality is also intersectional in nature, as not all impairment categorisation or impairment reality produces similar forms of disablism.

Acknowledging the intersectional nature of oppressions must go beyond identity recognition and involve dialogue around how we create inclusive spaces. This means making more visible and addressing the diversity of social relations and social restrictions. With no coordinated British Disabled People's Movement, and an increase in the number of impairment-specific groups springing up, not to mention the generational gaps that now exist since the 1990s, the need to find common ground, as well as acknowledging the diversity of experience, has never been greater.

While many disabled women were central to the decision-making of many national and local DPOs, it is shamefully clear now that gendered issues were not given the priority they merited. Similarly, other forms of oppression were 'acknowledged', but also inadequately addressed within the Movement. The early 1990s saw the British Council of Disabled People begin to address 'equality' within areas of policies and campaigning. Despite this, intersectional issues with the Movement continued to be marginalised, paradoxically, as the 'rights agenda' gained momentum. While issues specifically relevant to disabled women were marginalised within the majority of DPOs, it would be wrong to conclude there was a complete absence of these issues within disability politics.

Beckie Rutherford offered insights into disabled women's lives within both the Women's Liberation Movement and Disabled People's Movement.[19] Her summary includes Sisters Against Disablement (SAD), formed in 1982 with the aim of discussing and exploring the relationship between feminism and disablement. Rutherford informs us, 'Perhaps SAD's most striking intervention in feminist politics was their disruption of the Lesbian Sex and Sexuality Conference in 1983. SAD members boycotted the event and picketed the Conference venue on the grounds of it being inaccessible to disabled women.'[20]

Another important community of disabled women was the support group Gemma. Founded in 1976, its primary aim was to combat the isolation of disabled lesbians and bisexual women. Rutherford writes:

Some of the organisations that formed within the generative spirit of the Women's Liberation Movement – for example Gemma – are still running today and now exist alongside a myriad of other groups and projects run by disabled women. Some examples include the experimental collective, Sisters of Frida; the multi-racial self-help group, WinVisible; and the YouTube vloggers, the Triple Cripples.[21]

How do we address this situation? In the 1990s, we saw a challenge to 'the social model' [sic] from various sections of disabled communities; however, I believe much of this criticism was misplaced because it saw 'the model' as the sum total of disability politics or theory.[22] The previous two chapters sought to address aspects of this concern, but a major unanswered question that needs an answer is how and in what ways does the emancipation struggle – that is, ending oppression and creating inclusive societies – relate to personal experience of impairment reality? In seeking an answer, I believe it is necessary to consider Finkelstein's view that 'The central issue in our campaigns for a better life, therefore, ought to be concerned with issues around emancipation and this requires struggles for social change rather than concentrating on individual experiences, "rehabilitation", etc.'[23]

Taking control of impairment management and our own identities and lifestyles are outside the remit of the social model. There is a need for a clearer distinction between the emancipation struggle where a central demand is for social acceptance and engagement, including acknowledgement of impairment reality, and the struggles on a day-to-day basis of living with an impairment in a disablist society. Other 'models' or analytical tools are required; for example, I also would suggest both sites of struggle would benefit from an eco-social approach towards disability and a social model of impairment (discussed in Chapters 7 and 9). The latter would explore how impairment is a social product, the psycho-emotional consequences of disablism, and creating non-medicalised space for exploring impairment reality management.

We cannot ignore the psychological or emotional impact of disablism and how this in turn has consequences for issues such as taking control of impairment management and our own identities and lifestyles. It is necessary because these sites of struggle do inform and impact upon disability politics, because our personal space is often invaded by disablist ideologies and practice. The core feature of disability praxis must be to develop system change, as this would alter both public and private spheres.

Attempts have been made to discuss diverse encounters with oppressions by disabled people. Ayesha Vernon within 'The Dialectics of Multiple Identities and the Disabled People's Movement', for example, explains how race, gender and class intersect with disability in the experience of black women. Different notions were debated, ranging from 'double jeopardy' on to concepts such as 'triple disadvantage' and 'simultaneous oppression'.[24] Vernon states that Stuart and Begum applied the concept 'simultaneous oppression' to disabled black people's experience, 'rightly arguing that previous analyses of their experience being additive were inadequate. However, this, too, is verging on the additive, for it assumes that disability and race are invariably experienced at the same time.'[25] This was increasingly seen as problematic; however, Vernon herself refers to 'multiple oppression', which sees as the effects of being 'attributed several stigmatised identities are often multiplied (exacerbated) and they can be experienced simultaneously and singularly depending on the context.'[26]

Similarly, racism, sexism, homophobia, transphobia, classism, ageism, etc. all enter into relations with disablism. In relation to combating homophobia, transphobia and disablism, Regard was established as a national organisation of disabled lesbians, gay men, bisexuals and transgendered people. It highlights disability issues within the LGBTQI+ community and

LGBTQI+ issues within the disability community, campaigns on issues affecting disabled LGBTQI+ people, and works to combat social isolation amongst its membership. Regard was supportive of the British Council of Disabled People (BCODP), the Trade Union Disability Alliance (TUDA) and the National Centre for Independent Living (NCIL).[27]

The BBC's documentary, 'Silenced: The Hidden Story of Disabled Britain', sought to convey the historical treatment of disabled people in Britain since the nineteenth century.[28] Among the reviews was one by the Alliance for Inclusive Education (ALFIE) which pointed out:

> However, one of the shortfalls of the documentary is that it looks at Disabled people as a homogenous group ... It was clear that there was no room within the programme to give space to Black Disabled campaigners. The message for us and the future generation is it's 'ok' to do valuable work behind the scenes, but do not expect to get recognition.[29]

Among the invisible Black disabled campaigners mentioned by ALFIE were Millie Hill, Saâdia Neilson, Ossie Stuart and Nasa Begum. Others, such as Alia Hassan, who did feature in the documentary, could have been included in the list of absentees. BCODP were conscious of the lack of Black-led DPOs within our ranks, with only the Asian People's Disability Alliance having a representative on its National Council.[30] Many reasons existed for this absence including distrust and concerns about systemic racism.

Jaye Charles founded the Equalities National Council, which co-authored in 2012, 'Over-looked Communities, Over-due Change: How Services Can Better Support BME Disabled People'.[31] This report was part of Disability LIB, and Charles said the fact that it had been ignored highlighted how 'the British government had just "stood by and watched" as black disabled people's organisations have "disappeared" through lack of funding over the last decade.'[32] ALFIE's review concluded with 'We still have a long way to go for the inclusion of Black Disabled people and people of colour within our movement.'[33] While there are only fragments of a Disabled People's Movement remaining, any regeneration of the Movement must involve understanding intersectional issues within disability praxis.

While I am critical of many of the concepts and the language that has been entering British discussions around the politics of disability from the American Disability Rights Movement, Critical Disability Studies, and emerging Disability Justice, I acknowledge that the differences and similarities in opinions need to be engaged with if a new disability praxis is to emerge. In many modern social movements, the word 'justice' is deployed to signify a desire to create a fairer, more just and more equal world. Disability justice therefore is viewed as a social justice movement.[34]

ENGAGING WITH DISABILITY JUSTICE

Sins Invalid is an American disability justice-based performance project, which published a working definition of Disability Justice and its relationship to the Disability Rights Movement. According to one of its co-founders, Patty Berne, a 'second wave' of activists around 2005 noted that the Disability Rights' focus on litigation and bureaucracy often addressed symptoms but not root causes. Berne states, 'One cannot look at the history of US slavery, the stealing of indigenous lands, and US imperialism without seeing the way that white supremacy leverages ableism to create a subjugated "other".[35]

The definition of Disability Justice stems from a collective of disabled queer women of colour, including Patty Berne, Mia Mingus and the late Stacey Milbern. It is argued that Disability Justice takes a more comprehensive approach, going beyond securing rights for disabled people, by recognising the intersectionality of disabled people who belong to additional marginalised communities, and addressing the fact that the DRM was mainly led by white disabled people.[36]

The movement around Disability Justice is an important area to discuss in relation to disability praxis, as it has ten main principles around the inclusion of people who are marginalised on multiple fronts. Many of the unanswered questions that exist, the underdevelopment of theory and practice, and the shaping of a new disability praxis, could be explored via the deployment of these principles. What are they?

1. Intersectionality
The Disability Justice framework applies this concept by explaining that disabled people each have a different background and experience regarding race, class, sexuality, age, immigration status, and other issues. As stated previously, intersectionality recognises oppressive ideologies often operate together and empower one another.

2. Leadership of Those Most Impacted
Disability Justice makes the point that leadership must come from the people most impacted upon rather than coming from scholars and academics.

3. Anti-Capitalist Politics

This principle asserts that our worth as a person does not depend on how much we can produce. Disability Justice opposes the level of productivity a capitalist culture expects, as well as the systemic poverty that disabled people are forced into if they are unable to work. All people deserve to have their needs met, regardless of their ability to produce.

4. Cross-Movement Solidarity

Disability Justice combines with other movements seeking liberation – such as racial justice, environmental justice, anti-police terror, and others. Because every demographic of people includes those who are disabled, thus acknowledging liberation cannot be achieved with the success of each of these movements. This co-production and interdependency assists disabled people to become more united and comprehensive in our activism.

5. Recognizing Wholeness

Disability Justice movement holds that people have inherent worth outside of commodity relations and capitalist notions of productivity. Each person is full of history and life experience.

Challenging normality, creating social acceptance of living with impairments, has always been an aspect of disability politics and disability dialectics, but the notion of 'wholeness' is problematic as it tends to inform a form of 'idealism'.[37]

6. Sustainability

Another vital principle of the Disability Justice movement is sustainability. Disabled activists and advocates need to be in tune with their bodies to pace themselves long-term and continue steadily working toward justice over time without burning out. Additionally, the sustainability of the movement is dependent on the community, and cannot be pushed forward by individuals alone.

7. Commitment to Cross-Disability Solidarity

Disability Justice focuses on all disabled people, including those who are often left out.

8. Interdependence

Interdependence allows us to work side-by-side, creating a stronger community as we work to liberate all oppressed individuals. Instead of solely promoting independence, which was a focus of the Disability Rights and Independent Living movement, interdependence acknowledges that none of us can thrive without support. This principle is about building a sense of community among disabled people and organising to achieve liberation.

9. Collective Access
The collective access principle explains that Disability Justice creates methods of doing things outside of the dominant norms. [The] Disability Justice movement believes access needs ought to be welcomed, respected, and acknowledged.

10. Collective Liberation
Collective liberation means envisioning a world that can be created when disabled people with various backgrounds and lived experiences come together to enact a movement of change.[38]

Discussions in this book have revealed that conflicts and tensions exist relating to key issues such as definitions, and approaches towards identity and culture. The possibilities of negotiating the differences between US and British disability politics in relation to the principles of Disability Justice is discussed in the next chapter.

9

A Radical Eco-social
Approach Towards Sustainable
Community-based Services

In Chapter 4, it was argued that self-determination, de-institutionalisa-tion and promotion of self-directed living made up the third cornerstone of British disability politics, and the history of the development of Independent Living Movements was discussed. By the middle of the 1990s, theoretical, political and organisational differences emerged within both the British Disabled People's and Independent Living Movements. I was directly involved in the discussions around the detachment of the National Centre for Independent Living from the British Council of Disabled People as BCDOP's chairperson.[1] This took place against a backdrop of growing attacks upon the Welfare State.[2]

In 2005, New Labour launched its 'Improving the Life Chances of Disabled People' report which boldly claimed that:"By 2025, disabled people in Britain should have full opportunities and choices to improve their quality of life and will be respected and included as equal members of society."[3]

The vision forwarded a strategy of practical measures aimed at helping disabled people to achieve independent living by:

- moving progressively to individual budgets
- *drawing together the services to which they are entitled* (emphasis added)
- giving greater choice over the mix of support via the form of cash and/or direct provision of services.

The report noted the need for improving the advice services available, addressing existing problems with suitable housing and transport, and improving support for families with young disabled children by facilitating a smooth transition into adulthood. It was noted that the implementation of these measures should take account of the needs of older people who are dis-abled or who have 'care requirements' [sic].

Although not placed at the top of the priority list, it soon became clear that New Labour's own central target was improving support and incentives for getting and staying in employment.[4] Influential disabled people were involved in advising and writing this report which resulted in the produc-tion of a 'hybrid' strategy where 'progressive' ideas were incorporated into traditional and neoliberal market facing policies. The report was the basis of what I have termed 'Janus politics' and the selection process for disabled people to be involved in its implementation through Equality 2025 bears witness to the desire to exclude 'the usual suspects' [sic] from the waning Disabled People's Movement.[5]

Whilst the report spoke about achieving independent living and the need for an increase in the numbers of Centres of Independent Living, behind the rhetoric, the policymakers were transforming the language and concepts of the two Movements away from an emancipation agenda into a consum-er-rights one by rebranding it as 'personalisation'.[6]

Spicker writes:

Personalisation falls short, not just in terms of the wildly exaggerated claims that are made for it, but in terms of the theoretical benefits that consumerism is supposed to achieve, the extent to which it delivers tan-gible benefits and its delivery of services in practice. If, as the largest evaluation suggests, services for older people and people with learning disabilities are not actually improved by personalisation, and the gains for younger people with physical disabilities are marginal, then most of the people who are supposed to benefit from personalisation gain little or nothing from it.[7]

What followed from this period was the global economic crisis and the birth of the 'Age of Austerity'. The New Labour government from 1997 to 2010 ventured on a rightward shift towards an increasingly individualised and market-friendly approach to social policy, which resulted in greater condi-tionality within the welfare system. The economic downturn and financial crisis of 2008 was soon followed by the election of the Conservative/Liberal Democrat Coalition government in 2010 which hastened the transition to a more draconian relationship between the state and its citizens. The result was the sweeping away of the last foundations of post-war social democratic welfarist policies. The Coalition's austerity measures were extremely savage and left large sections of the community of disabled people in a state of shock, living in fear of losing their services and homes. Disabled people are on record as describing the process of applying for benefits as increasingly difficult and distressing, with fear of being plunged into poverty. During the age of austerity, numerous reports emerged of deaths and suicides linked to unsuccessful claims due to the assessments. In addition, disabled women and survivors of sexual violence and abuse found themselves failed by benefits system processes either because they re-ignited trauma through the additional requirements placed on rape survivors to access tax credits, or due to the failure to recognise the extra barriers faced by disabled women who were subjected to domestic abuse. All of this took place against political and media rhetoric about skivers and scroungers that has left disabled people feeling stigmatised, vulnerable and isolated. What little gains that were made by disabled people have largely been rolled back over the last twenty years and this is well documented.[8]

THE PRESENT SITUATION

In Britain today, there is broad agreement that there is a crisis within the system called 'Social Care'; however, there are vast differences of opinion in terms of the causes of the crisis and what is required to develop strategies to bring it to an end. In 2020, a Trade Union Congress press release reported that adult social care spending in England had started to rise again from 2016/17 due to a series of short-term funding boosts. However, current research indicated that the additions had not been enough to restore funding to 2010 levels, let alone address the rising demand. The TUC figures showed that councils in England had £7.8bn a year less to spend on key services in 2018/19, including social care, compared to 2010. Not untypically, the report focused on support for older people, which means it is difficult to obtain statistics for cuts to services for younger adult service users.[9]

There is still a stereotyped perception that 'Social Care' is simply about 'looking after older people', which means other groups of people in need of social support are either ignored or subjected to inappropriate services. Another major problem is that there is confusion and disagreement over what is understood by 'Social Care' and as a result, differing interests are being played off against each other. All the major political parties have misrepresented the crisis within so-called 'Social Care' due to the stereotyping of people in need of support via a crude collapsing together of health and social issues, hiding the impact of the implementation of cuts – for example, focusing on 'risk management' within criteria and undermining advocacy and independent living. People seeking services are finding their support needs are no longer considered to be significant enough to merit support or that the services they need no longer exist. Disabled people, for example, argue adult social care and independent living needs to be addressed outside of the outdated 'one size fits all' approach adopted by both the National Health Service and local authorities over the last forty years. Neoliberalism, marketisation and austerity have only made matters worse, with independent living virtually falling off the agenda.

In 2019, Reclaiming Our Futures Alliance, an alliance of disabled people and their organisations in England, published 'Independent Living for the Future: Our Vision for a National Independent Living Support System'. This vision paper had been shaped and developed through ongoing debate and discussion within the Independent Living Campaign, set up in 2011, in response to the then-planned closure of the Independent Living Fund (ILF) and other forums held to discuss the future direction of independent living.[10] Beresford and Harrison wrote:

> Disabled people of all ages are in the process of designing a new vision based on rights and the UN Convention on the Rights of Persons with Disabilities (CRPD). We, the users of social care, are planning a service that will be led by us, not service providers whose main focus has become to meet budget targets (cuts) and ration the care based on neo-liberal ideology – not rights or need. Personalisation policy is dead. The Care Act is as useful as a wet paper bag.[11]

WHAT DO DISABLED PEOPLE REALLY WANT?

What might disabled people seek to achieve as an outcome of their 'emancipation' struggle? The disabled people referred to in the question are those who are conscious of inequality and disablism. In 2018, it was reported that 'Nearly half of disabled people feel excluded from society and day to day life, according to a new report by disability charity Scope.'[12]

The report's findings confirmed that in the opinion of those canvassed, very little had substantially changed over the last forty years. How then do disabled people see the task of changing their social situation? Is it a question of campaigning for integration, inclusion, or transformation?

Right across the political spectrum, there are perspectives and campaigns considering the future of social support for older and disabled people. One such campaign began its life as Reclaim Social Care. The uniqueness of the group was that it involved activists and campaigners, professionals, academics, trade unionists and, most importantly, disabled people. Reclaim Social Care saw itself as a non-party political coalition of individuals and organisations. Under the influence of a small group of disabled activists, the campaign group adopted a new name: Act 4 Inclusion (A4I) and a radical, transformative vision.[13]

The A4I vision builds upon internal and external discussions including the work of Vic Finkelstein and other radical disabled activists, as well as acknowledging the importance of the looming ecological crisis. Unlike those who seek to 'reclaim', 'reinvigorate', or 'ditch' the social model of disability, A4I believes the model's methodology can be used to explore the current situation facing disabled people, thus paving the way for a more detailed eco-social approach to address disablement and disablism.

As the chief architect of the A4I vision, I have made space within this chapter to explain the thinking behind it. In order to embed the A4I vision and its concepts into the organisation, a series of members' meetings took place. One discussion revealed that there was a diversity of opinion surrounding people's interpretations of what integration and inclusion meant. A4I is not an organisation led by disabled people, but it is working in that direction by working in co-production with non-disabled allies to campaign for the development of a new national service capable of delivering community-based services via an eco-social system – a system that would work for all disabled people, of all ages, with all types of impairment, but also for everyone else in society.[14]

By exploring the question, 'What do disabled people really want?', we are forced to confront a major tension that exists within discussions associated with disabled people: who exactly are we talking about? This question carries with it a series of unspoken assumptions, as we are not only talking about individual needs or aspirations, but rather forging a collective conscious socio-political thought. It has been suggested that Mike Oliver's three-fold criteria for self-identification as a disabled person offers a framework for people with impairments, who politically self-identify as being 'disabled' through the imposition of social restrictions. The previous chapter did, however, acknowledge that the majority of older and Deaf people do not self-identify in this way for a variety of reasons and this, of course, has socio-political implications. People can be oppressed without knowing, understanding, or accepting they are oppressed.

Within the first part of this book, it was argued that the core of disability politics has been concerned with the struggle for emancipation of disabled people from social prisons. In simple terms, disability politics' original remit had a dual purpose: end segregation through de-institutionalisation and strive to build 'inclusive societies'. The concept of 'inclusion' had not been developed back in the 1970s and therefore, as we saw in Chapter 4, 'integration' was used by the early activists to signify the aspiration of disabled people to be full participants within society.

Finkelstein, as previously noted, argued that we can only talk about the social model of disability, independent living and the value of civil and human rights in a meaningful way, if we see them as interconnected elements of the struggle to overthrow disabled people's oppressive situation. In the US, there are people who have suggested a shift in language, moving away from 'independent' towards 'interdependent' living. Whatever term we employ to refer to the processes involved in establishing the means of self-directed living, it is essential that we acknowledge that social support will be a fundamental necessity for many people, due to either impairment reality and/or disabling barriers.

Challenging discriminatory practices against individuals assists our overall struggle, but this political activity is not the essence of disability politics or praxis. This statement needs placing within the context of the dialectics of disability. As previously stated, the nature of society in terms of its structures, systems, values, dominant thinking and practices, create and maintain disablement. Under these conditions, the relationship between the macro and micro levels of society and the differing environments involved in existing social relations impact upon disabled people's ability to participate in society. In Britain, the notion of institutional discrimination against disabled people has been rejected by the major political parties. As a consequence, 'disability discrimination' is reduced to being seen as 'when you are treated less well or put at a disadvantage for a reason that relates to your disability in one of the situations covered by the Equality Act'.[15]

This individualises the experience and defines 'treated less well or put at a disadvantage' within specific contexts – for example, policies, procedures and practice of employers and service providers. This narrow view of 'disability discrimination' has hindered our ability to identify the structural forms of disabled people's social oppression in depth, because the focus has always been on assisting the individual disabled person to fit into the status quo. This has been the legitimising force behind maintaining institutional living for those deemed 'too disabled' to live within the community.

The current crisis within Social Care in Britain cannot simply be resolved by increased resources or ending privatisation alone; the entire system is oppressive, not fit for purpose, and is in need of a complete transformation. The seven or twelve pillars of Independent Living are not solely about empowering individual choice and control, although that would be an outcome; they also relate to fighting for the means by which disabled people can fully participate within society. Getting this message across will not be easy as we are not all at the same point in the journey towards understanding what needs doing. In addressing the way forward and developing a new disability praxis, we need to consider the words of Paulo Freire: 'Leaders who do not act dialogically, but insist on imposing their decisions, do not organize the people – they manipulate them. They do not liberate, nor are they liberated: they oppress.'[16]

This process of working dialogically has been largely absent since the new century begun. A new praxis requires engagement in co-production based upon working via dialogue.

THE TASK OF DISABILITY JUSTICE, INCLUSION AND CO-PRODUCTION

In the previous chapter, the concept of disability justice was introduced in terms of intersectionality and how diverse systems of oppression amplify and reinforce one another. The term 'disability justice' is often used interchangeably with terms such as 'disability rights' and 'disability inclusion.'"

Inclusion is a broad term that describes policies, procedures and practice, alongside resources, which enable people who might otherwise be excluded or marginalised, such as those who have physical or mental impairments and members of other oppressed groups. Developing inclusion is not the same as integration. As previously argued, it is not possible to 'integrate' people into a service, system, or society that does not cater for their needs or lifestyles; only by transforming the structures, systems, services, through acting for inclusion, will everything become fairer, more equitable and healthy.

The concept of 'integration', as discussed within A4I and employed by Davis and Finkelstein, is different to the kind of integration that has more in common with assimilation in 'the absorption and integration of people, ideas, or culture into a wider society'".[17] It is also important to acknowledge that there are reformist and accommodationist approaches attached to the term 'inclusion'. However, within the context of this book, it is argued that in order to create social inclusion, active interventions to meet the needs, interests and lifestyles of diverse groups of people is required. Within A4I, it is suggested that the best way of achieving that aim would be through employing methods of co-production.

Co-production is a way of working 'whereby citizens and decision makers, or people who use services, family carers and service providers work together to create a decision or service which works for them all. The approach is value driven and built on the principle that those who use a service are best placed to help design it.'[18]

The other crucial concept is that of an eco-social approach. A tension within disability politics, as we have seen, is the positioning of the experiences of the disabled individual within the context of social oppression. As discussed earlier, Thomas argued that Finkelstein and UPIAS took a 'social relational' approach towards disability.[19] UPIAS, I would suggest, recognised disablement and disablism took place at both macro and micro levels of society.[20] Finkelstein in particular spoke of the interaction between the environment and the individual. This is not unlike the ideas within Ecological Systems Theory (EST).[21] EST was developed into a model by psychologist Urie Bronfenbrenner and applies the study of ecology to the social environment. In ecology, organisms are studied in relation to their environments. Therefore, EST places the individual at the centre of their social environment by recognising that they are surrounded by interacting environmental layers.[22]

The starting point within ecological theory is an acknowledgement that individuals, families, groups and communities do not operate in isolation but are influenced by their physical and social environments in which they live and interact. The vision therefore is to combine ecological theory with the radical social approach towards disability to develop a community-based eco-social system. A community-based eco-social system of support and self-directed living would require systems to see older and disabled people's lifestyles in relation to their homes, existing relationships and neighbourhoods, etc. from an asset perspective, and then to identify the appropriate services and support needed to overcome barriers to living in these familiar or chosen surroundings.

THE DEVELOPMENT OF AN ECO-SOCIAL APPROACH TOWARDS ESTABLISHING COMMUNITY-BASED SERVICES

Key aspects of Vic Finkelstein's work have been influential in assisting with my thinking in terms of advocating the developing of an eco-social approach towards establishing community-based services. By exploring the salient issues he raised, it is possible to see how they offer a framework for going forward.

In 1984, Finkelstein presented to the Medical Disability Society 'Schemes for Independent Living', a paper in which he outlined the social interpretation of disability to foreground the right to self-determination. The paper starts from UPIAS's view that disability is a particular form of social discrimination, but then goes on to say 'Human beings are, by nature, agents of change and the new organisations not only express the collective voice of disabled people against their discrimination, but are themselves increasingly the agents of social change.'[23]

He argued there was a lack of appropriate services and the role of professionals in terms of interventions resulted in enforced passivity in the community. As a result, disabled people were self-organising in an attempt to break out of this vicious circle by promoting and setting up centres for the provision of services in which they have a more direct role. His view was that the fundamental objectives of Centres for Independent Living (CILs) should be to 'enable disabled people to exercise much greater control over the services that they receive in the community'. Underpinning this would be to facilitate 'more direct involvement in all relevant decision-making'.[24]

The rationale behind this was the need to provide a framework for disabled people to become active in service provision which would, in turn, begin the process of affecting social change. He saw the development of a network of disabled people's organisations and CILs as a platform to 'become a communications channel for expressing the democratic voice of disabled people to central and local government, professional and voluntary workers and the general public'.[25] Finkelstein indicated that he believed CILs could be integrated into community support services. Although he saw these as inadequate, he saw the possibility of developing joint control between disabled people and the statutory services. He identified areas where joint control might be appropriate – information, counselling, housing, technical aids, personal assistance, transport, access and service planning – these, of course, corresponded to the pillars of independent living and existing campaigns.

The significance of this paper is that it links together self-determination, self-organisation, developing CILs and community support services – the same ingredients thought necessary for A4I's vision. In addition, there is acknowledgement that certain prerequisites need to exist for the development of collaboration between organisations of disabled people and the statutory services. Here lies the three interlocking elements that are required for taking a new eco-social way forward:

> Firstly, there is a need for national, regional and local organisations of disabled people to unite in a comprehensive network, to discuss the issues, to encourage and support a more active role for disabled people in service planning and delivery and to present a coherent policy on CILs to government and the professions ...
>
> Secondly, there is an urgent need for a change in prevailing professional attitudes [and approaches] towards service delivery in the community. These approaches need to be replaced by ones which support collaborative and joint work with disabled people ...
>
> Thirdly, there is a need for enabling legislation which will facilitate a new distribution and control of financial and other resources so that collaborative ways of working can materialise.[26]

The paper uses the term 'collaboration'; however, this can be viewed as articulating co-production. Finkelstein states:

> In this approach, professional and voluntary service providers have to learn how to place their expertise at the service of disabled people who, in turn, have to learn how to take an active role in making effective use of the support available to them. In this formulation those providing help and support become a resource, to be drawn upon by disabled people according to need.[27]

The landscape of course has dramatically changed since 1984, but the basic framework needed remains the same. Both in 1990 and 1991, Finkelstein presented further papers on what he calls the 'administrative model' of disability, which he saw as the bringing together of 'two critical components in the development of contemporary service interventions'.[28] Hence, he argues:

> Seen together the combined 'cure' (medical approach) and 'care' (welfare approach) offered by the 'Department of Health and Social Services' can be interpreted as being unconsciously guided by an 'administrative model' of disability. This can be regarded as the prevailing dominant approach to disability in the UK.[29]

He used his second paper as a platform to suggest that alternatives to current practice need to bring sector workers and disabled people together and share expertise in the process of barrier identification and removal at both 'the personal level (for the individual setting their own goals) and at the social level where public facilities need to be made truly public'.[30] In his outlining of collaborating in an active way, Finkelstein suggested a form of disability praxis by saying, 'agreeing to shift the focus from the disabled person as possessing the problem, will open up new experiences from which new and non-confrontational ideas can emerge.'[31] This also indicates the direction of travel he took in later papers.

The 'social barriers model' of disability and its associated 'integrated living support systems' approach were the bedrock for his praxis. Finkelstein believed the implementation of a social barriers model of disability approach involved various fundamental changes, which included shifting the base for disability-related service from 'health and welfare' to 'environment'-based services. Ending the culture of services being service-led would be a fundamental part of establishing 'integrated living support systems'. At the core of these systems would be CILs, which would provide 'the necessary central focus and guidance for all services used by disabled people including medical, educational, housing and transport services'.[32] To ensure these systems met the right of disabled people to access all required services the appropriate levels of resources would need to be available.

Integral to the approach advocated by Finkelstein would also be the cultural shift and redirection of education and training for all service providers. Key in this development would be improving the education and training of community-based service providers so that 'their analytical and organisational skills are better focussed on barrier identification and removal.'[33] Finally, legislation would have to be enacted as a framework for guiding the development of community based-support systems.

Seven years later, Finkelstein was asked by the World Health Organization to prepare a discussion document. The result was 'Re-thinking Care in a Society Providing Equal Opportunities for All'. A central message he offered was that:

> As long as community care is viewed in economic, managerial, professional and technical terms the cultural component of service provision and service utilisation tends to be neglected and this, in its own right, will undermine the best of policies. In this respect different national traditions need to be addressed in specific detail whatever global proposals are

made for the incorporation of cultural issues in the development of community care.[34]

Finkelstein spoke about a new community worker (Resource Consultant), who would operate within a lifestyle orientation that would be geared towards assisting people attain their personal goals and aspirations. To some extent, this is not unlike the notion of 'person-centred planning'.[35]

A year later, these ideas were developed further when he produced 'A Profession Allied to the Community: The Disabled People's Trade Union'. The piece is short and contrasts two professional stances toward disabled people. The first he describes as producing professions allied to medicine (PAMs), who have worked within the National Health Service and Social Services that are dominated by a culture of welfare provision – work in cure or care services – for the 'vulnerable'. He saw this as resulting in 'Control over the shaping and reshaping of social assistance [which] has not only enabled specific social groups to dominate others, but has also enabled them to define what is "normal" and, in so doing, label all assistance required by other groups as "special" and "compensatory".[36]

Finkelstein also addressed the developing relationship between the global disabled people's movement and the majority world. Firstly, he acknowledges that the development of disabled people's own approaches to assistance requires a dual method of working: there is a need to critique and address the imposed practices; while creating new forms of assistance based upon disabled people's lifestyles. He argues, 'Our constructing of systematic forms of help according to our own social model of disability will generate new services and service providers – professions allied to the community (PACs).'[37]

It is not clear which professions would be covered, but my reading is that any profession recruited to provide community-based services would be included. Interestingly, Finkelstein views these workers as constituting a trade union. I am assuming that these trade unionists are disabled people and non-disabled allies, because he speaks of them as being 'truly immersed in a disability culture' and being 'a vital engine for social change'.[38] The vision he presents is one where PACs 'will have a crucial role in promoting the national and international criticism of the dominant health and community care ideology that is not wanted by disabled people'.[39]

The second point he makes, which I concur with, is that it is already evident in the world, that 'the elaborate culture, language, policies of medicalising health (seeking to "cure" disability), community care policies, community-based variations of rehabilitation, and obsession with assessing and labelling us ... will be vigorously defended ... .'[40]

The third point made by Finkelstein, which flows from the second, echoes much of what has been argued in this book to date. The migration of the 'cure or care' culture and expertise developed by the minority world and exported or imposed upon the majority world are important tools for advancing the capitalist work ethic. Hence, 'Providing PAMs and welfare workers for our special needs enables the disabling societies of the minority world to further their control of the international economy – free of criticism from the majority world whose established supportive social relationships are being dismantled.'[41] In passing, it should be noted that 'capitalist work ethic' has been substituted for 'able-bodied', as it avoids endorsing the dominant ideological social construction that Finkelstein himself rightly criticises.[42]

Finkelstein does not detail his vision beyond simple description of the present and possible future. He writes, 'Community care services for disabled people based on the assessment of need and managed by PAMs demean both workers and users. They should be replaced by services based on the identification of aspirations managed by PACs in an alliance of workers and users.'[43] He also states:

The allying of service development with community-based aspirations requires substantially different worker attitudes and guidelines for providing professional assistance. Setting up CIL services transforms the way disabled people think about themselves and the public identity they wish to cultivate. In my view this is the beginning of a journey in which a whole new cultural matrix of human relationships is waiting to be discovered.[44]

There has always been an ambiguity in the British Disabled People's Movement, generally, and the Independent Living Movement, specifically, around the relationship between the need for personal assistance and what Finkelstein called 'barrier removal', and how he linked with this activity, with professional assistance. What comes into play here is the difference between the ideas that underpin independent living and those associated with integrated living. The latter was articulated as a more holistic and collective approach which placed an emphasis on interdependency, whereas independent living, as suggested by Ken Davis, focuses on individual and consumer rights.

It is also important to place Finkelstein's writing and ideas in historical context. He saw the beginning of the growing trend towards marketisation of 'care provision', the erosion of the welfare state, and the reduction of direct service provision. The trend towards neoliberal social policy fed into his vocal criticism of the development of direct payments and the rightward shift this married up with. In 2007, he complained that 'the disability movement is no longer setting the agenda for our emancipation – instead, we've become prisoners of a market that sets the agenda for our movement!'[45]

There is recognition of the need to get rid of the market in Act 4 Inclusion's vision; however, the next step must be for them and other campaigners seeking social change to address what this means for the future of 'direct payments' and 'personal budgets'. There is growing support for Finkelstein's view that the deployment of these schemes are:

> ... a capitalist dream come true – every single disabled person becomes an employer, pays personal assistants for their labour, is responsible for working conditions, ensures annual leave is provided, does the obligatory paperwork and checks taxes, etc. The only trouble is – capitalism doesn't stop here – competition means successful companies gobble up weaker groups, companies merge forming larger groups and those that fail, well, they go bankrupt and disappear.[46]

While it is understandable that these schemes are viewed as offering choice and control, the reality is very different for many in receipt of them. It is difficult to have dialogue around the issues involved because there is a genuine fear about the consequences.[47] The experience of people who use direct payments is particularly troubling because over recent years, the bureaucratic burden and increasingly rigid requirements imposed by the government and local authorities have left people with additional responsibilities. At the same time, these developments, coupled with imposed costs, have removed the freedom and control associated with direct payments. Innovation is not possible without choice and control, and therefore reform must promote a radical change in the approach, ensuring that restrictions are removed so that people are truly able to self-direct their support.

Within the British Disabled People's Movement, the praxis of UPIAS and Vic Finkelstein were viewed as laying the basis for disability politics; however, gradually these were eclipsed by Oliver's social model. As valuable as the social model is, there is a need to discuss the particular insights and theoretical ideas offered by Finkelstein as they go beyond addressing structural disablement. Within this book, I have drawn heavily on Finkelstein's work because so many of his arguments remain valid and needed airing once again. It is for others to judge to what degree arguments and concepts from thirty years ago are essential to developing a new radical disability praxis. Whether or not such a praxis is capable of emerging from the ashes of the old remains to be seen. It is hoped that the vision of A4I can contribute to this process. As part of this process, it is necessary to address tensions, contradictions and divisions that exist alongside developing concepts that will assist us. The following section points to some of these.

WHAT IS 'CLIMATE JUSTICE'?

Climate justice takes as its starting point the idea that the adverse impacts of a warming climate are not felt equitably among people; therefore key groups are differently affected. Climate impacts can exacerbate inequitable social conditions, which means there is growing momentum for seeking social and climate justice solutions globally. While international research is making a more concerted effort to actively include some populations in communication and strategies, the disability community have been consistently omitted. The wide-ranging exclusion is concerning, as climate change is expected to affect disabled people in three ways. They are:

1. most likely to have limited access to knowledge, resources, and services to effectively respond to environmental change;
2. more vulnerable to extreme climate events, ecosystem services loss, or infectious diseases;
3. more likely to have difficulties during required evacuations or migrations.[48]

In a United Nations Survey, a high proportion of disabled people were found to either be injured or even die during natural disasters. This was due to a lack of consultation with disabled people and governments that lacked necessary measures to support and protect them.[49] The needs of disabled people are often not considered – needs such as accessible evacuation centres, transport for the individual, any essential equipment they need to manage their impairment and health conditions, information in formats that they can read and understand, for example, communication tools for Deaf, deafened and visually impaired people.

In his article 'Social Ecology and Disability Justice: Making A New Society', American activist and writer Lateef H. McLeod explores commonalities between social ecology and disability justice in their respective visions for liberation. He explains, 'Focusing on the shared components of anti-capitalist critique, mutual aid or interdependence, and ecological sustainability ... I argue that social ecology and disability justice share a variety of values and goals that make them natural partners in struggles for collective liberation.'[50]

One of the messages that needs to be conveyed in discussions within disabled communities and among activists is the urgent need to acknowledge the interconnectedness between the climate, ecosystems and society.[51] Discussing the nature of society also requires an understanding what 'social' means within the context of 'social oppression'. 'Social' can be employed to mean:

- living or preferring to live in a community rather than alone;
- denoting or relating to human society or any of its subdivisions;
- of, relating to, or characteristic of the experience, behaviour and interaction of persons forming groups, and
- relating to or having the purpose of promoting companionship, communal activities, etc.

As already indicated, developing an eco-social approach draws upon two crucial influences. The first is the field of social ecology and what is understood to be the radical social interpretation of disability. The field of social ecology considers, for example, the physical environment, social and cultural environments, and personal attributes as a basis for addressing the interactions between individuals, groups and organisations. By providing context, we can gain a greater understanding of the complexity of human situations. Social ecology seeks to understand how we are dependent on nature for our existence, but also how humans have negative impacts on it. Physical environments include the natural world as well as the built world. The goal of social ecology is to create an ecology of freedom that promotes sustainability for both humans and nature. The second integral part of the approach is the radical social interpretation of disability, which articulates how disabled people's individual and collective disadvantages are due to complex forms of institutional and interpersonal discrimination.

The proposed approach is best articulated through acknowledging that the aspiration to change disabled people's social status through ending their oppression has to be situated within the context of what is achievable under capitalism. Is capitalism capable of meeting this aspiration? Addressing this question requires confronting the tensions and contradictions which exist when conflicting interests come to the fore. The dialectics of disability involve the body as a site of struggle precisely because the rejection of the impaired body has led to social exclusion of disabled people from society; which therefore stands in direct opposition to disabled people's aspiration. The emancipation struggle is grounded by this dialectic; thus, only by over-throwing capitalist means of production and living, will it be possible to rid society of disablement and meet disabled people's aspiration.

It has become common since the late 1980s to see the social model defini-tion of disability spoken of as 'the loss or limitation of opportunities to take part in the community on an equal level with others because of physical and social barriers'. There is, however, a tendency to view these social barriers as a result of environmental, organisational and attitudinal factors without always addressing their specificity or, conversely, their interconnectedness. This has resulted in descriptive rather than analytical usage of social models. I speak of 'social models' because I share the view that there is a range of models with differing socio-political sought outcomes attached to them.[52]

In previous chapters, we discussed the World Health Organization's ICF's definition of disability and noted it was referred to as a bio-psycho-social model. It is described this way because the definition acts as the umbrella term for impairments, activity, and participation restrictions, where the negative aspects of the interaction between an individual (with a health con-dition) and the individual's contextual factors (environmental and personal factors) can be observed. Nathan and Jones refer to this model as an example of interactionism because it:

> ... arguably solves the major problems with medical and social accounts, by recognizing that disabilities are triggered by a combination of biological and environmental conditions. Like the social approach, interactionists acknowledge the social dimension of disability. At the same time, inter-actionism incorporates the intuitive aspect of the medical model, by attributing a role to impairment in the production of disability, without committing to impairments being the sole, or even the primary factor.[53]

This quotation appears to mirror the claim, as noted earlier in this book, that it is possible to fuse the 'best bits' of medical and social accounts, a claim which has, of course, been contested.[54] Despite the fact there are already in existence eco-social models of disability drawing upon the bio-psycho-social approach from the WHO's ICF, it is possible to advocate the development of an eco-social approach in keeping with the historical materialist social inter-pretation of disability.[55]

THE TRANSFORMATIVE NATURE OF
THE ECO-SOCIAL APPROACH

By arguing for an eco-social approach to system change, we are not abandoning the foundations of the emancipation struggle of disabled people but instead, building upon them. Social ecology must be viewed as an additional component of the radical interpretation of disability. Transforming society into one that is inclusive to all, we must ensure that in recognising the interdependency that exists, attention is paid to how lifestyles, services, planning, etc. need to be based upon sustainability. The argument being that:

> Only with the inclusion and engagement of disabled populations as relevant stakeholders, will we be able to develop inclusive risk management and adaptation strategies, inclusive conservation policies, and sustainable just futures. Disability equality needs to become a key component of sustainability to make Agenda 2030 a reality.[56]

An eco-social approach to system change would employ inclusive practice through adopting co-production within design, planning and implementation of service delivery. Sharing power at national and local levels of society would be a progressive way to exercise choice and control. Our ability to construct an inclusive society turns on how feasible it will be to transform social relations. To end disabled people's social oppression requires us to address their 'unequal and differential treatment' and this cannot be done in isolation. Perhaps at a political rather than at a social level, there is a difference between what disabled people really want and what they actually need.[57]

In 1996, Finkelstein and Stuart advanced ideas on developing new services; however, over the last 25 years in particular, we have witnessed a reverse in providing 'what disabled people really want'.[58] I believe these words are as true as when they were first written:

> It is still at the earliest stage of speculation to consider what will be the future of services for disabled people when informed by the social model of disability. This is when the untravelled road from fantasy to reality is at its most confusing and daunting but, nevertheless, challenging, stimulating and exciting.[59]

I was drawn into disability politics through reading *A Life Apart* by F. J. Miller and G.V. Gwynne and speaking with Paul Hunt; therefore I will employ a quotation from Hunt as background to why the campaign group, Act 4 Inclusion, has embarked upon a radical journey at this difficult moment in history:

> What seems to me undeniable is that one of the factors in any progress towards a better society is the willingness of people to take theoretical and practical 'leaps' which sceptical common sense regards as unrealistic and idealistic. This is not to say that hard thinking, painstaking research and cautious experiment are not indispensable. The point is that they become sterile without imaginative vision and commitment.[60]

As stated earlier, developing an eco-social system for community-based services would involve making physical environments, housing, transport, information technologies, etc., more accessible to disabled people, whilst at the same time benefiting families, communities, and society as a whole. At the heart of the majority of campaigns concerned with the 'crisis within Social Care' [sic] is the call for the development of a new national service. The nature of this service is contested, with Act 4 Inclusion opposing the idea that it should be set up as 'a national care service', thus maintaining the administrative model approach. A community-based eco-social system would take an intersectional approach towards policymaking, considering the differential impact of universal and targeted policies across the diversity of disabled people – for example, people with different types of impairment, older people and younger disabled people, disabled women and from other oppressed groups. The firm belief is that self-directed living can be developed through a community based eco-social system ensuring civil and human rights.

An eco-social system would involve consideration of how people interact with their immediate and distant constructed and natural environments. Services would take a holistic approach using co-production to put individuals and groups at the centre of identifying and addressing barriers to self-directed living. Key to this development would be addressing a combination of various environmental and individual factors, thus allowing disabled people to have greater control over their own lives. This includes the opportunity to make real choices and decisions regarding where to live, with whom to live, and how to live.

Using a community-based eco-social approach for understanding the basic relationships between service users and their environments moves away from traditional need-led assessment procedures towards addressing how to create inclusive participation in both local communities and wider society. Having support to make decisions, and exercising choice and control are all aspects of inclusive participation. Effective inclusive participation enables individuals and communities to work together to build capacity in shaping and engaging in decision-making processes through co-production and the development of confidence, skills, knowledge and experience. What underpins all of these processes is establishing a new disability praxis.

10

From the Ashes:
A New Disability Praxis?

A key theme throughout this book has been the relationship between theory and action. Did disabled activists under-develop a disability praxis based upon a social understanding of disability by abandoning the foundations upon which disability politics were built? What lay behind the demise of the social movement and what lessons can be learnt? If a new disability praxis is to be developed from the ashes of the ideas and practice of the old, what needs to be done?

What can be developed from the ashes of the old British and global disabled people's movement? As a disabled historical materialist, I believe the insights offered by UPIAS's social interpretation of disability and Oliver's two models need to be reflected upon in the present, not simply assigned to the past. Taking this stance places me in conflict with many disabled scholar activists, academics and disabled communities across the globe. It will be said that I am displaying British arrogance by suggesting that only our social model has all the answers. Nothing could be further from the truth.

My starting point has always been to acknowledge 'disability' is not a fixed social construct that has shared meaning across the globe. From this recognition, I have argued that the historical materialist social approach still offers the most insightful way to see how those judged to be impaired have been seen and treated. This methodological approach, however, is not the only toolkit we can draw upon. I contend that disabled scholar activists and academics have paradoxically distorted disability praxis by using reductionist ways of implementing the social approach, which results in transforming Oliver's social model into a rigidly defined 'sacred cow', thus leading to it becoming defined as an all-singing and dancing 'grand theory' or 'ideology'. Elsewhere, I have expressed criticism of the way Oliver's 'models', designed to educate social workers, were inserted into disability politics in the manner they were. The shift not only undermined the purpose of 'the social model' in particular, but the crude insertion of the 'model' into disability politics also led to the abandonment of its original methodology. Even the most accommodating 'barrier removal' schemes are referred to as '*the social model*'.[1]

We see evidence of confused interpretations of 'the social model' in many Disability Studies schools, in both the global North and South. Gabel and Peters, in their article 'Presage of a Paradigm Shift? Beyond the Social Model of Disability Toward Resistance Theories of Disability', inform us that since the middle of the 1990s, 'a growing number of scholars in Disability Studies have begun to critique the social model of disability.'[2] The title of the article illustrates my point; what does 'beyond the social model' mean? What are they seeking to go beyond, as they both acknowledge a major problem? Gabel and Peters write:

> For the purposes of communication, we suggest generally that paradigms construct theories that use models in different ways and these models often lead to new theories that, in turn, can prompt new paradigms. In reviewing the literature on the social model, the first problem that becomes apparent is the conceptualization of a model. The language surrounding the social model complicates the issues. For example Donoghue (2003) variously describes social constructionism inherent in the social model as a paradigm, a theory, and a doctrine. Elsewhere, Shakespeare and Watson (1997) assert that the social model has been described as an ideology and a tenet.[3]

In passing, it should be noted that I disagree with all of these descriptions, and further, I do not support how Gabel and Peters view the social model either, as they perpetuate the claim by Tom Shakespeare and Nicholas Watson who argue that 'the "strong" social model itself has become a problem' and that 'a modernist theory of disability – seeking to provide an overarching meta-analysis covering all dimensions of every disabled person's experience – is not a useful or attainable concept.'[4]

This type of argument resulted in Richard Light, a British disabled scholar activist, seeking to address some of these issues in his article 'Social Model or Unsociable Muddle?':

> It is becoming increasingly clear that one of the key issues in disability activism – the Social Model of Disability – is subject to repeated attacks, particularly within the academic community ... Despite our concerns about harmful criticism of the social model, we wholeheartedly endorse

attempts to offer a more comprehensive or inclusive social theory of disability ... [This] is a heartfelt plea for theorists to understand the damage that is done by sweeping claims as to the social model's shortcomings, without proposing alternatives that are acceptable to the disability community.[5]

While I empathise with the sentiments expressed by Light, I believe to a degree, it was naïve to see these differences or attacks as 'muddled thinking' alone. There are theoretical and political differences at play which I have alluded to throughout this book. Within Disability Studies and other disciplines, there is an array of positions from materialist, postmodernist and feminist traditions. I have left it to others to outline and critique them, because I cannot do them justice in the space available. I have therefore focused primarily on disability politics from a British perspective; nonetheless, while having fundamental differences with the ideas of some North and South disability scholar activists, I recognise the importance of discussing their work, because it will impact upon any attempts to shape a new global disability praxis. This said, I am less accepting of the idea that it is possible to work towards 'a more comprehensive or inclusive social theory of disability', let alone a 'Grand Theory of Disability'.

Disability praxis does have the potential of rescuing disability-related theory and politics from the arid ivory towers of academic self-indulgence, returning them back into the communities who are seeking concrete solutions to material questions. As Soldatic informs us, 'Writers such as Grech (2011), Meekosha (2011) and Sherry (2007) have been arguing for a re-evaluation of disability praxis to reorient the movement's engagement towards a transnational frame of justice.'[6]

It is evident that an important element of disability praxis must include engaging with transnational justice because it is a major factor in the struggles against oppression, across the South in particular. Addressing global capitalism in all its manifestations is required, as it is the bedrock of disablement. Abberley's work points us in that direction when he talks about the production of impairments.[7] In turn, it can be linked to the definition of transnational justice used by former United Nations Secretary General Kofi Annan:

... the full range of processes and mechanisms associated with a society's attempts to come to terms with a legacy of large-scale past abuses, in order to ensure accountability, serve justice and achieve reconciliation.

These may include both judicial and non-judicial mechanisms, with differing levels of international involvement (or none at all) and individual prosecutions, reparations, truth-seeking, institutional reform, vetting and dismissals, or a combination thereof.[8]

However, Soldatic acknowledges:

... that while the CRPD has been a unifying force between the Global North and the Global South in terms of the transnational sphere of disability justice, it has also been about 'excluding in order to govern, so that the framing will, of course, attempt to render some issues non-political, while others are allowed to be raised within it' (Nancy Fraser in Nash and Bell 2007, 76). The limits of such exclusionary boundaries, as outlined above, have therefore made the production of impairment invisible within the transnational sphere and possibly within global disability movement politics.[9]

In Chapter 8, I stated that the movement around Disability Justice is an important area for discussion in relation to disability praxis; however, I believe the emphasis upon prejudice and what is called 'ableism' is misplaced. Neither notion addresses the root causes of disablism adequately. Too often, 'ableism' is reduced to being spoken of as 'the discrimination of and social prejudice against people with disabilities based on the belief that typical abilities are superior.'[10] Lewis defines ableism as:

A system that places value on people's bodies and minds based on societally constructed ideas of normality, intelligence, excellence, desirability and productivity. These constructed ideas are deeply rooted in anti-Blackness, eugenics, misogyny, colonialism, imperialism and capitalism. This form of systemic oppression leads to people and society determining who is valuable and worthy based on a person's language, appearance, religion and/or their ability to satisfactorily [re]produce, excel and 'behave.' You do not have to be disabled to experience ableism.[11]

There again, we find Kumari Campbell describing ableism as 'a network of beliefs, processes and practices that produces a particular kind of self and body (the corporeal standard) that is projected as the perfect, species-typical and therefore essential and fully human. Disability then, is cast as a diminished state of being human.'[12] Kumari Campbell's work is said to employ 'a relational-cultural model which sees disability in terms of an evolution; an interaction between the impairment and the environment, the person and others'.[13]

Those who developed Disability Justice do speak of the need to be anti-capitalist; however, the focus on discrimination and social prejudice as resulted from the corporeal standard – that is, 'projected as the perfect, species-typical and therefore essential and fully human' – does not address the issues adequately enough. I share Oliver's view, who writes:

> 'The production of disability therefore is nothing more or less than a set of activities specifically geared towards producing a good – the category disability – supported by a range of political actions which create the conditions to allow these productive activities to take place and underpinned by a discourse which gives legitimacy to the whole enterprise.[14]

My stance could be seen as being pedantic or splitting hairs; however, I believe these differences in approaches have long-term political significance. The abandonment of a materialist approach enabled the agenda to be switched towards focusing on discrimination and social prejudice, and therefore an over-reliance on calling for legal protection.

JANUS POLITICS AND THE LOSS OF RADICAL POLITICS OF DISABILITY

In earlier parts of this book, consideration was given to the nature of the British and global social movements. This posed the question: was the nature of these social movements, in the context of Britain, a contributory factor in its unpreparedness for the coming to power of the Conservative-Lib Dem Coalition government and all that has followed since? Elsewhere, I have spoken about how the decline in the radicalism of British disability politics can be related to how some of the Movement's founders during the 1990s were critical of the focus on obtaining 'anti-discrimination legislation', and how issues such as independent living, direct payments and rights were being viewed as detached from the social approach towards disability. It was argued that the emerging 'rights approach' not only shifted the focus away from the original social one, but it also paved the way for sections of the Movement to collude with New Labour's neoliberal 'rights with responsibilities' mantra.[15] The term 'Janus politics' was employed to describe looking back to the concepts of the old Disabled People's Movement, but empty them of their original radical meanings, and replace them with reformist ideas that sat comfortably with neoliberal policies which furthered self-reliance and individualism.[16] The adoption of Janus politics gave rise to a new 'Disability Movement', comprised of the traditional disability charities and market-orientated disabled people's organisations. This produced a sharp distinction between the broad 'politics of disability' that exists within society, and disability politics which has been articulated in this book as the roots of praxis coming from the historical materialists' approach to defining disability.

By acknowledging the divisions that emerged within the Movement, it is possible to ask to what extent disabled people and their organisations were ill equipped for the Age of Austerity – did they miss vital clues that might have 'armed' them better? The mid-1990s onwards saw a tendency emerge that focused on accommodating to the service sector and solely engaging with protecting disabled people from 'discrimination' and seeking to promote a better life through exercising rights and obtaining social inclusion within society. The passing of the Disability Discrimination Act was viewed as a victory; however, Finkelstein addressed this when he wrote, 'The ideological problem facing the ... movement ... from the 1990s onwards was whether the social model ... was still relevant in guiding our struggle or whether social changes had advanced so far that the original model no longer reflected the social context in which it had been created?'[17]

When we consider the political task of developing a new disability praxis, it is necessary to recognise the role of disabled people who called for, and continue to campaign for, civil and human rights. This call, as argued earlier, should have been viewed as a means to an end, rather than an end in itself. By shifting the focus entirely on 'Rights', the Movement lost sight of the bigger picture, which halted any critical evaluation of capitalist society. As a result, the 'leadership', through BCODP and Rights Now, tied the Movement to a reformist agenda which centred primarily upon 'Rights' as the key to unlocking the disabling barriers at the micro level of society. On a personal and political level, as a leading activist, I am implicated in the direction of travel taken. The disabling barriers at a macro level – the structures and systems of capitalist society itself – were as a consequence played down. Suddenly, 'inclusive practices' were viewed as capable of removing disabling barriers and addressing disablism.

An important turning point was the establishment of New Labour's Task Force and the willingness of disabled activists from the centre-right, at the exclusion of the left, to work with New Labour. From 1996 onwards, BCODP and later UKDPC and the National Centre for Independent Living began to 're-invent' the Disabled People's Movement as a 'rights-based movement', and in the process left more radical disability politics behind. The Movement began to lose sight of its aims and New Labour isolated large sections of it, whilst incorporating others into the revisionist agenda. The significance of this is two-fold: firstly, it led to the Movement becoming only a rump of its former self and, over time, it lost sight of its original aims and methodological approach. What this means is the Movement offered no leadership to disabled people because it became trapped within a static time warp until it fizzled out. The UKDPC, for example, employed the same language used in the 1990s, but with little or no reference to the current struggles facing disabled people. The majority of disabled activists therefore fell into two broad camps. One was a radical resistance current which continued to hold onto a disjointed political perspective hewn from disability politics. The other was a reformist current that employs 'fusion politics', which is basically a mixture of the dominant approach to disability coated with reformist versions of the social model of disability. Currently, there is no serious challenge to the Government or disablism.

Secondly, it seems highly questionable to speak about a Disabled People's Movement under these conditions because the original aims have been 'lost', or placed upon a back burner. Over the last decade, there have been numerous calls from DPOs and activists to breathe new life into the Movement, but nothing concrete emerged as a result until Disabled People Against Cuts, Inclusion London and ALFIE established Reclaiming Our Futures Alliance, which remains small and marginal.[18] Reference has been made to disability rights throughout the book, but at no time has this term been clarified. To address disability praxis requires dialogue on what we mean when we speak of disability rights. The following section opens with the background to the demand by disabled people for human and civil rights and outlining some of the issues involved, before proceeding on to questioning what is meant by the term 'disability rights'.

HUMAN RIGHTS LAWS AND ANTI-DISCRIMINATION LEGISLATION: PART OF THE STRUGGLE AND PART OF THE SOLUTION?

In Britain, since the middle of the 1980s, there has been a call for disabled people to have full human and civil rights. In my opinion, there remains far too little understanding as to why the demand for 'Rights Not Charity' ended up as mainly being about campaigning for legislation. As someone who was involved from almost the beginning, I want to provide some historical background to this campaigning and in the process suggest that there are two differing ways of interpreting what 'disability rights' means.

The starting point is acknowledging campaigns for anti-discrimination legislation and demands for protection of disabled people's human rights laws as being only part of the struggle to bring about the end of the inequality they encounter through their positioning within society. During the last quarter of the twentieth century, disabled people challenged how social and welfare policies maintained their inequality. The growth of the Independent Living Movement also witnessed a clamour for greater rights.[19] In Chapter 3, it was stated that a major influence on British disability politics was the American breakthrough, when disabled people were given basic rights with the passing of the Rehabilitation Act (1973). However, it was not until the 1990s that the legal case for legislation in terms of anti-discrimination legislation and civil and human rights beyond employment and social care was put forward effectively in Britain.[20]

The reason it took so long can be partly explained by the fact that disabled people were largely viewed as 'invisible'. In Britain, for example, there appears to be a conflict between those who see citizenship as a platform for 'rights for all', and the more traditional view propagated by Marshall who expressed the view that 'Citizenship is a status bestowed on those who are full members of a community. All who possess the status are equal with respect to the rights and duties with which the status is endowed.'[21]

Marshall spoke of three types of rights – those being civil, political and social – none of which he saw as applying to disabled people.[22] Western societies today, for example through the United Nations and European Union, do speak of disabled people as having rights; however, evidence would suggest that current practices and issues of accessibility prevent the majority of disabled people worldwide from being able to exercise their rights.[23]

This is the background as to why disabled activists through Disabled People's International began to press the United Nations for a Convention on the Rights of Disabled People. The aim of the Convention was not to grant disabled people 'new rights' but instead offer a framework, based (initially) upon the social approach towards disability, which would enable governments to apply human rights in meaningful ways for disabled people.[24] We now have a Convention; however, there remain many outstanding issues. It needs to be remembered that the term 'people with disabilities' is used differently to how it is applied in the UK. This problem is compounded by the fact that there is a certain ambiguity at play: does the United Nations actually work within the social approach, or have they fallen in line with the World Health Organization's definition of 'disabilities' which collapses together impairment, body functioning and social restrictions?[25] Add to the mix the way in which the UN's committee on the UNCRDP criticised the British government for violating disabled people's rights. What does this tell us about enforcement?[26]

The concept of 'rights' is not straightforward. Hurst suggests the talk of legal protection for disabled people have involved three themes – 'human rights', 'civil rights' and 'anti-discrimination legislation' – because they share a common objective. However, she explains there are differences between them. Human rights, she points out 'are all those rights that are inherent in an individual's humanity'.[27] This begs the question, for example, in the context of the European Convention on Human Rights, how can people be seen as having these rights or access to the legal processes involved, if they are not even seen as being 'human'?[28]

The notion of 'inherent in an individual's humanity' could also be judged as highly questionable when placed in the context of social oppression.[29] For example, Hurst goes on to say civil rights are what citizens can expect through national laws interpreted by courts; therefore, anti-discrimination legislation ensures that the human right not to be discriminated against is grounded in civil law. However, because the premise on which this legislation is based is social change, it does not give an absolute right not to be discriminated against. Decisions are qualified by 'the effect that these changes might have on an employer or service provider'.[30] Given this situation, the ability of legislation to deliver the goods for disabled people can be called into question. In the US, experts point out that many of the ADA's promises of universal accessibility have not come to pass. As Beth Ziebarth is quoted as saying: 'The mechanism for actually implementing the ADA, in many respects, is the process of somebody with a disability filing a complaint about the lack of accessibility … [that] … leads to spotty compliance across the country.'[31]

This raises another weakness with the civil rights approach. It may be worth considering that the law 'is not, therefore, an actor in itself but only the instrument of the human actors whose interests it represents'.[32] The ADA was a blueprint for much of the anti-discrimination legislation across Western societies and as a result, the focus is on the treatment of individuals, thus combining the dominant ideologies based on individualism within the law and current practices as they relate to disabled people.[33] Speaking of the research he undertook for his book *Disabled People in Britain and Discrimination: A Case for Anti-discrimination Legislation*, Barnes said, 'It shows that the negative attitudes and discriminatory practices which effectively deny basic human rights to disabled people are ingrained in the core institutions of our society.'[34]

The case put forward in the book did not focus primarily on individual forms of discrimination, but rather the institutional form because 'institutional discrimination is evident when the policies and activities of all types of modern organisations result in irregularity between disabled people and non-disabled people.'[35] When Britain did adopt legislation in the form of the Disability Discrimination Act in 1995, it was not along the lines advocated by Barnes or the Disabled People's Movement. Gooding states, despite the fact it was a historic step towards recognising disabled people's rights, that it nevertheless 'failed to establish the clear principle of equal treatment which should be the essence of law countering discrimination.'[36]

In the US, Marta Russell argued that the ADA felt a backlash prompted by capitalist opposition which she concluded 'not only stifled any potential benefits that might have resulted from ADA enforcement, [but] it has promoted the backlash among groups of workers who have become fearful that their own interests are in jeopardy as a result of the Act's enforcement powers.'[37] Russell thus puts forward the case that under capitalist economic and social policies, whether from a progressive or conservative form, they will fail to adequately create the conditions necessary for economic and social justice for disabled people. In a similar fashion, Barnes states, 'even fully comprehensive and enforceable civil rights legislation, will not, by itself, solve the problem of discrimination against disabled people.'[38]

How then should the campaigns for 'rights' be appraised? Vic Finkelstein argues that the radical (materialist) social model is about creating a society which enables disabled people to be 'human', whereas the idealistic rights models merely seeks to help access 'rights' within the existing competitive market society. Within this book, it has been suggested that there exists a conflicting interpretation of what constitutes social oppression. The radical social model argues that what happens to disabled people 'is an integral part of the way our society is organised and structured.'[39] Only by overthrowing the very nature of society itself can people with impairments be liberated, along with humanity as a whole. The alternative approach, through legal 'rights', seeks to 'free' disabled people by transforming existing structures and granting them an equality of opportunities by dismantling disabling barriers.[40]

Whilst it is understandable for disabled people to want to end their social exclusion and be rid of discriminatory practices, one must question the politics behind the belief that the entitlement to rights would automatically confer 'social acceptance', or lead to an end to social oppression. Richardson states that disabled people over the past two decades have challenged traditional ways of seeing and responding to disability by 'arguing that disability is created by social barriers and barriers in the built environment'.[41] This appears to be an inadequate watered-down version of the original radical description of disablement.

In attempting to make the concept of social oppression understandable, disabled activists have simplified it to one of being a question of encountering or removing 'disabling barriers'. The implications of this are many. Taking this approach can reduce 'the problem of disability' to be simply about obtaining 'rights' and removing disabling barriers. This simplistic approach has also spawned the idealistic notion of a 'barrier-free' society which has been used to undermine the social model.[42] What the campaigns for rights achieved was to politicise disabled people by galvanising them into a social movement which meant that they, and their issues, became more visible within mainstream socio-political circles.[43] The shift from passive acceptance of what is done to them to a visible struggle for empowerment has also helped change the existing landscape in social policy and practice to some degree.[44] Depending upon one's analysis of the problem of disability, campaigns for civil and human rights can be viewed in a variety of ways. Governments have addressed these campaigns as being a plea for 'fairer treatment' within the status quo, and therefore little concrete action has been taken to resolve the real problems created by disablement and disablism.

The weakness of seeing disabled people as automatically having a 'shared agenda' is that it does not address the fact that people with impairments come from an array of socio-political backgrounds. This distorts how disability activists address the implications of differing interpretations of what disability is, what social oppression means and therefore results in conflicting views regarding what campaigns for 'rights' could achieve. As disabled activists, I believe we need to combine fighting for improvements within existing structures, whilst at the same time seeking ways to transform them beyond the confines of capitalism. Recognising both of these tasks is extremely difficult in the present climate, but we must look at ways, despite its shortcomings, we can employ the Convention on the Rights of Disabled People as leverage when putting our demands for social justice forward and resisting the ongoing attacks upon our rights. Soldatic and other writers have begun to interrogate the strengths and weaknesses of the Convention.[45] It may be time once again to ask: to what extent are human rights laws and anti-discrimination legislation part of the struggle and part of the solution?

As someone who sees the problem of disability as being the social restrictions imposed upon people with impairments, my take on 'disability rights' differs from the way, for example, American disabled people employed the term in their struggles, or how it has come to be co-opted into the British way of thinking.

The idea of reclaiming our futures is a good one, but it requires greater clarity. Developing a new disability praxis will be an essential element of this process, but another crucial part of the exercise of 're-claiming' the ground secured by the original Disabled People's Movement must involve the task of distinguishing between the broad self-defined meaning given to 'disability rights' by disabled activists, and the more specific meaning associated with the struggle to obtain civil and human rights. The latter should be viewed as a legal set of demands, as the two are not synonymous.

Because of the reformist perspective that existed within the Disabled People's Movement, we have been left with re-interpretations of the social model of disability as a 'rights-based approach' and this needs challenging. In my opinion, the attractiveness of this approach stems from how many disabled activists have come to articulate their understanding of what is meant by 'disability rights'. In an online discussion around this subject, one disabled activist wrote, 'For me rights should be at every level all aspects of life so that individuals can choose how to use them in their own lives with support of communities and structures. We just have to lobby to get them right or at least hold on to what we've got these days.'[46]

This articulation combines the desire to have, and to hold onto, civil and human rights, with the drive for what I would call 'self-determination'. In other words, 'the free choice of one's own acts without external compulsion', which would fit into what the disabled activist was articulating.[47] It is this definition of self-determination that is used here in relation to exploring what is meant by disability rights. From a radical social [model] perspective, 'disability rights' means 'self-determination' – that is, the right not to be subjected to discriminatory practice or social exclusion, the right not to be dependent upon charity, and the right not to be de-humanised. There is a dialectical relationship between positive and negative rights. Hence, 'the definition of a negative right is the freedom to have something without interference. Negative rights say that no one can get in the way of your liberties as long as you don't get in the way of theirs.'[48]

These rights do not require legislation; they require social change and greater respect for the whole of humanity, and for the planet we inhabit. Finkelstein is correct when he says, 'we cannot understand or deal with disability without dealing with the essential nature of society itself. To do this disabled people must find ways of engaging in the class struggle where the historical direction of society is fought, won or lost.'[49]

The definition of self-determination can be applied to both an individual and a collective of 'peoples'. Leaving to one side the issue of the individual's right to self-determination, let us focus on what self-determination means in a collective sense. It has already been argued that within mainstream society, the label 'the disabled' [sic] represents disabled people as a collection of individuals rather than as an identifiable social group. In this book, the term 'disabled communities' includes any people with impairments who are defined as 'disabled' via any definitions employed within British society. In sociological terms, 'the disabled' would be classed as a social category, because they would be viewed as a collection of people who do not interact but who share similar characteristics. Similarly, 'disabled communities' might also be regarded as a social category to a degree; however, within these broad 'communities', there are groups and individuals who do interact with each other and share similar characteristics and a sense of unity and, therefore as a result, could be considered as constituting a social group.

Writing from a psychological perspective in relation to social roles, McLeod states:

We do not expect people to behave randomly but to behave in certain ways in particular situations. Each social situation entails its own particular set of expectations about the 'proper' way to behave. Such expectations can vary from group to group ... Social roles are the part people play as members of a social group. *With each social role you adopt, your behaviour changes to fit the expectations both you and others have of that role.*[50]

UPIAS was quite clear in its belief that what united disabled people was not the actual existence of impairments, but rather the oppressive social relations people experienced as a result of having impairments.[51] Finkelstein suggested that an understanding of the psychology of disability must start from the principle that 'we make sense of our world according to the way we experience it':

If disabled people are denied access to normal social activities, we will not only have different experiences to that of our able-bodied peers but we will interpret the world differently; we will see it, think about it, have feelings about it and talk about it differently. The question is, however, 'from what standpoint should this psychological experience be interpreted?'[52]

Finkelstein argued:

> ... [that as most things are] 'made sense of' through the lived experiences of non-disabled people, this means the development of an understanding of the psychology of disability has been prevented. Disabled people's own interpretations of the world have been ignored, not allowed to develop or simply denied because they are regarded as subjective and therefore not valid.[53]

How is this relevant to understanding what disability rights are? I want to suggest disabled people's experience of 'unequal and differential treatment' goes beyond encountering barriers or discriminatory practices. It includes the denial of their social worth and often results in invalidating their existing social roles within society. It is within this context that the political significance of 'disability rights' have the greatest purchase. The Disabled People's Movement, by distorting the social model's usage with an emphasis on 'removing disabling barriers', underemphasised the structural nature of 'being disabled by society' and moved away from exploring how disabled people are materially excluded from and marginalised within capitalist societies. Disabled people's social situation stems from their oppression – that is, being made invisible, externally defined, often actively excluded and marginalised – and assists in disabling their ability to combat it. By seeing 'disability' as a social situation, UPIAS revealed the dialectics of disability, whereby disability rights are about the sets of demands furthered by disabled people to exercise self-determination and in opposition to their social oppression. This understanding of disability rights underpins how disability praxis should evolve because it articulates disability rights as being primarily about disabled people fighting to establish:

- control over defining who and what they are;
- control over what is done to their own bodies;
- the means and decision making capacity to fully participate within social activities without confronting unnecessary restrictions, and

- that people with impairments are not seeking 'sameness', but rather recognition and acceptance of differing lifestyles.

Disability rights must involve addressing 'disabled identities', internalised oppression and disabled people's social status within a disablist society.

The articulation of what disability praxis should involve has, of course, come from my own interpretations of theory and practice. It was stated from the beginning that much of this grounding is contested and as a result, we are confronted by tensions, contradictions and differing ways of viewing disability, disabled people and their oppression. Developing a new disability praxis requires ways of mediating how we co-produce moving forward.

DEVELOPING A NEW DISABILITY PRAXIS: IS IT POSSIBLE?

The current political, economic and social climate makes the prospect of developing a new disability praxis in Britain look bleak. After a decade of trying to resist the punitive state, many disabled activists have withdrawn into comfort zones, trying to survive and intervene where possible. The demise of the Movement has left a vacuum and, as I write, no network of disabled people's organisations is making headway in terms of shaping any disability political agenda. There is also a disconnect between academics within Disability Studies, scholar activists and ordinary disabled people. Globally, the fracturing of Disabled People's International, and the tensions between the global North and South in terms of envisioning both theory and practice, has increased divisions and reinforced an international state of uncertainty. Meekosha, for example, calls 'intellectual decolonization', thinking differently about disability studies', in part to the need to acknowledge what she sees as 'privileged discourses and the excluded discourses in disability'.[54] This has prompted writers such as Grech to advocate for 'a global disability studies grounded in and conversant with local contexts, socio-economics, micro-politics, cultures, issues of poverty and global dimensions of power (e.g. neoliberal globalisation and coloniality)'.[55] He believes these are the issues constituting and confronting the South and its peoples, but are generally ignored or underplayed by disabled scholar activists in the North.

Whether or not a project along these lines is possible remains to be seen; however, the issues raised are pertinent to discussions relating to developing disability praxis on a global scale. Gabel and Peters have already been mentioned in terms of seeking to go beyond the social model of disability and toward resistance theories of disability. This was viewed as developing a paradigm shift. Their paper illustrates a range of theoretical, conceptual and methodological confusions; nevertheless, it should not be ignored. While disagreeing with much of what they write, it is still possible, at the same time, to suggest these 'visible' confusions and interpretative accounts of other people's work reveal areas that require discussion. Gabel and Peters refer to Young because she argues that 'disagreements are more likely to be addressed and overcome when a group includes differently situated voices that "speak across their differences and are accountable to one another".[56]

They go on to say, 'Specifically, justice claims must "draw on the situated knowledge of the people located in different [group] positions as resources for enlarging the understanding of everyone and moving them beyond their own parochial interests".[57]

This has been described as a deliberative approach to political action.[58] It can be argued this approach corresponds with Freire's notion of conscientisation which is, as indicated previously, 'learning to perceive social, political, and economic contradictions, and to take action against the oppressive elements of reality'.[59] This is an urgent task in the development of any new disability praxis, be that in Britain or globally. Gabel and Peters also argue:

> Our analysis of … responses and reactions to the social model indicate a shift in assumptions about theory and praxis. Today, a growing number of disabled people and theoreticians are using eclectic theories that move across and operate between paradigms while they are identifying their work as within the social model. Rather than weakening the social model, this trend actually strengthens it.[60]

Whether I agree with this or not is immaterial. What matters is creating space for dialogue. Without doubt there have been paradigm shifts, and we can question how many of them have proved progressive or not. The work of A. J. Withers and Robert McRuer, for example, have opened up new lines of enquiry that have caught the imagination of disabled scholar activists. McRuer has contributed to fields in transnational queer and disability studies.[61]

The differences that exist around theory and practice relating to defining what disability is, what disabled people want, and addressing impairment reality, need articulating within the development of a new praxis.

Whether or not people will consider my approach towards disability politics and praxis as too parochial remains to be seen. What I have sought not to do is use this book to impose a future agenda on those engaged in the disabled people's struggle for emancipation. Instead, I have attempted to employ a critical critique and signpost towards possibilities. The book has been written by a British disability activist endeavouring to be reflective and challenging – with an eye on the past, present, and future.

Notes

PREFACE

1. I am using the term 'disability praxis' to refer to bringing theory and practice together to challenge disabled people's oppression.
2. Vic Finkelstein, 'The Social Model of Disability and the Disability Movement' (Leeds: University of Leeds, 2007), 6, https://disability-studies.leeds.ac.uk/wp-content/uploads/sites/40/library/finkelstein-The-Social-Model-of-Disability-and-the-Disability-Movement.pdf (last accessed June 2023).
3. Mike Oliver, 'Disabled People and the Inclusive Society: or The Times They Really Are Changing' (Public Lecture, Strathclyde Centre for Disability Research and Glasgow City Council, 1999).

CHAPTER 1   SETTING THE SCENE

1. Frances Hasler, 'Philosophy of Independent Living' (Independent Living Institute, 2003), www.independentliving.org/docs6/hasler2003.html (last accessed June 2023).
2. Finkelstein, 'The Social Model', 6.
3. Judy Hunt, *No Limits* (Manchester: TBR Imprint, 2019), 99.
4. Ibid.
5. Paul Abberley, 'The Concept of Oppression and the Development of a Social Theory of Disability', in *Disability Studies: Past Present and Future*, Len Barton and Mike Oliver, eds (Leeds: The Disability Press, 1997), 160–78, 162–3.
6. Colin Barnes and Geof Mercer, 'Breaking the Mould? An Introduction to Doing Disability Research', in *Doing Disability Research*, Colin Barnes and Geof Mercer, eds (Leeds: The Disability Press, 1997) 3–4.
7. Carol Thomas, 'Rescuing a Social Relational Understanding of Disability' (Stockholm: Stockholm University Press, *Scandinavian Journal of Disability Research*, Vol. 6, No. 1, 2004), 22–36, 33.
8. Elizabeth Walter, ed., 'Emancipation', *Cambridge Dictionary* (Cambridge: Cambridge University Press, 2005), https://dictionary.cambridge.org/dictionary/english/emancipation (last accessed June 2023).
9. Abberley, 'Concept of Oppression', 165.
10. Mark Priestley, Vic Finkelstein and Ken Davis, 'Fundamental Principles of Disability' (Union of the Physically Impaired Against Segregation, 1975), 4,

https://disability-studies.leeds.ac.uk/wp-content/uploads/sites/40/library/UPIAS-fundamental-principles.pdf (last accessed June 2023).

11. 'International Classification of Functioning, Disability and Health (ICF)' (World Health Organization, 2001), www.who.int/classifications/icf/en/ (last accessed June 2023).

12. Mike Oliver, 'Capitalism, Disability and Ideology: A Materialist Critique of the Normalization', (Leeds: University of Leeds, 1994), https://disability-studies.leeds.ac.uk/wp-content/uploads/sites/40/library/Oliver-cap-dis-ideol.pdf (last accessed June 2023).

13. Gerry Zarb and Mike Oliver, 'Ageing with a Disability: What Do They Expect After All These Years?' (London: University of Greenwich, 1992); Nirmala Erevelles and Andrea Minear, 'Unspeakable Offenses: Untangling Race and Disability in Discourses of Intersectionality' (*Journal of Literary & Cultural Disability Studies*, Vol. 4, No. 2, 2010).

14. Alison Sheldon, 'One World, One People, One Struggle? Towards the Global Implementation of the Social Model of Disability', in *The Social Model of Disability: Europe and the Majority World*, Colin Barnes and Geof Mercer, eds (Leeds: The Disability Press, 2005), 119; Tom Shakespeare, 'Cultural Representation of Disabled People: Dustbins for Disavowal?' (*Disability & Society*, Vol. 9, No. 3, 1994), 283–99.

15. Elizabeth Walter, ed., 'Praxis', *Cambridge Dictionary* (Cambridge: Cambridge University Press, 2005). https://dictionary.cambridge.org/dictionary/english/praxis (last accessed June 2023).

16. Mike Oliver and Jane Campbell, *Disability Politics: Understanding Our Past, Changing Our Future* (London: Routledge, 1996); Diane Driedger, *The Last Civil Rights Movement: Disabled People's International* (York: St. Martin's Press, 1989).

17. Paulo Freire, *Pedagogy of the Oppressed* (New York: Continuum, 1986), Ch. 4.

18. Karen Soldatic, 'The Transnational Sphere of Justice: Disability Praxis and the Politics of Impairment' (*Disability & Society*, Vol. 28, No. 6, 2013), 744–55; Melinda C. Hall, 'Critical Disability Theory', *The Stanford Encyclopedia of Philosophy*, Winter 2019 ed., Edward N. Zalta, ed., https://plato.stanford.edu/archives/win2019/entries/disability-critical/ (last accessed June 2023); Christopher Johnstone, 'Disability and Identity: Personal Constructions and Formalized Supports' (*Disability Studies in Public Health and the Health Professions*, Vol. 24, No. 4, 2004).

19. 'Praxis', *Collins English Dictionary – Complete & Unabridged*, 10th ed. (Glasgow: HarperCollins, 2009); A. B. Cryer, 'Praxis (Process) Explained' (*Everything Explained Today*, 2022), http://everything.explained.today/Praxis_(process)/ (last accessed June 2023).

20. Oliver Quinlan, 'Praxis: Bringing Theory and Practice to Learning' (2012), www.oliverquinlan.com/blog/2012/10/23/praxis/ (last accessed June 2023).

21. Bob Williams-Findlay, 'The Disabled People's Movement in the Age of Austerity: Rights, Resistance and Reclamation', in *Resist the Punitive State: Grassroots Struggles Across Welfare, Housing, Education and Prisons*, Emily Luise Hart, Joe Greener and Rich Moth, eds (London: Pluto Press, 2019).

22. Jenny Morris, 'Why Have So Many Disabled People Died of Covid-19?' (2021), https://jennymorrisnet.blogspot.com/2021/03/why-have-so-many-disabled-people-died.html?m=1 (last accessed June 2023).

23. 'Disability and the Climate Crisis' (Climate Reality Project, 2021), www. climaterealityproject.org/blog/disability-and-climate-crisis (last accessed June 2023); John Pring, 'Met Apologises for Failing to Consult Disabled Advisers Over XR Protests' (*Disability News Service*, 2019), www. disabilitynewsservice.com/met-apologises-for-failing-to-consult-disabled-advisers-over-xr-protests/ (last accessed June 2023).

24. 'New Network Aims to Unite Disability Movement' (*Disability News Service*, 2012), www.disabilitynewsservice.com/new-network-aims-to-unite-disability-movement/ (last accessed June 2023).

25. 'Updated: National Disabilities Conference 2013 4th July 2013 at One Drummond Gate, Victoria, SW1V 2QQ' (*DPAC*, 2013), https://dpac. uk.net/2013/05/national-disabilities-conference-2013-4th-july-2013-at-one-drummond-gate-victoria-sw1v-2qq/ (last accessed June 2023).

26. Bob Williams-Findlay, 'Personalisation and Self-determination: The Same Difference?' (*Critical and Radical Social Work*, Vol. 3, No. 1, Bristol: Policy Press, 2015), 67–87.

CHAPTER 2   THE FIRST CORNERSTONE:
THE FUNDAMENTAL PRINCIPLES OF DISABILITY

1. Mike Oliver and Jane Campbell, *Disability Politics: Understanding Our Past, Changing Our Future* (London: Routledge, 1996), 21–2.

2. 'Disablement Income Group', Wikipedia, last modified 5 May 2023. https:// tinyurl.com/3xen2a77 (last accessed June 2023).

3. Steven Dodd, 'Challenges Facing the Disabled People's Movement in the UK: An Analysis of Activist's Positions', PhD diss. (University of Central Lancashire, 2014).

4. Judy Hunt, *No Limits* (Manchester: TBR Imprint, 2019), 96.

5. Ibid., 97.

6. Ibid.

7. Ibid., 98.

8. Paul Hunt, 'Letter to Magic Carpet' (*Magic Carpet*, Vol. XXV, No. 1, 1973), 36. https://disability-studies.leeds.ac.uk/wp-content/uploads/sites/40/library/ Hunt-Hunt-2.pdf (last accessed June 2023).

9. Hunt, *No Limits*, 101.

10. Ibid.

11. Ibid.

12. Oliver and Campbell, *Disability Politics*, 66.

13. 'Union of the Physically Impaired Against Segregation: Policy Statement' (Union of the Physically Impaired Against Segregation, 1974), 1, 2, 5. https://disability-studies.leeds.ac.uk/wp-content/uploads/sites/40/library/UPIAS-UPIAS.pdf (last accessed June 2023).

14. Mark Priestley, Vic Finkelstein and Ken Davis, 'Fundamental Principles of Disability' (Union of the Physically Impaired Against Segregation, 1975), 4, https://disability-studies.leeds.ac.uk/wp-content/uploads/sites/40/library/UPIAS-fundamental-principles.pdf (last accessed June 2023).

15. Ibid.

16. Amelia I. Harris, Judith R. Buckle, Elizabeth Cox and Christopher R.W. Smith, 'Handicapped and Impaired in Great Britain, Part 1,' 'Office of Population Censuses and Surveys, Social Survey Division, Work and Housing of Impaired Persons in Great Britain, Part II' (London: HMSO, 1971), 'UPIAS' (1975) 20.

17. *Disability Challenge 1* (Union of the Physically Impaired Against Segregation, 1981), 6.

18. Miranda Yardley, 'Discrimination and Oppression' (*#CounterCulturalGeek*, 2015),https://mirandayardley.com/en/discrimination-and-oppression/(last accessed June 2023).

19. Brendan J. Gleeson, 'Disability Studies: a historical materialist view,' (*Disability & Society*, Volume 12, Issue 2, 1997), 179-202, 196.

20. Michael Oliver, *The Politics of Disablement* (London: Macmillan, 1990), 26.

21. Nirmala Erevelles, 'Re-Constituting the "Disabled" Other: Historical Materialism and the Politics of Schooling' (New York: Syracuse University, 1997), 5.

22. Oliver, *Politics of Disablement*, 26

23. Anthony Forder, Terry Caslin, Geoffrey Ponton and Sandra Walklate, *Theories of Welfare* (Milton Keynes: Routledge & Kegan Paul, 1984), 89.

24. Vic Finkelstein, 'Disability and the Helper/Helped Relationship: An Historical View', in Ann Brechin, Penny Liddiard and John Swain, eds, *Handicap in a Social World* (London: Hodder and Stoughton, the Open University, 1981), 58–62.

25. John Lye, 'Ideology: A Brief Guide' (St. Catharines: University of Brock, 1997).

26. Antonio Gramsci, *Selections from the Prison Notebooks*, Quintin Hoare, Geoffrey Nowell-Smith, eds, trans (London: Lawrence and Wishart, 1971).

27. Peter Hamilton, 'Editor's Foreword', in Robert Bocock, *Hegemony* (London: Tavistock Hamilton, 1987), cited in Oliver, *Politics of Disablement*, 43.

28. Oliver, *Politics of Disablement*, 22.

29. Ibid., 15.

30. Gary L. Albrecht and Judith A. Levy, 'Constructing Disabilities as Social Problems', in Gary L. Albrecht, ed., *Cross National Rehabilitation Policies: A Sociological Perspective* (London: Sage, 1981).
31. Erevelles, ' Re-Constituting the "Disabled" Other', 5.
32. Ibid.
33. Gareth Stedman Jones, 'History: the Poverty of Empiricism', in Robin Blackburn, ed., *Ideology in Social Science* (Bungay: Fontana Press, 1972), 98.
34. Joanna Ryan and Frank Thomas, *The Politics of Mental Handicap* (London: Free Association Books, 1987); Andrew T. Scull, *Museums of Madness: Social Organization of Insanity in 19th Century England* (London: Routledge & Kegan Paul, 1979).
35. A. L. Beier, *The Problem of the Poor in Tudor and Early Stuart England* (New York: Methuen, 1983), 5.
36. Carol Thomas, 'Developing the Social Relational in the Social Model of Disability: A Theoretical Agenda', in Colin Barnes and Geof Mercer, eds, *Implementing The Social Model of Disability: Theory and Research* (Leeds: Disability Press, 2004), 35.
37. Thomas, 'Developing the Social Relational' , 36.
38. Mike Oliver, 'Capitalism, Disability and Ideology: A Materialist Critique of the Normalization' (Leeds: University of Leeds, 1994), 4.
39. Pauline Morris, *Put Away* (London: Routledge & Kegan Paul, 1969).
40. Stuart Hall, 'Racism and Reaction,' cited in *Five Views of Multi-Racial Britain* (London: Commission for Racial Equality, 1978), 26.
41. Oliver, *Politics of Disablement*, 44; Dan Goodley, *Disability Studies: An Interdisciplinary Introduction*, 2nd ed. (London: SAGE, 2016), 11.
42. Oliver, *Politics of Disablement*, 47; Michel Foucault, *Discipline and Punish: The Birth of the Prison* (Harmondsworth: Penguin, 1977); Shelley Tremain, ed. *Foucault and the Government of Disability*, (Ann Arbor: University of Michigan Press, 2005).
43. Bill Hughes, 'The Constitution of Impairment: Modernity, and the Aesthetic of Oppression', (*Disability & Society*, Vol. 14, No. 2, 1999), 155–72, 167.
44. Wendy McElroy, 'You Are What You Read?' (*LewRockwell.com*, 2000), www.lewrockwell.com/mcelroy/mcelroy14.html (last accessed June 2023).
45. Bob Williams-Findlay, 'The Historical Roots of Defining Disability' in *Disability in Employment – Training Material*, S. Maynard, ed. (Bristol: Equal Ability Ltd, 1999), 19.
46. Lennard J. Davis, *Enforcing Normalcy: Disability, Deafness, and the Body* (New York: Verso, 1995).
47. R. Moore, 'Class and Underclass', in Digby Tantam and M. J. Birchwood, eds., *Seminars in Psychology and the Social Sciences* (London: RCPsych Publications, 1994), 296.
48. Findlay, 'Defining Disability', 19.

49. Pablo V. Gejman and Ann Weilbaecher, 'History of the Eugenic Movement' (*Israel Journal of Psychiatry and Related Sciences*, Vol. 39, No. 4, 2002), 217–31.

50. Maria Berghs, Karl Atkin, Hilary Graham, Chris Hatton and Carol Thomas, 'Implications for Public Health Research of Models and Theories of Disability: A Scoping Study and Evidence Synthesis' (*Public Health Research*, 2016 No.4.8.), www.ncbi.nlm.nih.gov/books/NBK378951/ (last accessed June 2023); Louis Gooren and Luk Gijs, 'Medicalization of Homosexuality', in *The International Encyclopedia of Human Sexuality*, A. Bolin and P. Wheleham, eds (Wiley-Blackwell, 2015); Parin Dossa, *Racialized Bodies, Disabling Worlds* (Toronto: University of Toronto Press, 2009).

51. Mike Mantin, 'Coalmining and the National Scheme for Disabled Ex-Servicemen after the First World War' (*Social History*, Vol. 41, No. 2, 2016), 155–70.

52. Findlay, 'Defining Disability'; Tom Shakespeare, *Disability Rights and Wrongs* (London: Routledge, 2006).

53. Mike Oliver, 'The Social Model in Action: If I had a Hammer', in *Implementing the Social Model of Disability: Theory and Research,* Colin Barnes and Geof Mercer, eds (Leeds: The Disability Press, 2004), 18–31, 2.

54. Mike Oliver, 'The Individual and Social Models of Disability' (Joint Workshop of the Living Options Group, Research Unit of the Royal College of Physicians, 1990), 3.

55. Oliver, 'Capitalism, Disability', 3.

56. Gleeson, 'Disability Studies', 167.

57. Oliver, *Politics of Disablement*, 3.

58. Thomas, 'Developing the Social Relational', 6.

CHAPTER 3 THE SECOND CORNERSTONE: THE SELF-ORGANISATION OF DISABLED PEOPLE

1. 'A Brief History Of Disabled People's Self-Organisation' (Manchester Coalition of Disabled People, 2010), 3.

2. '1890: British Deaf Association (BDA)' (British Deaf Association, n.d.), www.deafhistory.eu/index.php/component/zoo/item/1890-british-deaf-association-bda (last accessed June 2023).

3. David Ludden, 'Is Deafness Really a Disability?' (*Psychology Today*, 1 February 2018).

4. 'The Cultural Model of Deafness' (Inclusion London, n.d.), www.inclusionlondon.org.uk/disability-in-london/cultural-model-of-deafness/the-cultural-model-of-deafness/ (last accessed June 2023).

5. 'National League of the Blind' (TUC100, n.d.), https://tuc150.tuc.org.uk/stories/national-league-blind/ (last accessed June 2023).

6. Bob Williams-Findlay, 'The Falsification of History: The Twenty Year Burial of the Civil Rights Bill' (Disabled People Against Cuts, 2015), https://dpac.uk.net/2015/11/the-falsification-of-history-the-twenty-year-burial-of-the-civil-rights-bill/ (last accessed June 2023).

7. 'National League of the Blind' (n.d.).

8. History of the British Legion (British Legion, 2023), https://tinyurl.com/3s8s6zvc (last accessed June 2023); 'Home From the War: What Happened to Disabled First World War Veterans' (*Heritage Calling*, 2018), https://heritagecalling.com/2018/12/14/home-from-the-war-what-happened-to-disabled-first-world-war-veterans/ (last accessed June 2023).

9. Deborah Cohen, *The War Come Home: Disabled Veterans in Britain and Germany, 1914–1939* (Berkeley: University of California Press, 2001).

10. Judy Hunt, *No Limits* (Manchester: TBR Imprint, 2019), 8.

11. Ibid., 33.

12. 'Paul Hunt' (National Disability Arts Collection and Archive, n.d.), https://the-ndaca.org/the-people/paul-hunt/ (last accessed June 2023); Paul Hunt, *Stigma: The Experience of Disability*, Geoffrey Chapman, ed. (London: Catholic Book Club, 1966).

13. Hunt, *No Limits*, 64.

14. Diane Driedger, *The Last Civil Rights Movement: Disabled People's International* (York: St. Martin's Press, 1989), 1.

15. Ibid., 35.

16. 'Inclusive language' (gov.uk, n.d.), www.gov.uk/government/publications/inclusive-communication/inclusive-language-words-to-use-and-avoid-when-writing-about-disability (last accessed June 2023).

17. 'Taking a User-led Approach' (*Compass Disability Services*, 2011), www.scie.org.uk/publications/guides/guide36/resources/ (last accessed June 2023); 'Improving Life Chances of Disabled People. Final Report' (Prime Minister's Strategy Unit, 2006), https://webarchive.nationalarchives.gov.uk/ukgwa/+/http:/www.cabinetoffice.gov.uk/media/cabinetoffice/strategy/assets/disability.pdf (last accessed June 2023).

18. Henry Enns, 'The Role of Organizations of Disabled People: A Disabled Peoples' International Discussion Paper' (n.d.), www.independentliving.org/docs5/RoleofOrgDisPeople.html (last accessed June 2023); 'Disabled Peoples International,' (People with Disability Australia, n.d.), https://pwd.org.au/about-us/our-history/disabled-peoples-international/ (last accessed June 2023).

19. Edward Roberts, 'When Others Speak For You, You Lose', in *When Others Speak for You, You Lose*, Jeff Heath, ed. (Adelaide: Disabled Peoples' International Australia, 1983), 7.

20. Enns, 'Role of Organizations of Disabled People'.

21. Ibid.

22. Ibid.

23. Mike Oliver, *Understanding Disability: From Theory to Practice* (London: Macmillan Press, 1996), 166–7.

24. Ibid.

25. Paulo Freire, *Pedagogy of the Oppressed*, trans. Myra Bergman Ramos (New York: The Seabury Press, 1970), 39.

26. Enns, 'Role of Organizations of Disabled People'.

27. Ibid.

28. Ibid.

29. Mike Oliver and Jane Campbell, Disability Politics, (1996), 90.

30. Marta Russell, 'Disablement, Oppression, and Political Economy' (*MROnline*, 2019), https://mronline.org/2019/08/10/disablement-oppression-and-political-economy/ (last accessed June 2023); Steve Haines and David Ruebain, eds, *Education, Disability and Social Policy* (Bristol: Bristol University Press, 2011).

31. Bob Findlay, 'Disability Information or Misinformation?' (*NDIP Newsletter*, No. 9:1, 1994).

32. Enns, Organizations of Disabled People, (n.d.).

33. Ralph H. Turner, Neil J. Smelser and Lewis M. Killian, 'Social Movement' (*Encyclopaedia Britannica*, 2023), www.britannica.com/topic/social-movement (last accessed June 2023); Sidney Tarrow, *Power in Movement* (Cambridge: Cambridge University Press, 2006), 4.

34. Tom Shakespeare, 'Disabled People's self-organisation: A New Social Movement?' (*Disability, Handicap and Society*, Vol. 8, No. 3, 1993), 249–64, 257.

35. Srilatha Batliwala, *Changing their World: Concepts and Practices of Women's Movements* (2nd ed.) (Toronto, Mexico City and Cape Town: AWID, 2012).

36. Julia Hamaus, 'Bridge Gender and Social Movements Cutting Edge Programme: Stories of Influence' (Brighton: Institute of Development Studies, 2015), 22.

37. Batliwala, *Changing their World*, 3; Srilatha Batliwala, 'All About Movements' (Kathmandu: CREA South Asia, Movement Building and Human Rights Institute, 2010).

38. Michael Oliver and Colin Barnes, *The New Politics of Disablement* (London: Palgrave Macmillan, 2012) 174–5.

39. Alison Sheldon, 'One World, One People, One Struggle? Towards the Global Implementation of the Social Model of Disability', in *The Social Model of Disability: Europe and the Majority World*, Colin Barnes and Geof Mercer, eds (Leeds: The Disability Press, 2005), 120.

40. Kenneth Cloke, 'Conflict and Movements for Social Change' (*Mediate*, 2013), www.mediate.com/articles/ClokeK16.cfm (last accessed June 2023).

41. Ibid.

42. Disability Discrimination Act, 1995 c. 50; Bob Williams-Findlay, 'The Disabled People's Movement in the Age of Austerity: Rights, Resistance and Reclamation', in *Resist the Punitive State: Grassroots Struggles Across Welfare,*

Housing, Education and Prisons, Emily Luise Hart, Joe Greener and Rich Moth, eds (London: Pluto Press, 2019).

43. Julia Hamaus, 'Bridge Gender and Social Movements Cutting Edge Programme: Stories of Influence' (Brighton: Institute of Development Studies, 2015), 27–30.

44. Oliver, *Understanding Disability*; Oliver and Barnes, *Politics of Disablement*.

45. Oliver and Barnes, *Politics of Disablement*, 173.

46. Shakespeare, 'Disabled Self-organisation', 249.

47. Ibid., 254.

48. Vic Finkelstein, 'The Social Model of Disability and the Disability Movement' (Leeds: University of Leeds, 2007), 10.

49. Ibid., 1.

50. Micheline Mason, 'Internalized Oppression', in *Disability Equality in Education*, Richard Rieser and Micheline Mason, eds (London: Inner London Education Authority, 1990); Donna Reeve, 'Psycho-emotional Disablism and Internalised Oppression', in *Disabling Barriers – Enabling Environments*, 3rd ed., John Swain, Sally French, Colin Barnes and Carol Thomas, eds (London: SAGE, 2014), 92–8.

51. Shakespeare, 'Disabled Self-organisation', 258.

52. Ibid.

53. Ronald Franklin Inglehart, 'Postmaterialism' (*Encyclopaedia Britannica*, 2023), www.britannica.com/topic/postmaterialism (last accessed June 2023).

54. Oliver and Barnes, *Politics of Disablement*, 173.

55. Shakespeare, 'Disabled Self-organisation' (1993), 258.

56. Ibid.

57. 'BRIDGE, Social Movements: Evolution, Definitions, Debates And Resources' (Brighton: Institute of Development Studies, n.d.), 19, https://socialmovements.bridge.ids.ac.uk/socialmovements.bridge.ids.ac.uk/sites/socialmovements.bridge.ids.ac.uk/files/07.%202.%20Social%20Movements.pdf (last accessed June 2023).

58. Colin Barnes, *Disabled People in Britain and Discrimination* (London: Hurst & Company, 1991), 224.

59. Shakespeare, 'Disabled Self-organisation', 261.

60. Alan Scott, *Ideology and New Social Movements* (London: Routledge, 1990).

61. Sharon Smith, 'Mistaken Identity – Or Can Identity Politics Liberate the Oppressed?' (*International Socialism*, Spring 1994, No. 62).

62. 'Identity Politics' (Springfield, MA: Merriam Webster Dictionary, n.d.), www.merriam-webster.com/dictionary/identity%20politics (last accessed June 2023).

63. Cressida Heyes, 'Identity Politics', *The Stanford Encyclopedia of Philosophy*, Fall 2020 ed., Edward N. Zalta, ed., https://plato.stanford.edu/entries/identity-politics/ (last accessed June 2023).

64. Vic Finkelstein, 'The Social Model Repossessed' (Manchester Coalition of Disabled People, 2001), 5.
65. Heyes, 'Identity Politics'.
66. Iris Marion Young, *Justice and the Politics of Difference* (Princeton, NJ: Princeton University Press, 1990).
67. Heyes, 'Identity Politics'.
68. Tom Shakespeare, *Disability Rights and Wrongs* (London: Routledge, 2006), Ch. 4.
69. Heyes, 'Identity Politics'.
70. Ibid.
71. Ibid.
72. Ibid.
73. Sonia Kruks, *Retrieving Experience: Subjectivity and Recognition in Feminist Politics* (Ithaca, NY: Cornell University Press, 2001), 85.
74. Heyes, 'Identity Politics' (2020).
75. Helen Liggett, 'Stars Are Not Born: An Interpretative Approach to the Politics of Disability' (*Disability, Handicap and Society*, Vol. 3, No. 3, 1988), 263–76; Shakespeare, *Disability Rights*, 78.
76. Dan Goodley, *Disability Studies*, 2nd ed. (London: Sage Publications Ltd, 2017), 13.
77. Lori Marso, [2014] 'Sonia Kruks, Simone de Beauvoir and the Politics of Ambiguity, Review' (*Contemporary Political Theory*, Vol. 13, No. 4), review of Sonia Kruks, *Simone de Beauvoir and the Politics of Ambiguity* (Oxford: Oxford University Press, 2012), 53.
78. Ibid., 66.
79. Sonia Kruks, *Retrieving Experience: Subjectivity and Recognition in Feminist Politics* (New York: Cornell University Press, 2012), 35.
80. Ibid.
81. Tom Shakespeare, 'The Social Model of Disability', in *The Disability Studies Reader*, Lennard J. Davis, ed. (New York: Routledge, 2010), 266–73, 279.
82. Shakespeare, 'Disabled Self-organisation', 253.
83. Finkelstein, 'Social Model', 5.
84. Heyes, 'Identity Politics'.
85. Williams-Findlay, 'Falsification of History'.

CHAPTER 4   THE THIRD CORNERSTONE:
SELF-DETERMINATION, DE-INSTITUTIONALISATION
AND PROMOTION OF SELF-DIRECTED LIVING

1. Chava Willig Levy, 'A People's History of the Independent Living Movement' (Independent Living Institute, 1998).
2. Judy Hunt, *No Limits* (Manchester: TBR Imprint, 2019), 28.

3. John Evans, 'Independent Living and Centres for Independent Living as an Alternative to Institutions' (European Network of Independent Living, 2001), 3.

4. Paul Hunt, Letter to *The Guardian* (1972).

5. S. Graby, 'Neurodiversity: Bridging the Gap Between the Disabled People's Movement and the Mental Health System Survivors' Movement?', in *Madness, Distress and the Politics of Disablement*, Helen Spandler, Jill Anderson, and Bob Sapey, eds.(Bristol: Policy Press, 2015).

6. Peter Durrant, 'Reflections' (*Community Care*, 2002), www.communitycare.co.uk/2002/08/07/reflections-8/ (last accessed June 2023).

7. 'A Memorial to Ed Roberts, Born January 23, 1939' (Dakota Center for Independent Living, 2018), https://dakotacil.org/2018/01/22/a-memorial-to-ed-roberts-born-january-23-1939/ (last accessed June 2023).

8. Scot Danforth, 'Becoming the Rolling Quads: Disability Politics at the University of California, Berkeley, in the 1960s' (*History of Education Quarterly*, Vol. 58, No. 4, 2018).

9. Kitty Cone, 'Short History of the 504 Sit-in' (Disability Rights Education & Defense Fund, 1993).

10. Shirley Wilcher, 'The Rehabilitation Act of 1973: 45 Years of Activism and Progress' (INSIGHT, 2018).

11. Maggie Shreve, *The Independent Living Movement: History and Philosophy to Implementation and Practice* (Chicago, IL: IL NET, 1994), 48.

12. Ibid., 52.

13. Gerben DeJong, 'Independent Living: From Social Movement to Analytic Paradigm' (*Archives of Physical Medicine and Rehabilitation*, Vol. 60, No. 10, 1979).

14. Shreve, *Independent Living*, 129.

15. Ibid.

16. Ravi Malhotra, 'Empowering People With Disabilities' (*New Politics*, Vol. XI, No. 1, Whole Number 41, 2006).

17. Shreve, *Independent Living*, 49.

18. Ibid., 50.

19. Ibid., 50–51.

20. Ibid., 48.

21. Ibid., 52.

22. Ibid., 53.

23. Colin Barnes, 'Independent Living for Disabled People: A Policy Initiative That Can No Longer Be Ignored' (*Community Care*, 1992), 2, https://disability-studies.leeds.ac.uk/wp-content/uploads/sites/40/library/Barnes-Article8.pdf (last accessed June 2023).

24. Ibid.

25. John Evans, 'The Independent Living Movement in the UK' (Independent Living Institute, 2003).

26. 'Making a Reality of Community Care: A Report by the Audit Commission' (London: Audit Commission, 1986).

27. John Evans, 'Independent Living in the UK: Developments, Accomplishments and Impact on Government Social Policy and Legislation' (Independent Living Institute, 2008).

28. Ibid.

29. Evans, 'Independent Living' (2003).

30. Bob Williams-Findlay, 'Personalisation and Self-determination: The Same Difference?' (*Critical and Radical Social Work*, Vol. 3, No.1, Bristol: Policy Press, 2015), 67–87.

31. Ken Davis, 'Notes on the Development of the Derbyshire Centre for Integrated Living (DCIL)' (Derbyshire Coalition of Disabled People, 1984), 1, https://disability-studies.leeds.ac.uk/wp-content/uploads/sites/40/library/DavisK-earlydcil.pdf (last accessed June 2023).

32. Peter Millington and Hazel Wood, 'Forward: The History of Birmingham Disability Resource Centre' (Birmingham: Birmingham Disability Resource Centre, 2010).

33. Davis, 'Notes on the DCIL', 1.

34. Ibid., 2.

35. Ibid.

36. Vic Finkelstein, 'The Social Model of Disability and the Disability Movement' (Leeds: University of Leeds, 2007), 10.

37. Davis, 'Notes on the DCIL', 3.

38. Ibid.

39. Ibid., emphasis added.

40. Ibid.

41. Ibid.

42. Ibid.

43. Vic Finkelstein, 'A Profession Allied to the Community: The Disabled People's Trade Union' (Leeds: The Disability Press, 1999); Vic Finkelstein (1998) 'Re-thinking Care in a Society Providing Equal Opportunities For All' (Maidenhead: Open University Press, 1998).

44. Finkelstein, 'Re-thinking Care', 26.

45. Ibid.

46. Davis, 'Notes on the DCIL', 3–4.

47. A. J. Withers, 'Self-determination, Disability and Anti-Colonialism or Self-Determination as Disablism and Colonialism' (*Still My Revolution*, 2015), https://stillmyrevolution.org/2015/01/25/self-determination-disability-and-anti-racism-or-self-determination-as-disablism-and-racism/ (last accessed June 2023).

48. Mike Oliver, 'The Disability Movement and the Professions' (Leeds: University of Leeds, 1999), 3.

49. Vic Finkelstein, 'Phase 3: Conceptualising New Services' (Lancaster: Lancaster University, 2004), 29.

50. 'Independent Living' (European Network for Independent Living, n.d.), https://enil.eu/independent-living/ (last accessed June 2023).

CHAPTER 5   THE FOURTH CORNERSTONE: DISABILITY CULTURE AND IDENTITY

1. Vic Finkelstein, 'Disabled People and Our Culture Development' (*DAIL*, No. 8, 1987), 1.
2. Ibid., 4.
3. Vic Finkelstein 'Experience and Consciousness' (Liverpool Housing Authority, 1990), 1.
4. Peter Weinreich and Wendy Saunderson, *Analysing Identity* (London: Routledge, 2002).
5. 'Self-identity' (Oxford, Lexico UK Dictionary, n.d.), www.lexico.com/definition/self-identity (last accessed June 2023); 'Personhood' (Oxford: Lexico UK Dictionary, n.d.), www.lexico.com/definition/personhood (last accessed June 2023).
6. David S. Meyer, Nancy Whittier and Belinda Robnett, eds, *Social Movements: Identity, Culture, and the State* (Oxford: Oxford University Press, 2002), 319.
7. Finkelstein, 'Disabled People and Our Culture Development', 4.
8. Mary Chayko, *Socialization, Self, and Identity* (SuperConnected, 2021), https://superconnectedblogdotcom.files.wordpress.com/2018/01/6-techno-socialization-and-the-self.pdf (last accessed June 2023).
9. Isabel Gonzalez-Prendergast, 'Identity is Ruled by Stereotypes' (*Litro*, 2015), www.litromagazine.com/arts-and-culture/identity-is-ruled-by-stereotypes/ (last accessed June 2023).
10. Margaret Wangui Murugami, 'Disability and Identity' (*Disability Studies Quarterly*, Vol. 29, No. 4, 2009).
11. Mike Oliver and Gerry Zarb, 'Personal Assistance Schemes' (Greenwich Association of Disabled People's Centre for Independent Living, 1992); Liz Crow, 'Including All of Our Lives: Renewing the Social Model of Disability', in *Exploring the Divide*, Colin Barnes and Geof Mercer, eds (Leeds: The Disability Press, 1996), 55–72.
12. Kendra Cherry, 'What Is Self-Concept?' (*Verywell Mind*, 2022), www.verywellmind.com/what-is-self-concept-2795865 (last accessed June 2023).
13. Wangui Murugami, 'Identity'.
14. Ryan J. Voigt, 'Who Me? Self-Esteem for People with Disabilities' (*Brain Line*, 2009), www.brainline.org/article/who-me-self-esteem-people-disabilities (last accessed June 2023).
15. Heikki Ikäheimo, 'Personhood and the Social Inclusion of People With Disabilities: A Recognition-theoretical Approach', in *Arguing about Disability: Philosophical Perspectives*, Kristjana Kristiansen, Simo Vehmas and Tom Shakespeare, eds (London: Routledge, London, 2009).

16. Kate Sullivan, 'Otherness and the Power of Exclusion' (Stockholm International Peace Research Institute, 2015), www.sipri.org/commentary/blog/2015/otherness-and-power-exclusion (last accessed June 2023); Bob Williams-Findlay, *More Than a Left Foot* (London: Resistance Books, 2020), Ch. 7.

17. Carol Thomas, *Sociologies of Disability and Illness: Contested Ideas in Disability Studies and Medical Sociology* (Basingstoke: Palgrave Macmillan, 2007), 73.

18. Fiona Kumari Campbell, 'Exploring Internalised Ableism Using Critical Race Theory' (*Disability & Society*, Vol. 23, No. 2, 2008), 151–62.

19. Micheline Mason, 'Internalized Oppression', in *Disability Equality in Education*, Richard Rieser and Micheline Mason, eds (London: Inner London Education Authority, 1990), x.

20. Vic Finkelstein, 'Outside, "Inside Out"' (Manchester: Manchester Coalition of Disabled People, 1996), 30–36.

21. Williams-Findlay, *More Than a Left Foot*, 135–6; Vic Finkelstein, 'The Commonality of Disability', in *Disabling Barriers – Enabling Environments*, John Swain, Vic Finkelstein, Sally French and Mike Oliver, eds (London: SAGE, 1993).

22. Colin Hambrook, 'Colin Cameron Talks About the Affirmative Model of Disability' (*Disability Arts Online*, 2013), https://disabilityarts.online/magazine/opinion/towards-affirmative-model-disability/ (last accessed June 2023).

23. Paul Abberley, 'The Concept of Oppression and the Development of a Social Theory of Disability', in *Disability Studies: Past Present and Future*, Len Barton and Mike Oliver, eds (Leeds: The Disability Press, 1997), 160–78, 176.

24. Yasmin Sheikh and Harun Tulunay, 'Disability, Race and Sexuality Intersectionality Conversation – Part Two' (*The Law Society Podcast*, 2019), www.lawsociety.org.uk/Topics/Lawyers-with-Disabilities/Podcasts/disability-race-and-sexuality-intersectionality-part-two (last accessed June 2023).

25. Finkelstein, 'Commonality of Disability'; Bob Williams-Findlay, 'The Disabled People's Movement in the Age of Austerity: Rights, Resistance and Reclamation', in *Resist the Punitive State: Grassroots Struggles Across Welfare, Housing, Education and Prisons*, Emily Luise Hart, Joe Greener and Rich Moth, eds (London: Pluto Press, 2019).

26. Nick Watson, 'Well, I know this is going to sound very strange to you, but I do not see myself as a disabled person' (*Disability & Society*, Vol. 17, No. 5, 2002).

27. Antonio Gramsci, *Selections from the Prison Notebooks*, Quintin Hoare and Geoffrey Nowell-Smith, eds and trans (London: Lawrence and Wishart, 1971).

28. Mike Oliver, 'Capitalism, Disability and Ideology: A Materialist Critique of the Normalization' (Leeds: University of Leeds, 1994), 3.

29. Abberley, 'The Concept of Oppression', 172.

30. Tom Shakespeare and Nicholas Watson, 'The Social Model of Disability: An Outdated Ideology?' (*Research in Social Science and Disability*, Vol. 2, 2002); Carol Thomas, 'Developing the Social Relational in the Social Model of Disability: A Theoretical Agenda', in *Implementing The Social Model of Disability: Theory and Research*, Colin Barnes and Geof Mercer, eds (Leeds: Disability Press, 2004), 35.

31. David Hevey, *The Creatures Time Forgot: Photography and Disability Imagery* (London: Routledge, 1992), 118.

32. Colin Barnes, 'Effecting Change; Disability, Culture and Art' (Liverpool Institute for the Performing Arts, 2003), https://disability-studies.leeds. ac.uk/wp-content/uploads/sites/40/library/Barnes-Effecting-Change.pdf (last accessed June 2023).

33. Elspeth Morrison and Vic Finkelstein, 'Broken Arts and Cultural Repair: The Role of Culture in the Empowerment of Disabled People', in *Disabling Barriers – Enabling Environments*, John Swain, Vic Finkelstein, Sally French and Mike Oliver, eds (London: Sage Publications in association with the Open University, 1993), 122–8; Vic Finkelstein, 'The Commonality of Disability', also in *Disabling Barriers – Enabling Environments*, 9–15; Hevey, *Creatures Time Forgot*.

34. Lois Bragg, quoted in Susan Peters, 'Is There a Disability Culture? A Syncretisation of Three Possible World Views' (*Disability & Society*, Vol. 15, No. 4, 2000), 584.

35. Peters, 'Is There a Disability Culture?', 593; Peter Mclaren, *Revolutionary Multiculturalism: Pedagogies of Dissent for the New Millennium* (London: Routledge, 1997).

36. Paulo Freire, *Pedagogy of the Oppressed*, Myra Bergman Ramos, trans. (New York: Continuum, 1986).

37. Len Barton, 'Disability, Difference and the Politics of Recognition' (University of Sheffield, 1993), 3, https://disability-studies.leeds.ac.uk/wp-content/uploads/sites/40/library/Barton-inaugral-lecture-barton.pdf (last accessed June 2023).

38. Bob Findlay, 'Disability Information or Misinformation?', in *Quality and Equality in Education: The Denial of Disability Culture*, P. Ribbins and E. Burridge, eds (London: Cassell Publishers, 1994).

39. Anne Austin, 'Bob Williams-Findlay interviewed by Anne Austin, Sounds Collection: Speaking for Ourselves: An Oral History of People With Cerebral Palsy' (British Library, 2005), https://sounds.bl.uk/sounds/bob-williamsfindlay-interviewed-by-anne-austin-1001358206000x000019 (last accessed June 2023).

40. Morrison and Finkelstein, "Broken Arts," (1993b).

41. H. Hahn, 'Towards a Politics of Disability: Definitions, Disciplines, and Policies' (*The Social Journal*, Vol. 22, 1985), 87.

42. 'Models of Disability: Types and Definitions' (*Disabled World*, 2010), www. disabled-world.com/definitions/disability-models.php (last accessed June 2023).

43. Steven E. Brown, 'What Is Disability Culture?' (*Disability Studies Quarterly*, Vol. 22, No. 2, 2002); Doris Fleischer and Frieda Zames, *The Disability Rights Movement* (Philadelphia, PA: Temple University Press, 2001).

44. *Disability Challenge 1* (Union of the Physically Impaired Against Segregation, 1981), 7.

45. John Swain and Sally French, 'Towards an Affirmation Model of Disability' (*Disability & Society*, Vol. 15, No. 4, 2000).

46. Helen Liggett, 'Stars are not born: An Interpretative Approach to the Politics of Disability' (*Disability, Handicap and Society*, Vol. 3, No. 3, 1988), 189.

47. Tom Shakespeare, *Disability Rights and Wrongs* (London: Routledge, 2006), 82; Liggett, 'Stars are not born'; N. Shilpa, 'Identity Politics in India – Its Various Dimensions' (*International Journal of Research in Engineering, IT and Social Sciences*, Vol. 11, No. 2, 2021), 36.

48. Erving Goffman, *Stigma* (London: Penguin, 1963).

49. G. Pratt, 'Identity politics', in *The Dictionary of Human Geography, 4th Edn.*, R. J. Johnston, Derek Gregory, Geraldine Pratt and Michael Watts, eds (Oxford: Blackwell. 2000), 367.

50. Vic Finkelstein, 'The Evolution of Disability Awareness' (Leeds: University of Leeds, 1989), 7.

51. Ibid., 8.

52. Cressida Heyes, 'Identity Politics' *The Stanford Encyclopedia of Philosophy*, Edward N. Zalta, ed. (Fall 2020 ed.), https://plato.stanford.edu/entries/identity-politics/ (last accessed June 2023).

53. William E. Connolly, *Identity/Difference: Democratic Negotiations of Political Paradox,* (Minneapolis: University of Minnesota Press, 2002), 64.

54. Ibid.

55. Shakespeare, *Disability Rights and Wrongs.*

56. Gurminder K. Bhambra and Victoria Margree, 'Identity Politics and the Need for a "Tomorrow"' (*Economic and Political Weekly*, Vol. 45, No. 15, 2010), https://cris.brighton.ac.uk/ws/portalfiles/portal/324590/Identity_politics.pdf (last accessed 3 July 2023).

57. Ibid.

58. Carol J. Gill, 'A Psychological View of Disability Culture' (*Disability Studies Quarterly*, Vol. 15, No. 4, 1995), 16–19.

59. Simon Brissenden, 'What is Disability Culture?' (*Disability Arts in London Magazine*, 1988).

60. Ibid.

61. Elspeth Morrison and Vic Finkelstein, 'Culture as Struggle: Access to Power', in *Disability Arts and Culture Papers*, Sarag Leeds, ed. (London: Shape, 1992), 124.

62. Rose Galvin, (2003) 'The Paradox of Disability Culture: The Need to Combine Versus the Imperative to Let Go' (*Disability and Society*, Vol. 18, No. 5), 675–90.

63. Gill, '"A Psychological View of Disability Culture,"', 18 (1995).

64. Bob Williams-Findlay, 'The Representation of Disabled People in the News Media', in *Disabling Barriers – Enabling Environments*, John Swain, Sally French, Colin Barnes and Carol Thomas, eds (London: SAGE, 2014).

65. 'The Incorrigibles: Perspectives on Disability Visual Arts in the 20th and 21st Centuries: Tony Heaton contribution entitled "Different Shoes"', www.tonyheaton.co.uk/writings---interviews.html?fbclid=IwAR3btcwFmzGwQ 5qYvhvQlladiRtne1zLS2pOZpkz8EKqbBXIABznMuD-Vcg (last accessed 4 July 2023); Allan Sutherland, *Electric Bodies – Travels In Life History: Personal Stories of the Emergence of the Disability Arts Movement* (London: Disability Art Online, 2021), Foreword.

66. Linda Rocco, 'Reflections on the Disability Arts Movement,' interviews Tony Heaton, David Hevey and Jo Verrent (Shape Arts, 2019), www.shapearts.org.uk/blog/reflections-on-the-disability-arts-movement (last accessed June 2023).

CHAPTER 6 IMPAIRMENT AND OPPRESSION: THE BATTLEGROUND REVIEWED

1. Paul Abberley, 'The Concept of Oppression and the Development of a Social Theory of Disability', in *Disability Studies: Past Present and Future*, Len Barton and Mike Oliver, eds (Leeds: The Disability Press, 1997), 160–78, 172.

2. David Wasserman and Sean Aas, 'Disability: Definitions and Models', Edward N. Zalta, ed. (*The Stanford Encyclopedia of Philosophy*, Summer 2022 ed.), https://plato.stanford.edu/archives/sum2022/entries/disability/ (last accessed June 2023).

3. Marilee Hanson, 'Elizabethan Poor Laws' (*English History*, 2022), https://englishhistory.net/tudor/life/elizabethan-poor-laws/ (last accessed June 2023).

4. John Pratt, David Brown, Mark Brown, Simon Hallsworth and Wayne Morrison, eds, *The New Punitiveness: Trends, Theories, Perspectives* (Portland: Willan Publishing, 2005).

5. Marta Russell and Ravi Malhotra, 'Capitalism and Disability' (*Socialist Register*, Vol. 38, 2002).

6. Liza Morton, 'Every choice has been dictated by my health condition' (*British Psychology Society*, Vol. 33, 2020), 6.

7. Allan St J. Dixon, Beatrix Milburn and Julia K. Wood, 'Philip Henry Nicholls Wood' (*BMJ Clinical Research*, Vol. 339, 2009); Vic Finkelstein, 'Phase 2: Discovering the Person In "Disability" and "Rehabilitation"' (*Magic Carpet*, Vol. 7, No. 1, 1975), 33.
8. Michael Oliver, *The Politics of Disablement* (London: Macmillan, 1990), 2.
9. Amelia I. Harris, Judith R. Buckle, Elizabeth Cox and Christopher R.W. Smith, 'Handicapped and Impaired in Great Britain, Part 1,' 'Office of Population Censuses and Surveys, Social Survey Division, Work and Housing of Impaired Persons in Great Britain, Part II' (London: HMSO, 1971); Alfred Morris, 'Office of Population Censuses and Surveys (Social Survey Division)' (*Hansard*, 1981), https://hansard.parliament.uk/Commons/1981-07-02/debates/b249c75f-9445-4309-9959-377345e3a931/OfficeOfPopulationCensusesAndSurveys(SocialSurveyDivision) (last accessed June 2023).
10. Bob Sapey, '*Politique du handicap: un modèle basé sur l'autonomie individuelle*' (*Informations Sociales*, No. 159, 2010).
11. J. Martin, H. Meltzer and D. Elliot, *OPCS Surveys of Disability in Great Britain: Report 1 - The Prevalence of Disability Among Adults* (London: HMSO, 1988).
12. Judy Hunt, *No Limits* (Manchester: TBR Imprint, 2019), 106.
13. Vic Finkelstein, 'Phase 2', 33.
14. A. J. Withers, *Disability Politics and Theory* (Black Point: Fernwood Publishing, 2012).
15. 'Handicap' (Springfield, MA: Merriam-Webster Dictionary, n.d.), www.merriam-webster.com/dictionary/handicap?msclkid=22e3e169cf7c11ec8087ac3023453d1a (last accessed June 2023).
16. E. Barnett and M. Casper, 'A Definition of "Social Environment"' (*American Journal of Public Health*, Vol. 91, No.3, 2001).
17. Vic Finkelstein, *Barriers To Community Life* (Maidenhead: Open University Press, n.d.).
18. Mike Oliver, *Understanding Disability: From Theory to Practice* (London: Macmillan Press, 1996), 22; emphasis added.
19. Irving Kenneth Zola, 'Medicine as an Institution of Social Control' (*Sociological Review*, Vol. 20, No. 4, 1972).
20. 'Disability in the 19th Century' (*Historic England*, n.d.), https://historicengland.org.uk/research/inclusive-heritage/disability-history/1832-1914/ (last accessed June 2023).
21. Philip H.N. Wood, and Elizabeth M. Badley, 'People With Disabilities: Toward Acquiring Information Which Reflects More Sensitively Their Problems and Needs' (*World Information Fund*, 1980).
22. 'International Classification of Impairments, Disabilities, and Handicaps – A Manual of Classification Relating to the Consequences of Disease' (World Health Organization, 1980), 28.

23. 'International Classification of Functioning, Disability and Health (ICF)' (World Health Organization, 2001), 287–305.

24. Arika Okrent, 'Why Did "Disabled" Replace "Handicapped" As the Preferred Term?' (*Mental Floss*, 2015), www.mentalfloss.com/article/69361/why-did-disabled-replace-handicapped-preferred-term (last accessed June 2023).

25. 'Northern Officers Group Defining Impairment and Disability' (*Disability Studies*, 1999), https://disability-studies.leeds.ac.uk/wp-content/uploads/sites/40/library/Northern-Officers-Group-defining-impairment-and-disability.pdf (last accessed June 2023).

26. Vic Finkelstein, 'Disability: An Administrative Challenge?', in *Social Work – Disabling People and Disabling Environments*, Michael Oliver, ed. (London, Jessica Kingsley Publishers, 1991).

27. Giulio Amerigo Caperchi, 'Occupy Hegemony: Gramsci, Ideology and Common Sense' (*GoCBlog*, 1992), https://thegocblog.com/2012/04/07/occupy-hegemony-gramsciideology-and-common-sense/ (last accessed October 2020).

28. Talcott Parsons, *The Social System* (Glencoe, IL: Free Press, 1951); S.E. Smith, 'The "Sick Role" and Perceptions of Disability' (2010), https://urocyon.wordpress.com/2012/06/30/when-roles-have-you-living-in-their-parents-basement/ (last accessed June 2023).

29. Ibid.

30. Martin Powell, 'New Labour and the Third Way in the British Welfare State: A New and Distinctive Approach?' (*Critical Social Policy*, Vol. 20, No. 1, 2000); John Offer, *An Intellectual History of British Social Policy*, (Bristol: Bristol University Press, 2006); Irene Gedalof, 'Work Yourself Better: The Disabled Person as Benefit Scrounger', in *Narratives of Difference in an Age of Austerity. Thinking Gender in Transnational Times*, idem, ed. (London: Palgrave Macmillan, 2018).

31. Vic Finkelstein, 'The Commonality of Disability' in *Disabling Barriers – Enabling Environments*, John Swain, Vic Finkelstein, Sally French and Mike Oliver, eds (London: SAGE, 1993), 2.

32. Stuart Hall, 'Cultural Studies and its Theoretical Legacies' in *Cultural Studies*, Lawrence Grossberg, Cary Nelson and Paula Treichler, eds. (New York: Routledge, 1992), 278.

33. Maria Barile, 'Globalization and ICF Eugenics: Historical Coincidence or Connection? The More Things Change the More They Stay the Same' (*Disability Studies Quarterly*, Vol. 23, No. 2, 2003), 211; E. S. Solomon, 'Women With a Physical Disability: A Review of Literature and Suggestions for Intervention', in *Women with Disabilities: Found Voices*, Mary Willmuth and Lillian Holcomb, eds (New York: Harrington Press, 1993).

34. David Pfeiffer, 'Disabling Definitions: Is the World Health Organization Normal?' (*New England Journal of Human Services*, Vol. 11, 1992); David Pfeiffer, 'The ICIDH and the Need for its Revision' (*Disability & Society*, Vol. 13, No. 4, 1998); David Pfeiffer, 'The Devils are in the Details: The

ICIDH2 and the Disability Movement' (*Disability & Society*, Vol. 15, No. 7, 2000).

35. 'The ICF: Overview' (Centers for Disease Control and Prevention, n.d.), www.cdc.gov/nchs/data/icd/icfoverview_finalforwho10sept.pdf (last accessed June 2023).

36. Rob Imrie, 'Demystifying Disability: A Review of the International Classification of Functioning Disability and Health' (*Sociology of Health & Illness*, Vol. 26, No. 3, 2004).

37. Debbie Jolly, 'Tale of Two Models: Disabled People vs Unum, Atos, Government and Disability Charities' (*Disabled People Against Cuts*, 2012), https://dpac.uk.net/2012/04/a-tale-of-two-models-disabled-people-vs-unum-atos-government-and-disability-charities-debbie-jolly/ (last accessed June 2023); Chris Grover and Karen Soldatic, 'Neoliberal Restructuring, Disabled People and Social (In)Security in Australia and Britain' (*Scandinavian Journal of Disability Research*, Vol. 15, No. 3, 2013); Simoni Symeonidou, 'New Policies, Old Ideas: The Question of Disability Assessment Systems and Social Policy' (*Disability & Society*, Vol. 29, No. 8, 2014).

38. Jolly, 'Tale of Two Models'.

39. 'Ingeus Recruiting Health Advisors for DWP Forced Biopsychosocial Health Assessments' (A Latent Existence, 2013), https://ingeus.co.uk/resources/news/ingeus-to-deliver-dwp-functional-health-assessments (last accessed 3 July 2023).

40. Abberley, 'The Concept of Oppression', 176.

41. Ibid., 161.

42. Paul Abberley, *Handicapped by Numbers: A Critique of the OPCS Survey* (Bristol: Bristol Polytechnic, 1991), 6, https://disability-studies.leeds.ac.uk/wp-content/uploads/sites/40/library/Abberley-occ-paper.pdf (last accessed June 2023).

43. Mike Oliver, *Understanding Disability: From Theory to Practice* (London: Macmillan Press, 1996), 139.

44. Abberley, 'The Concept of Oppression', 162.

45. Ibid., 164.

46. Ibid.

47. Andreas Reckwitz, 'Toward a Theory of Social Practices' (*European Journal of Sociology*, Vol. 5, No. 2, 2002), 243–63.

48. Abberley, 'The Concept of Oppression', 164.

49. Finkelstein, 'Commonality of Disability', 10.

50. Karen Soldatic, 'The Transnational Sphere of Justice: Disability Praxis and the Politics of Impairment' (*Disability & Society*, Vol. 28, No. 6, 2013), 747.

51. Ibid., 748; Maria Berghs, 'Coming to Terms with Inequality and Exploitation in an African State: The Case of Sierra Leone' (*Disability & Society*, Vol. 25, No. 7, 2010), 861–5; Emma Stone, 'Disability and Development' (Leeds: Disability Press, 1999).

52. Soldatic, 'Transnational Sphere', 748.
53. Abberley, 'The Concept of Oppression', 169.
54. 'The Prevention of Occupational Diseases' (International Labour Organization, 2013), 5, https://tinyurl.com/53p76exx (last accessed June 2023).
55. Abberley, 'The Concept of Oppression', 164.
56. Ibid., 165.
57. Soldatic, 'Transnational Sphere', 747.
58. Russell and Malhotra, 'Capitalism and Disability', 214.
59. Nicki Lisa Cole, 'What Is Cultural Hegemony?' (*ThoughtCo.*, 2020), www.thoughtco.com/cultural-hegemony-3026121 (last accessed June 2023).
60. Abberley, 'The Concept of Oppression', 175.
61. Peter Leonard, *Personality and Ideology: Towards a Materialist Understanding of the Individual* (London: Palgrave Macmillan, 1984), Ch. 8.
62. John Pring, 'BBC's Disabled-led "Benefit Cheat" Drama Causes Anger and Disbelief,' (*Disability News Service*, 2010), www.disabilitynewsservice.com/bbcs-disabled-led-benefit-cheat-drama-causes-anger-and-disbelief/ (last accessed June 2023).
63. Abberley, 'The Concept of Oppression', 176.

CHAPTER 7 LOCATION OF IMPAIRMENT WITHIN DISABILITY POLITICS: IMPAIRMENT EFFECTS AND IMPAIRMENT REALITY

1. Colin Barnes and Geof Mercer, *Disability* (Cambridge: Polity Press, 2003), 65–86.
2. Nick Watson, 'The Dialectics of Disability: A Social Model for the 21st Century?', in *Implementing the Social Model of Disability: Theory and Research*, Colin Barnes and Geof Mercer, eds (Leeds: The Disability Press, 2004), 101–17.
3. Mike Oliver, 'A Sociology of Disability or a Disablist Sociology?', in *Disability and Society: Emerging Issues and Insights*, L. Barton, ed. (London: Longman, 1996), 38.
4. Mara Barile, 'Globalization and ICF Eugenics: Historical Coincidence or Connection? The More Things Change the More They Stay the Same' (*Disability Studies Quarterly*, Spring, Vol. 23, No. 2, 2003), 208–23.
5. A model is 'a schematic description of a system, theory, or phenomenon that accounts for its known or inferred properties and may be used for further study of its characteristics' (*American Heritage Dictionary*, 2011).
6. Barnes and Mercer, *Disability*, 67, citing Vic Finkelstein, 'Outside, "Inside Out"' (*Coalition*, April, GMCDP, 1996), 30–36, 34.
7. Finkelstein, 'Outside, "Inside Out"', 31.
8. Jenny Morris, 'Feminism, Gender and Disability' (Paper presented at a seminar in Sydney, Australia, February 1998), 5.

10. The question of the relationship between the public and private spheres goes beyond issues concerned with the impairment and disability relationship. Neither side fully acknowledged the differing sites of struggle involved with living with impairment reality and the intersectionality issues that underpin the encountered oppression, at a personal and collective level of consciousness.

11. Christopher J. Kelly, "'The Personal is Political'" (*Encyclopedia Britannica*, 2022) www.britannica.com/topic/the-personal-is-political (last accessed June 2023).

12. Carol Thomas, *Female Forms: Experiencing and Understanding Disability* (Buckingham: Open University Press, 1999), 42; emphasis added.

13. Jenny Morris, 'Feminism and Disability' (*Feminist Review*, Vol. 43, Spring, 1993), 57–70, 68.

14. Sally French, 'Disability, Impairment or Something in Between?', in *Disabling Barriers – Enabling Environments*, John Swain, Sally French, Colin Barnes and Carol Thomas, eds (London: Sage, 1993), 17.

15. Finkelstein, 'Outside, "Inside Out"', 31.

16. Ibid.

17. Vic Finkelstein, 'Modelling Disability' (based on a presentation at the workshop organised for the 'Breaking The Moulds' conference, Dunfermline, Scotland, 16–17 May 1996).

18. Finkelstein, 'Outside, "Inside Out"', 32.

19. See, for example, Liz Crow, 'Including All of Our Lives: Renewing The Social Model Of Disability', in *Exploring the Divide: Illness and Disability*, C. Barnes and G. Mercer, eds (Leeds: The Disability Press, 1996); Sally French, 'Disability, Impairment or Something in Between?', 17–25; Jenny Morris, 'Personal and Political: A Feminist Perspective on Researching Physical Disability' (*Disability, Handicap and Society*, Vol. 7, No. 2, 1992), 157–66; Thomas, *Female Forms*.

20. Liz Crow, 'Including All of Our Lives', 6.

21. The notion of 'living with an impairment' is of course contested by many postmodernists.

22. Mike Oliver, 'Capitalism, Disability and Ideology: A Materialist Critique of the Normalization Principle', https://disability-studies.leeds.ac.uk/wp-content/uploads/sites/40/library/Oliver-cap-dis-ideol.pdf (last accessed June 2023).

23. Disabled People Against Cuts, 'Reinvigorating the Social Model of Disability' (2020), https://dpac.uk.net/2020/07/reinvigorating-the-social-model-of-disability/ (last accessed June 2023).

24. Finkelstein, 'Modelling Disability', 18.

25. Carol Thomas, 'Developing the Social Relational in the Social Model of Disability: A Theoretical Agenda', in *Implementing the Social Model of Disability: Theory and Research*, Colin Barnes and Geof Mercer, eds (Leeds: The Disability Press, 2004), 32–47.

26. Thomas, 'Developing the Social Relational', 33.
27. UPIAS, 'Fundamental Principles of Disability' (London: Union of the Physically Impaired Against Segregation, 1976).
28. Thomas, 'Developing the Social Relational', 33.
29. Ibid., 34.
30. See: Finkelstein, 'Outside, "Inside Out"'; 'Modelling Disability', and this volume, Chapters 8, 9 and 10.
31. Mike Oliver, *Understanding Disability: From Theory to Practice* (Houndsmills, UK: Macmillan Press, 2nd ed., 2009).
32. Carol Thomas, 'Theorising Disability and Chronic Illness: Where Next for Perspectives in Medical Sociology?' (*Social Theory and Health*, Vol. 10, No. 3, 2012), 209–28, 211.
33. Carol Thomas, 'Disability and Impairment' in *Disabling Barriers – Enabling Environments*, 3rd ed., John Swain, Sally French, Colin Barnes and Carol Thomas, eds (London: SAGE Publications Ltd, 2014).
34. Thomas, *Female Forms: Experiencing and Understanding Disability*, (1999), 37; Susan Wendell, *The Rejected Body* (New York: Routledge, 1996), 57.
35. Susan Wendell, (1989) 'Toward a Feminist Theory of Disability' (*Hypatia, Feminist Ethics & Medicine*, Vol. 4, No. 2, 1996), , 104–24, 108.
36. Ibid.
37. Ibid.
38. Thomas, *Female Forms*, 37.
39. David L. Hosking, 'Critical Disability Theory' (Paper presented at the 4th Biennial Disability Studies Conference at Lancaster University, UK, 2–4 September 2008), 8. www.lancaster.ac.uk/fass/events/disabilityconference_archive/2008/papers/hosking2008.pdf (last accessed June 2023).
40. Mike Oliver, 'The Social Model of Disability: Thirty Years On' (*Disability & Society*, Vol. 28, No. 7, 2013),1024–1026.
41. Colin Barnes and Geof Mercer, 'Introduction', in *Exploring the Divide: Illness and Disability*, idem, eds (Leeds: The Disability Press, 1996); Thomas, *Female Forms*, 39.
42. Pam Thomas, Lorraine Gradwell and Natalie Markham, 'Defining Impairment Within the Social Model of Disability' (*Coalition*, GMCDP, 1997).
43. UPIAS, 'Fundamental Principles of Disability', 4.
44. American International Academy of Education, 'Impairments, Activity Limitations, and Participation Restrictions, Disability and Health Overview' (2021), https://aie-edu.academy/2021/01/19/impairments-activity-limitations-and-participation-restrictionsdisability-and-health-overview/ (last accessed June 2023).
45. Thomas, *Female Forms*, 43; Carol Thomas, 'How Is Disability Understood? An Examination of Sociological Approaches' (*Disability & Society*, Vol. 19, No. 6, 2004), 569–83.

46. Vic Finkelstein, 'Emancipating Disabling Studies', in *The Disability Reader: Social Sciences Perspectives*, Tom Shakespeare, ed. (London: Cassell, 1998). Finkelstein was a tutor on the OU's groundbreaking disability course P853, 'The Handicapped Person in the Community', which began in 1975.

47. Thomas, 'Developing the Social Relational', 41.

48. Finkelstein, 'Modelling Disability', 11.

49. Ibid.

50. Thomas, 'Disability and Impairment', 14.

51. *Mind*, 'Disability Discrimination' (2023), www.mind.org.uk/information-support/legal-rights/disability-discrimination/disability/ (last accessed June 2023).

52. Janine Owens, Barry John Gibson, Karthik Periyakaruppiah, Sarah Ruth Baker and Peter Glen Robinson, 'Impairment Effects, Disability and Dry Mouth: Exploring the Public and Private Dimensions' (*Health*, Vol. 18, No. 5, 2014), 509.

53. 'Reality' (*Oxford Living Dictionary*, 2016), https://en.oxforddictionaries.com/definition/reality (last accessed June 2023).

54. Shelly Tremain, 'Foucault, Governmentality, and Critical Disability Theory: An Introduction', in *Foucault and the Government of Disability*, idem, ed. (Ann Arbor, MI: University of Michigan Press, 2005), 1–24; Mairian Corker and Tom Shakespeare, *Disability/Postmodernity: Embodying Disability Theory*, idem, eds (London: Bloomsbury Publishing, 2002); Margrit Shildrick, 'Critical Disability Studies: Rethinking the Conventions for the Age of Postmodernity', in *Routledge Handbook of Disability Studies*, Nick Watson, Alan Roulstone and Carol Thomas, eds (London: Routledge, 2012), 30–41; Dan Goodley; Kirsty Liddiard and Katherine Runswick-Cole, 'Feeling Disability: Theories of Affect and Critical Disability Studies' (*Disability & Society*, Vol. 33, No. 2, 2018), 197–217.

55. Thomas, 'Disability and Impairment', 12.

56. Melinda C. Hall, 'Critical Disability Theory' (*Stanford Encyclopedia of Philosophy*, 2019), https://plato.stanford.edu/entries/disability-critical/ (last accessed June 2023).

57. Sami Schalk, 'Critical Disability Studies as Methodology' (*Lateral, Journal of the Cultural Studies Association*, 2017), http://csalateral.org/issue/6-1/forum-alt-humanities-critical-disability-studies-methodology-schalk/ (last accessed June 2023).

CHAPTER 8   DISABILITY PRAXIS: UNANSWERED QUESTIONS

1. Chris Costello, 'How Capitalism Contributes to Ableism' (*The Mighty*, 2017), https://themighty.com/topic/disability/how-capitalism-contributes-to-ableism (last accessed June 2023).

2. Nirmala Erevelles, 'Disability and the Dialectics of Difference' (*Disability & Society*, Vol. 11, No. 4, 1996), 519–38; Ayesha Vernon, 'The Dialectics

of Multiple Identities and the Disabled People's Movement' (*Disability & Society*, Vol. 14, No. 3, 1999), 385–98; Gareth H. Williams, 'Review Article: Bodies on a Battlefield. The Dialectics Of Disability' (*Sociology of Health & Illness*, Vol. 21, No. 2, 2001), 242–52.

3. Eric Ruder, 'The Dialectics and Why They Matter to Marxists' (*Socialist Worker.Org*, 2015), https://socialistworker.org/2015/07/09/the-dialectic-and-why-it-matters (last accessed June 2023).

4. Brendan J. Gleeson, 'Disability Studies: A Historical Materialist View' (*Disability & Society*, Vol. 12, No. 2, 1997), 179–202; Marta Russell, M., *Capitalism and Disability: Selected Writings*, K. Rosenthal, ed. (London: Haymarket Books, 2019).

5. Paul Abberley, 'The Concept of Oppression and the Development of a Social Theory of Disability', in *Disability Studies: Past Present and Future*, Len Barton and Mike Oliver, eds (Leeds: The Disability Press, 1997), 160–78, 163–4.

6. See Chapter 9.

7. Claus Offe, *Contradictions of the Welfare State* (London: Taylor and Francis, 2018).

8. Barbara M. Montgomery and Leslie A. Baxter, *Dialectical Approaches to Studying Personal Relationships* (New York: L. Erlbaum Associates, 1998).

9. Mike Oliver, *Understanding Disability: From Theory to Practice* (London: Macmillan Press, 1996); Ken Davis, 'Notes on the Development of the Derbyshire Centre for Integrated Living' (Derby: DCIL, 1984).

10. Mike Clear and Brendan Gleeson, 'Disability and Materialist Embodiment' (*Journal of Australian Political Economy*, Vol. 49, 2002).

11. Vic Finkelstein, 'The Social Model Repossessed' (Manchester Coalition of Disabled People, 2001), 5.

12. Disability LIB, *Thriving or Surviving: Challenges and Opportunities for Disabled People's Organisations in the 21st Century* (Disability LIB, 2008). See Chapter 5, 'A Statement of Common Understanding', 47.

13. Ibid.

14. Teodor Mladenov, 'Disability and Austerity' (*Cost of Living*, 2014), www.cost-ofliving.net/disability-and-austerity/#:~:text=Austerity%20measures%20have%20had%20a%20strong%20impact%20on,people%E2%80%99s%20cultural%20recognition%20and%20political%20representation%20as%20well (last accessed June 2023).

15. Vic Finkelstein, 'The Social Model of Disability and the Disability Movement' (Leeds: University of Leeds, 2007), 12.

16. BCODP nevertheless had a good relationship with leading Deaf activists, although the movements were separate: Penny Beschizza, Jen Dodds and Andrew Don, 'Campaigning for a Better Life' (*British Deaf Association*, 2015), https://bda.org.uk/campaigning-for-a-better-life/ (last accessed June 2023).

17. Ann Phoenix, 'What is Intersectionality?' (The British Academy, 2018), www.thebritishacademy.ac.uk/blog/what-is-intersectionality/ (last accessed June 2023).

18. Peggy McIntosh, 'White Privilege: Unpacking the Invisible Knapsack' (Wellesley Centres for Women, 2010), https://nationalseedproject.org/images/documents/Knapsack_plus_Notes-Peggy_McIntosh.pdf.

19. Beckie Rutherford, 'Disabled Women and the Women's Liberation Movement' (*Reteach.org*, 2020), https://reteach.org.uk/subject/history/disabled-women-and-the-women-s-liberation-movement (last accessed June 2023).

20. Ibid.

21. Ibid.

22. Oliver, *Understanding Disability*, 41.

23. Finkelstein, 'The Social Model Repossessed' (Manchester Coalition of Disabled People, 2001), 2.

24. Vernon, 'The Dialectics of Multiple Identities', 387.

25. Ibid.; Ossie Stuart, 'Race and Disability: Just a Double Oppression?' (*Disability and Society*, Vol. 7, 1992), 177–88; N. Begum, 'Mirror, Mirror on the Wall', in *Reflections: The Views of Black Disabled People on Their Lives and Community Care*, N. Begum, M. Hill and A. Stevens, eds (London: CCETSW, 1994); Hazel Carby, 'White Woman Listen! Black Feminism and the Boundaries of Sisterhood', in *Empire Strikes Back: Race and Racism in 70s Britain*, Centre For Contemporary Cultural Studies, eds (London: Hutchinson, 1994 [1982]).

26. Vernon, 'The Dialectics of Multiple Identities', 395.

27. Regard is a national organisation of lesbians, gay men, bisexuals, transgender and queer people (LGBTQI+) who self-identify as disabled:. http://regard.org.uk/about-us/ (last accessed June 2023).

28. BBC, 'Silenced: The Hidden Story of Disabled Britain' (2021), www.bbc.co.uk/programmes/p094nhsl (last accessed June 2023).

29. The Alliance for Inclusive Education, 'What More Can We Achieve? A Critical Review of "Silenced: The Hidden Story of Disabled Britain"' (*Inclusion Now*, Vol. 58, 2021), www.allfie.org.uk/news/inclusion-now/inclusion-now-58/what-more-can-we-achieve-a-critical-review-of-silenced-the-hidden-story-of-disabled-britain/ (last accessed June 2023).

30. Asian People's Disability Alliance (APDA) was founded as a Pan-Disability Organisation (DPO), to provide culturally specific care for South Asian elderly and disabled communities, https://apda.org.uk/aims-and-objectives (last accessed June 2023).

31. Robert Trotter, 'Over-looked Communities, Over-due Change: How Services Can Better Support BME Disabled People' (London, *Scope*, 2012), https://lx.iriss.org.uk/content/over-looked-communities-over-due-change-how-services-can-better-support-bme-disabled-people (last accessed 1 July 2023).

32. John Pring, 'Black disabled people "must protest at invisibility and discrimination" – quotation from Charles on report' (*Disability News Service*, 2020), https://www.disabilitynewsservice.com/black-disabled-people-must-protest-at-invisibility-and-discrimination/ (last accessed June 2023).

33. Alliance for Inclusive Education, 'What more can we achieve?'.

34. Social justice is defined as 'justice in terms of the distribution of wealth, opportunities, and privileges within a society' (*Bruce on politics*, 2015), www.bruceonpolitics.com/2015/04/09/social-justice/ (last accessed June 2023).

35. Sins Invalid, 'Skin, Tooth, and Bone – The Basis of Movement is Our People: A Disability Justice Primer' (*Reproductive Health Matters*, Vol. 25, No.50, 2017), 149–50.

36. Maia Goodell, 'Disability Rights and Disability Justice' (*ADA Update Disability Law News & Analysis*, 2021), https://ada-update.com/2021/04/30/disability-rights-and-disability-justice/ (last accessed June 2023).

37. Idealism and wholeness are semantically related. Sometimes you can use 'idealism' instead of the noun 'wholeness'– social acceptance and 'wholeness' are not one and the same. People determine individually what self-love means to them; it cannot be externally constructed: Paul Guyer and Rolf-Peter Horstmann, 'Idealism', (*The Stanford Encyclopedia of Philosophy*, Spring 2023 ed.), Edward N. Zalta and Uri Nodelman, eds, https://plato.stanford.edu/archives/spr2023/entries/idealism/ (last accessed June 2023).

38. Sins Invalid, '10 Principles of Disability Justice' (2015), www.sinsinvalid.org/blog/10-principles-of-disability-justice (last accessed June 2023).

CHAPTER 9   A RADICAL ECO-SOCIAL APPROACH TOWARDS SUSTAINABLE COMMUNITY-BASED SERVICES

1. National Centre for Independent Living, https://en.wikipedia.org/wiki/National_Centre_for_Independent_Living (last accessed June 2023); Hannah Morgan; Colin Barnes and Geof Mercer, *Creating Independent Lives: An Evaluation Of Services Led By Disabled People, Conference Report and Findings* (Leeds: The Disability Press, 2000), https://disability-studies.leeds.ac.uk/wp-content/uploads/sites/40/2011/10/report1.pdf (last accessed June 2023).

2. Emma Briant, Nick Watson and Gregory Philo, 'Bad News for Disabled People: How the Newspapers are Reporting Disability: Project Report' (Strathclyde Centre for Disability Research and Glasgow Media Unit, University of Glasgow, Glasgow, 2011), https://www.gla.ac.uk/media/Media_214917_smxx.pdf (last accessed June 2023).

3. Prime Minister's Strategy Unit, *Improving the Life Chances of Disabled People* (London: Cabinet Office, Prime Minister's Strategy Unit, 2005), 7.

4. Debbie Jolly, 'A Tale of two Models: Disabled People vs Unum, Atos, Government and Disability Charities', *Disabled People Against Cuts* (DPAC, 2013).

5. John Pring, 'End of the Road for Equality 2025' (*Disability News Service*, 2013), www.disabilitynewsservice.com/end-of-the-road-for-equality-2025/ (last accessed June 2023).

6. Peter Beresford, '*Compass* Think Piece 47: Whose Personalisation?' (London: *Compass*, 2009).

7. Paul Spicker, 'Personalisation Falls Short' (*British Journal of Social Work*, Vol. 43, No. 7, 2013), 1259–75.

8. Alison Thewliss, 'No Woman Should Have to Prove They Were Raped to Claim Child Benefit. What is This Madness?' (*The Telegraph*, 6 April 2017), www.telegraph.co.uk/women/politics/no-woman-should-have-to-prove-they-were-raped-to-claim-child-ben/ (last accessed June 2023); Frances Ryan, 'Domestic Violence and Disabled Women: An Abuse of Power' (*The Guardian*, 9 November 2012), www.theguardian.com/society/2012/nov/19/domestic-violence-disabled-women-abuse (last accessed June 2023); Inclusion Scotland, 'Welfare Reform Impacts On Disabled People' – The Facts by Inclusion Scotland' (*Inclusion Scotland*, 2015), http://inclusionscotland.org/welfare-reform-impacts-on-disabled-people-the-facts/# (last accessed June 2023); Frances Ryan, *Crippled: Austerity and the Demonization of Disabled People* (London: Verso, 2019).

9. Trade Union Congress, 'Social Care Spending in England Still £600m Lower than in 2010' (*Trade Union Congress*, 2020), www.tuc.org.uk/news/councils-england-spending-ps78bn-year-less-key-services-2010-says-tuc (last accessed June 2023).

10. Reclaiming our Futures Alliance, 'Independent Living for the Future: Our Vision for a National Independent Living Support System' (*Reclaiming our Futures Alliance*, 2019), www.rofa.org.uk/independent-living-for-the-future/ (last accessed June 2023); Inclusion London, 'One Year On: Evaluating the Impact of the Closure of the Independent Living Fund' (*Inclusion London*, 2016), www.inclusionlondon.org.uk/campaigns-and-policy/facts-and-information/independent-living-social-care-and-health/ilf-one-year-on/ (last accessed June 2023).

11. Peter Beresford and Mark Harrison, 'Social Care is Broken Beyond Repair – So What Should Replace It?' (*Labour Briefing*, 2017), https://labourbriefing.org/blog/2017/11/24/ayugootu1ts3hj752d342uv1wn9778 (last accessed June 2023).

12. Rahul Verma, '49% of Disabled People Feel Excluded From Society' (*Each Other*, 2018), https://eachother.org.uk/49-of-disabled-people-feel-excluded-from-society/ (last accessed June 2023).

13. Act 4 Inclusion, 'Vision and Strategy – Choice. Control. Independence. Campaigning for All Involved with Social Care' (*Act 4 Inclusion*, 2021), https://act4inclusion.org/vision-and-strategy/ (last accessed June 2023).

14. Ibid.
15. Equality and Human Rights Commission, 'Disability Discrimination', www.equalityhumanrights.com/en/advice-and-guidance/disability-discrimination (last accessed June 2023).
16. Paulo Freire, *Pedagogy of the Oppressed* (New York: Continuum, 2000), Chapter 4.
17. Ask Difference, 'Assimilation' (definition), www.askdifference.com/assimilation-vs-adaptation/ (last accessed June 2023).
18. Social Care Institute for Excellence, 'Co-production: What It Is And How To Do It' (*Social Care Institute for Excellence*, 2022), www.scie.org.uk/co-production/what-how/ (last accessed June 2023).
19. Carol Thomas, *Female Forms: Experiencing and Understanding Disability* (Buckingham: Open University Press, 1999).
20. UPIAS, 'Disability Challenge No.1' (UPIAS, 1981), 5, https://disability-studies.leeds.ac.uk/wp-content/uploads/sites/40/library/UPIAS-Disability-Challenge1.pdf (last accessed June 2023).
21. Margot C. Howe and Ann K. Briggs, 'Ecological Systems Model for Occupational Therapy' (*American Journal of Occupational Therapy*, Vol. 36, No. 5, 1982), 322–7.
22. Ibid., 327.
23. Vic Finkelstein, 'Schemes for Independent Living' (*Medical Disability Society*, 1984) https://disability-studies.leeds.ac.uk/wp-content/uploads/sites/40/library/finkelstein-indepliv.pdf (last accessed June 2023).
24. Ibid., 2.
25. Ibid.
26. Ibid., 4.
27. Ibid.
28. Vic Finkelstein, 'Services for Clients or Clients for Services' (*North Regional Association for the Blind*, Annual Course: 'Working Together', 1990), 1, https://disability-studies.leeds.ac.uk/wp-content/uploads/sites/40/library/finkelstein-finkelstein7.pdf (last accessed June 2023).
29. Ibid., 2.
30. Vic Finkelstein, 'Disability: An Administrative Challenge? (The Health and Welfare Heritage)', in *Services for Clients or Clients for Services: Social Work – Disabling People and Disabling Environments*, M. Oliver, ed. (London: Jessica Kingsley Publishers, 1991), 12.
31. Ibid.
32. Ibid., 13.
33. Ibid.
34. Vic Finkelstein, 'Re-thinking Care in Society Providing Equal Opportunities for All' (Discussion Paper by Vic Finkelstein, Honorary Senior Research Fellow, School of Health and Social Welfare, The Open University, 3 March 1998), 1.
35. Ibid., 2.

36. Pete Ritchie, Helen Sanderson, Jackie Kilbane and Martin Routledge, *People Plans and Practicalities – Achieving Change Through Person-Centred Planning* (Edinburgh: Scottish Human Services Trust, 2003).

37. Vic Finkelstein, 'A Profession Allied to the Community: The Disabled People's Trade Union', in *Disability and Development: Learning From Action and Research on Disability in the Majority World*, Emma Stone, ed. (Leeds: The Disability Press, 1991), 1, https://disability-studies.leeds.ac.uk/wp-content/uploads/sites/40/library/finkelstein-PAC-Trade-Union.pdf (last accessed June 2023).

38. Ibid., 2.

39. Ibid.

40. Ibid.

41. Ibid.

42. Vic Finkelstein, (1999b) 'Professions Allied to the Community (PACs) I and II', https://disability-studies.leeds.ac.uk/wp-content/uploads/sites/40/library/finkelstein-pacall.pdf (last accessed June 2023).

43. Ibid., 3.

44. Ibid., 6.

45. Vic Finkelstein, 'The Social Model of Disability and the Disability Movement' (Leeds: University of Leeds, 2007), 13.

46. Ibid.

47. Sheila Riddell, Mark Priestley, Charlotte Pearson, Geof Mercer, Colin Barnes and Debbie Jolly, 'Personal Assistance Policy in the UK: What's the Problem With Direct Payments?' (*Disability Studies Quarterly*, Vol. 25, No. 1, 2005); Anne Pridmore, 'Disability Activism, Independent Living and Direct Payments' (Independent Living and Direct Payments: The National Picture Conference, 2006), https://disability-studies.leeds.ac.uk/wp-content/uploads/sites/40/library/pridmore-direct-payments-conference-paper-11.pdf (last accessed June 2023).

48. A. Kosanic, I. Kavcic, M. van Kleunen and S. Harrison, 'Climate Change and Climate Change Velocity Analysis Across Germany' (*Scientific Reports*, Vol. 9, No. 2196, Nature Publishing Group, 2019), www.nature.com/articles/s41598-019-38720-6 (last accessed 1 July 2023).

49. United Nations Development Programme (UNDP), 'The Peoples' Climate Vote' (University of Oxford et al., 2021), www.undp.org/publications/peoples-climate-vote (last accessed June 2023).

50. Lateef H. McLeod 'Social Ecology and Disability Justice: Making A New Society' (*Harbinger: a Journal of Social Ecology*, Institute for Social Ecology, 2019), https://harbinger-journal.com/ (last accessed June 2023).

51. Sandra Daniels and Bob Williams-Findlay, 'The Principle of Collective Access' (*Anti-Capitalist Resistance*, 2021), https://anticapitalistresistance.org/the-principle-of-collective-access (last accessed June 2023).

52. Mark Priestley, 'Constructions and Creations: Idealism, Materialism and Disability Theory' (*Disability and Society*, Vol. 13, No. 1, 1998), 75–94.

53. Anne-Marie Callus and Sue Vella, 'The Independent Living Movement and Capitalism: Challenges and Contributions' (*Studies in Social Wellbeing*, Vol. 1, No. 1, 2021), 12–25.
54. Marco Nathan and Jeffrey Brown, 'An Ecological Approach to Modeling Disability' (*Bioethics*, Vol. 32, No. 9, 2018), 593–601, https://onlinelibrary.wiley.com/doi/10.1111/bioe.12497 (last accessed June 2023).
55. David Pfeiffer, 'The Devils are in the Details: The ICIDH2 and the Disability Movement' (*Disability & Society*, Vol. 15, No. 7, 2000), 1079–1082; Maria Barile, 'Globalization and ICF Eugenics: Historical Coincidence or Connection? The More Things Change the More They Stay the Same' (*Disability Studies Quarterly*, Spring, Vol. 23, No. 2 (Spring), 2003), 208–23.
56. Karrie A. Shogren, Michael L. Wehmeyer, Jonathan Martinis and Peter Blanck, 'Social-Ecological Models of Disability', in *Supported Decision-Making: Theory, Research, and Practice to Enhance Self-Determination and Quality of Life*, Cambridge Disability Law and Policies Policy Series (Cambridge: Cambridge University Press, 2018), 29–45; Aleksandra Kosanic, Jan Petzold, Berta Martin-Lopez and Mialy Razanajatovo, 'An Inclusive Future: Disabled Populations in the Context of Climate and Environmental Change' (*Current Opinion in Environmental Sustainability*, Vol. 55:101159, 2022), 9, www.sciencedirect.com (last accessed June 2023); United Nations, 'Realization of the Sustainable Development Goals by, for and with Persons with Disabilities: UN Flagship Report on Disability and Development 2018' (Disability and the 2030 Agenda for Sustainable Development, 2018), 387, https://digitallibrary.un.org/record/1641068?ln=en (last accessed 1 July 2023).
57. Finkelstein, 'The Social Model of Disability and the Disability Movement', 11.
58. Vic Finkelstein and Ossie Stuart, 'Developing New Services', in *Beyond Disability: Towards an Enabling Society*, G. Hales, ed. (London: Sage, 1996).
59. Finkelstein, 'The Social Model of Disability and the Disability Movement', 9.
60. Paul Hunt, 'Parasite People: A Critique of *A Life Apart* by F. J. Miller and G. V. Gwynne' (*Cheshire Smile*, Vol. 18, Autumn 1972, 3); Eric John Miller and Geraldine V. Gwynne, *A Life Apart: A Pilot Study of Residential Institutions for the Physically Handicapped and the Young Chronic Sick* (London: Tavistock Publications, 1972).

CHAPTER 10 FROM THE ASHES: A NEW DISABILITY PRAXIS?

1. Fleur Perry, 'Social Model of Disability: Who, What and Why' (*Disability Horizons*, 2019), https://disabilityhorizons.com/2019/05/social-model-of-disability-who-what-and-why/ (last accessed June 2023).
2. Susan L. Gabel and Susan Peters, 'Presage of a Paradigm Shift? Beyond the Social Model of Disability Toward Resistance Theories of Disability' (*Disability & Society*, Vol. 19, No. 6, 2004), 585–600, 585, 587; Christopher

Donoghue 'Challenging the Authority of the Medical Definition of Disability: An Analysis of the Resistance to the Social Constructionist Paradigm' (*Disability & Society*, Vol. 18, No. 2, 2003), 199–208.

3. T. Shakespeare and N. Watson, 'The Social Model of Disability: An Outdated Ideology?', in *Exploring Theories and Expanding Methodologies: Where We Are and Where We Need To Go*, S. Barnartt and B. Altman, eds (London: JAI, 2001), 9–28.

4. Ibid., 13–19.

5. Richard Light, 'Disability Theory: Social Model or Unsociable Muddle?' (*Disability Tribune*, December 1999/January 2000), 10–13, 10.

6. Karen Soldatic, 'The Transnational Sphere of Justice: Disability Praxis and the Politics of Impairment' (*Disability & Society*, Vol. 28, No. 6, 2013), 744–55, 745; S. Grech, 'Recolonising Debates or Perpetuated Coloniality? Decentring the Spaces of Disability, Development and Community in the Global South' (*International Journal of Inclusive Education*, Vol. 15, No. 1, 2011), 87–100; H. Meekosha, 'Decolonising Disability: Thinking and Acting Globally' (*Disability &Society*, Vol. 26, No. 6, 2011), 667–82; M. Sherry, '(Post)Colonising Disability' (*Wagadu*, Vol. 4, 2007), 10–22.

7. Paul Abberley, 'The Concept of Oppression and the Development of a Social Theory of Disability' (*Disability, Handicap & Society*, Vol. 2, No. 1, 1987), 5–19, 13.

8. United Nations, 'Report of the Secretary-General on the Rule of Law and Transitional Justice in Conflict and Post-Conflict Societies' (*UN Doc.*, S/2004/616), 4.

9. Soldatic, 'The Transnational Sphere of Justice', 749; Kate Nash and Vikki Bell, 'The Politics of Framing: An Interview with Nancy Fraser' (*Theory, Culture & Society*, Vol. 24, No. 4, 2007), 73–86.

10. A.J. Withers, 'Disablism or Ableism?' (*Stillmyrevolution*, 2013), https://stillmyrevolution.org/2013/01/01/disablism-or-ableism/ (last accessed June 2023); BBC *Ouch*, 'First There was Racism and Sexism, Now There's Ableism' (*BBC*, 2014), www.bbc.co.uk/news/blogs-ouch-27840472 (last accessed June 2023).

11. Talila Lewis, 'Working Definition of Ableism' (January 2021), www.talilalewis.com/blog/january-2021-working-definition-of-ableism (last accessed June 2023).

12. Fiona Campbell, 'Inciting Legal Fictions: Disability's Date with Ontology and the Ableist Body of the Law' (*Griffith Law Review*, Vol. 10, 2001), 42–62, 44.

13. Ibid.

14. Mike Oliver, 'Capitalism and Ideology: A Materialist Critique of the Normalization Principle' (1994), 3, https://disability-studies.leeds.ac.uk/wp-content/uploads/sites/40/library/Oliver-cap-dis-ideol.pdf (last accessed June 2023).

15. Mike Oliver and Colin Barnes, 'Disability Politics and the Disability Movement in Britain: Where did it all go Wrong?' (2006), http://pf7d7vi 404s1dxh27mla5569.wpengine.netdna-cdn.com/files/library/Barnes-Coalition-disability-politics-paper.pdf (last accessed June 2023).

16. Jenny Morris, 'Rethinking Disability Policy' (*Viewpoint*, 2011), www.jrf.org. uk/report/rethinking-disability-policy (last accessed June 2023).

17. Vic Finkelstein, 'The Social Model of Disability and the Disability Movement' (Leeds: University of Leeds, 2007), 14, https://disability-studies. leeds.ac.uk/wp-content/uploads/sites/40/library/finkelstein-The-Social-Model-of-Disability-and-the-Disability-Movement.pdf (last accessed June 2023).

18. Bob Williams-Findlay, 'The Disabled People's Movement in the Age of Austerity: Rights, Resistance and Reclamation', in *Resist the Punitive State, Grassroots Struggles Across Welfare, Housing, Education and Prisons*, Emily Luise Hart, Joe Greener and Rich Moth, eds (London: Pluto Press, 2019).

19. France Hasler, 'Philosophy of Independent Living' (2003), http://www. independentliving.org/docs6/hasler2003.html#2 (last accessed 2 July 2023).

20. Colin Barnes, *Disabled People in Britain and Discrimination: A Case for Anti-discrimination Legislation* (London: C. Hurst & Co., University of Calgary Press in association with the British Council of Organisations of Disabled People, 1991).

21. Thomas H. Marshall, *The Right to Welfare and Other Essays* (London: Heinemann, 1981), 28.

22. Sally Witcher, 'Disabled People Citizenship And Public Life' (Discussion paper to Disability Working Group, Satellite Group 3, Scottish Executive's Equality Unit, 2005), www.scotland.gov.uk/Topics/People/Equality/ disability/dwg3paperjun05 (last accessed June 2023).

23. Equality and Human Rights Commission, 'UK Independent Mechanism Update Report to the UN Committee on the Rights of Persons with Disabilities' (*EHRC*, 2018, written in conjunction with Scottish, Welsh, and Northern Ireland bodies). www.equalityhumanrights.com/sites/default/ files/progress-on-disability-rights-in-the-uk-crpd-shadow-report-2018_0. pdf (last accessed June 2023).

24. Katerina Kazou, 'Analysing the Definition of Disability in the UN Convention on the Rights of Persons with Disabilities: Is it Really Based on a 'Social Model' Approach?' (*International Journal of Mental Health and Capacity Law*, Vol. 23, 2017), 25.

25. World Health Organisation, *International Classification of Functioning, Disability and Health (ICF)* (Geneva: WHO, 2001), www.who.int/ classifications/icf/en/ (last accessed June 2023).

26. Stammeringlaw, 'Convention on the Rights of Persons with Disabilities (CRPD)' (*Stammeringlaw*, 2021), www.stammeringlaw.org.uk/disability-equality-law/european-union-human-rights-un/cprd/#cttee (last accessed June 2023).

27. Rachel Hurst, 'Legislation and Human Rights', in *Disabling Barriers – Enabling Environments*, John Swain, Sally French, Colin Barnes and Carol Thomas, eds (London: SAGE Publications, 2004), 195–200, 197.

28. Luke Clements and Janet Read, 'The Dog That Didn't Bark', in *Disability Rights in Europe: From Theory to Practice*, Anna Lawson and Caroline Gooding, eds (Oxford and Portland, OR: Hart Publishing, 2005), 26.

29. Felicity Armstrong and Len Barton, 'Is There Anyone There Concerned With Human Rights?' Cross-cultural Connections, Disability and the Struggle for Change in England', in *Disability, Human Rights and Education: Cross-cultural Perspectives*, F. Armstrong and L. Barton, eds (Buckingham: Open University Press, 1999).

30. Hurst, 'Legislation and Human Rights', 297.

31. Nora McGreevy, 'The ADA was a Monumental Achievement 30 Years Ago, but the Fight for Equal Rights Continues' (*Smithsonian Magazine*, 2020), www.smithsonianmag.com/history/history-30-years-since-signing-americans-disabilities-act-180975409/ (last accessed June 2023).

32. Caroline Gooding, *Disabling Laws, Enabling Acts* (London: Pluto Press, 1994), 29.

33. Caroline Gooding, *Blackstone's Guide to the Disability Discrimination Act 1995* (London: Blackstone Press).

34. Barnes, *Disabled People in Britain and Discrimination*, 2.

35. Ibid.

36. Gooding, *Disabling Laws, Enabling Acts*, 1.

37. Marta Russell, 'Backlash, the Political Economy, and Structural Exclusion' (*Berkeley Journal of Employment and Labor Law*, University of California, Vol. 21, No. 1, 2000), 1.

38. Colin Barnes, 'Disability Rights: rhetoric and reality in the UK' (*Disability & Society*, Vol. 10, No. 1, 1995), 111–16, 114.

39. Vic Finkelstein, 'The Social Model Repossessed' (Manchester Coalition of Disabled People, 2001), 4.

40. Hasler, 'Philosophy of Independent Living'.

41. Malcom Richardson, 'Addressing Barriers: Disabled Rights and the Implications for Nursing of the Social Construct of Disability' (*Journal of Advanced Nursing*, Vol. 25, No. 6, 1997), 1269–75, 1269.

42. Tom Shakespeare, *Disability Rights and Wrongs* (Oxford: Routledge, 2006).

43. Oliver and Barnes, 'Disability Politics and the Disability Movement in Britain'.

44. Damon Arik Young and Ruth Quibell, 'Why Rights are Never Enough: Rights, Intellectual Disability and Understanding' (*Disability and Society*, Vol. 15, No. 5, 2000), 747–64, 748.

45. Soldatic, 'The Transnational Sphere of Justice'.

46. I attribute this quotation to Mark Lynes, who made a comment on Bob Williams-Findlay's Facebook page on 27 July 2012.

47. 'Self-determination', definition, www.merriam-webster.com/dictionary/self-determination (last accessed June 2023).

48. Alex, 'Negative Rights: A Definitive Guide on What They Are' (*Libertas Bella*, 2022), https://blog.libertasbella.com/glossary/negative-rights/#:~:text=The%20simplest%20definition%20is%20a%20negative%20right%20is,for%20someone%20to%20vote%20without%20interference%20or%20persuasion (last accessed June 2023).

49. Finkelstein, 'The Social Model Repossessed', 5.

50. Saul McLeod, 'Social Roles' (*Simply Psychology*, 2008), https://www.simplypsychology.org/social-roles.html?source=post_page- (last accessed 2 July 2023); emphasis added.

51. UPIAS, 'Disability Challenge 1' (1981), 4–5, https://disability-studies.leeds.ac.uk/wp-content/uploads/sites/40/library/UPIAS-Disability-Challenge1.pdf (last accessed 3 July 2023).

52. Vic Finkelstein, 'Experience And Consciousness' (Notes for 'Psychology of Disability' Talk, *Liverpool Housing Authority*, 1990).

53. Ibid. See also Peter Leonard, *Personality and Ideology: Towards a Materialist Understanding of the Individual* (London: Macmillan, 1984).

54. Meekosha, 'Decolonising Disability'.

55. Shaun Grech, 'Recolonising Debates or Perpetuated Coloniality?, 98.

56. Iris M. Young, *Inclusion and Democracy*, Oxford Political Theory (Oxford: Oxford University Press, 2000), 107.

57. Gabel and Peters, 'Presage of a paradigm shift?', 593, citing Young, *Inclusion and Democracy*, 109.

58. James Bohman, *Public Deliberation: Pluralism, Complexity and Democracy* (Cambridge, MA: MIT Press, 1996).

59. Paulo Freire, *Pedagogy of the Oppressed* (New York: Continuum, 1986), 19.

60. Gabel and Peters, 'Presage of a paradigm shift?', 597.

61. A. J. Withers, *Disability Politics and Theory* (Halifax and Winnipeg:Fernwood Publishing, 2012); Robert McRuer, *Crip Times: Disability, Globalization, and Resistance* (New York: NYU Press, 2018).

Index

For topics relating to disability and disabled people, *see* the topic, e.g. identity; oppression

n refers to a note

Thanks to our Patreon subscriber:

Ciaran Kane

Who has shown generosity and
comradeship in support of our publishing.

Check out the other perks you get by subscribing
to our Patreon – visit patreon.com/plutopress.

Subscriptions start from £3 a month.

The Pluto Press Newsletter

Hello friend of Pluto!

Want to stay on top of the best radical books
we publish?

Then sign up to be the first to hear about our
new books, as well as special events,
podcasts and videos.

You'll also get 50% off your first order with us
when you sign up.

Come and join us!

Go to bit.ly/PlutoNewsletter